BYZANTIUM FOR ROME

Byzantium for Rome

THE POLITICS OF NOSTALGIA

IN UMBERTIAN ITALY, 1878–1900

BY RICHARD DRAKE

The University of North Carolina Press *Chapel Hill*

© 1980 The University of North Carolina Press
All rights reserved
Manufactured in the United States of America
ISBN 0-8078-1405-9

Library of Congress Catalog Card Number 79-16578
Drake, Richard, 1942–
  Byzantium for Rome.

  Bibliography: p.
  Includes index.
  1. Italy—Politics and government—1870–1915. 2. Politics and culture—Italy. 3. Italy—Civilization—1789–1900. 4. Umberto I, King of Italy, 1844–1900. 5. Annunzio, Gabriele d', 1863–1938.
  I. Title.
DG564.D66   320.9′45′09   79-16578
ISBN 0-8078-1405-9

For my parents,

Floyd Wilbur Drake and

Ornella Maria De Franceschi Giovitto Drake,

who taught me to love Italy

CONTENTS

viii   *Contents*

ACKNOWLEDGMENTS

I started to think about this book in 1971, and since then I have accumulated a large number of intellectual and professional debts, the most outstanding of which I would like to mention here.

First, Robert Wohl, of the history department at UCLA, worked several miracles in gaining financial support for me in the form of fellowships and university positions from 1971 to 1975, and without them it would have been impossible to go ahead with this work. Moreover, he had faith in my project from the beginning and never wavered in that faith, even when I began to doubt that anyone could make sense out of D'Annunzio. Slowly the book evolved, and at every stage of the writing process he offered me advice that was both penetrating and constructive. He read every line of what I wrote, it seems a half-dozen times or more, and I could always count on a close, critical reading from him. No student could ever ask for a more demanding or perceptive mentor than I had in Robert Wohl.

Two other people at UCLA read my earlier draft, professor Eugen Weber, also of the history department, and professor Marga Cottino-Jones of the Italian department. Both of them provided me with valuable suggestions on how the work might be improved in terms of organization and of literary criticism. Professor Cottino-Jones's bibliographical suggestions were particularly helpful.

I owe a very special debt of gratitude to professor Franco Masciandaro of the UCLA Italian department who assisted me in translating several selections of D'Annunzio's poetry into English. I must accept full responsibility, however, for any imperfections in the prose translations.

In its present form, *Byzantium for Rome* has bene-fited enormously from the detailed critique that Pro-fessor Benjamin F. Brown gave it. From the beginning of his association with my book he put his profound knowledge of the Umbertian period in Italian history completely at my disposal. Professor Brown lavished more attention on this project than I had a right to expect, and his wise comments saved me from errors too numerous and embarrassing to mention.

No less helpful was Clara M. Lovett, professor of history at Baruch College, C.U.N.Y. She also read the entire manuscript in its present form. Her trenchant questions forced me to reconsider some of my most cherished assumptions about the Umbertian period, and in particular I learned much from her about how to approach the difficult problems of politics and eco-nomics in the history of *trasformismo*.

Professor Alexander J. De Grand of Roosevelt Uni-versity in Chicago, who knows more about Enrico Cor-radini than any man living, gave a very thoughtful reading on my ninth chapter in which Corradini is a prominent figure. Professor Frank J. Coppa, of St. John's University in New York, read a different ver-sion of the same material when he served as the com-mentator for a paper that I delivered on D'Annunzio and Corradini at the American Historical Association convention in December 1977. Our jousting in Dallas helped me to see some implications in my research that I had missed, and in the long run I was per-suaded to modify arguments that had been advanced perhaps a little too stridently.

Several institutions and organizations aided my re-search at key points in the project. First, the staff in the Inter-Library Loan department at the UCLA Re-search Library heroically persevered against the uncertainties of the Italian postal system and managed to secure valuable materials for me from Italy. Second, a patent fund grant from the UCLA Academic Senate enabled me to spend part of a summer doing research at Harvard's Widener Library and at Columbia's Casa Italiana. Third, I was privileged to receive in the same year, 1972–73, the Aldo Moro fellowship for summer study in Italy and a Fulbright grant, enabling me to spend fifteen continuous months in Rome, Florence, and Venice. While there I was given full and free access to vital research material in all the major libraries, primarily the Biblioteca Universitaria Alessandrina, the Biblioteca del Senato della Repubblica, the Biblioteca dell'Istituto di Storia Moderna e Contemporanea, and the Biblioteca della Camera dei Deputati in Rome, the Biblioteca Nazionale Centrale in Florence, and the Biblioteca Nazionale Marciana in Venice.

Two Italian scholars helped me while I lived in Italy: professor Renzo De Felice of the University of Rome and Dr. Emilio Mariano, superintendent of the Vittoriale. Dottoressa Ines Monti-Ottolenghi, a more recent acquaintance, has given generously of her time in rounding up important source materials for me in Milan. My good friend, Nicholas Bufalino, has provided the same service in another part of the world, Berkeley, California.

Finally, I want to express my deep appreciation to my wife, Megen Thompson Drake, who assisted me in preparing the final manuscript for my demanding and meticulous editors at The University of North Carolina Press, Lewis Bateman, Gwen Duffey, and Ann Weir. Without her loving help this book would have been less than it is.

R. D.

When I think of the twentieth-century historian who will wear out his eyes and his health in order to understand truly the century of Pius IX and of Garibaldi, I feel full of respect and admiration for his useless courage.

T. L. Roncisvalle, *Nabab*, 28 December 1884

INTRODUCTION

*". . . the horizontally specialized student of a certain
literary current will have to come to grips with the
careers and the mobility of the literati who espouse it,
the incentive system under which they work, the
nature of the public to which they address themselves,
the channels of communication available to them, and
the social orientation of their patrons."*
—Karl Mannheim, *Essays on the Sociology of Culture*

A word about the title. At first glance, *Byzantium for Rome* may appear confusing or
misleading, but I hope the subtitle, *The
Politics of Nostalgia in Umbertian Italy,
1878–1900*, will help direct the reader's attention toward the book's object, which is to examine the relationship between politics and culture in Italy during
the reign of Umberto I. I chose this title because,
despite first impressions, it fits the story better than
any other that I or anyone else could think of in
the seven years it took me to write this book. For the
generation of Italian intellectuals who came to maturity around 1880, Byzantium and Rome were powerful
symbols, charged with a meaning both historical and
political. Byzantium represented the decadent, effemi-
nate past of Latin corruption and decline; Rome symbolized the glorious, virile past of Latin strength and
conquest. Mazzini and the Risorgimento generation of
Italian intellectuals had promised a new Rome for
united Italy, but for the generation of 1880 all visible
signs pointed instead toward a new Byzantium. In
their minds, Byzantium for Rome was more than a
poetic metaphor; it was a nauseating political reality,
producing disgust with existing society and a simul-

taneous nostalgia for a classical past whose stone and marble vestiges loomed as constant reminders that post-Risorgimento Italians were degenerate mutations in a race once prolific of heroes. The politics of nostalgia developed in an atmosphere of increasing despair over the tragic disjunction between Risorgimento rhetoric and post-Risorgimento reality; it was Mazzinianism gone sour. By 1880 these ideas were already hardening into a convention among literary intellectuals with political interests, and it is quite in keeping with the spirit of the times that this generation found its representative figure in the good but feckless King Umberto I, "the mediocre exponent of a mediocre age."[1] To understand his unique place in Italian history, one must know something about the circumstances of his accession and about the quite extraordinary power and prestige of his father, King Vittorio Emanuele II.

When Vittorio Emanuele suddenly died on 9 January 1878, the age of regal paramountcy in Italian politics passed with him. He was only fifty-eight and had been in robust health almost up to the moment of his collapse. The king's death shocked his adoring subjects. Alongside Cavour, Garibaldi, and Mazzini, the "Re galantuomo" held a place of heroic eminence in the affections of the Italian people as the patriot king, the father of his country, "the redeemer of the most glorious of nations." Scarcely a hint of this future greatness was apparent to onlookers at the time of his coronation, for the young monarch's succession to the crown of Piedmont-Sardinia in 1849 had taken place in the most depressing circumstances imaginable to the political mind of that generation. The war with Austria—the First War of the Risorgimento—had been lost at Custoza and Novara, leaving the Piedmontese with a treasury as bankrupt as the government's "l'Italia farà da sé" foreign policy. In his humiliation and impotence King Carlo Alberto had abdicated in favor of his son, the Duke of Savoy, shortly to become Vittorio Emanuele II.

Nearly as galling to the departing monarch was a concession that he had made in the previous year to the constitutional spirit of the age, the *Statuto* of 1848, considerably diluting his hitherto absolute authority. This document provided for the basic elements of Italy's post-Risorgimento parliamentary life; but, Carlo Alberto's grudging bestowal of power on a bicameral legislative body notwithstanding, the king's office was far from purely ceremonial. The king was commander-in-chief of the armed forces. He had sole right to declare war and make treaties, and his power in foreign affairs was virtually supreme. He alone nominated members of the upper house, and he chose and dismissed ministers who were responsible to him, not to Parliament. He enjoyed broad prerogatives in the use of royal decrees. The *Statuto* was quite explicit on all of these points, and for good measure contained the unambiguous statement, "To the King alone belongs the executive power." [2]

Vittorio Emanuele possessed the will, if not always the tact and intelligence, to defend these privileges and even to augment them. Despite a justly deserved reputation for low-brow vulgarity and fustian posturing, the Piedmontese king was one of the two most politically powerful men in the country during the Risorgimento period, sharing and contesting the spotlight with Cavour. After Cavour's death in 1861, the king's political role swelled in importance. Vittorio Emanuele dwarfed his ministers—Ricasoli, Rattazzi, Farini, Minghetti, Lamarmora, Menebrea, and Lanza. As they came and went, he always remained at the center of power, ever in the public eye and consciousness. These ministers never knew when the king might undercut them with a court policy of his own, separate and distinct from the policy of Parliament. Though parliamentary power was real, it was divided, and this factionalism played into the ambitious king's hands. In the confusion of the parties and interest groups, the king appeared to be the nation's only source of political coherence.

Vittorio Emanuele enjoyed the best in the best of all possible worlds: a power that was large and impressive, coupled with what amounted in practice to a parliamentary escape clause, enabling him to point an accusing finger at Montecitorio when things went seriously wrong as they often did after 1861. Not until 1946, with the abolition of the monarchy, would the impenetrable frontier zone between the king's prerogatives and Parliament's authority be cleared away at last. Though many deplored these dense thickets of constitutional ambiguity, everyone in Italian political life took advantage of them to find cover from final responsibility for anything. This was not a system to produce Harry Trumans—the lira, so to speak, never stopped anywhere. Since no clear and precise definition or allotment of power existed, this ramshackle political apparatus hardly worked well even in comparatively good times, and during a crisis it became utterly and often tragically useless, as the country's spectacular failures from 1861 to 1945 reveal: Africa always, the 1915 declaration of war, the postwar fascist takeover, and, most pitifully of all, the confused and inept policies of the government after the first fall of fascism in 1943.

The future pattern of relations between king and Parliament, characterized chiefly by an unstable balance between legislature and executive, became established during the reign of Vittorio Emanuele. After 1861 his preponderance in foreign affairs hardly drew a challenge from Parliament. He had forced Cavour to send troops to the Crimea in 1855, but in General Lamarmora the king had a pliant prime minister who eagerly fell in with royal schemes for war against Austria in 1866. Vittorio Emanuele correctly judged that the aristocracy had no use in society aside from war; however, his delusions about being a gifted general had disastrous consequences for the Italian people. When the Italians, with greatly superior forces, suffered humiliating defeats at Custoza and Lissa, General Lamarmora in the government and Admiral Persano in the military became the principal scapegoats. The real cause of these calamities lay in an Italian problem as old as the battle of Fornovo in 1495 and brought right up to date by Vittorio Emanuele: the failure to establish a clear chain of command. Although the fault belonged to the king, he deftly fobbed off responsibility for the lost war on Parliament, which, as an institution, would always be pathetically impotent about defending itself, and would never find enthusiastic defenders in the rest of society. The deputies at Montecitorio made an ideal collective whipping boy; if they had not existed, the king would have had to create them.

For the last twelve years of his life Vittorio Emanuele spent lavishly on the army and navy, trying to enhance the absolutist traditions of the Casa Savoia, to live up to one minister's description of him as "the last of the conquistadors."[3] After 1870, with the conquest of Rome, the ageless monuments of his new capital hauntingly proclaimed a radiant imperialist past, reinforcing the king's perfervid desire for glory and conquest. The extreme poverty of the country and the niggardly economic policies of the old right's conservative ministers put a brake on these ambitions, but in the heady atmosphere of classical Rome the swashbuckling Vittorio Emanuele at last had found an historically appropriate setting for his martial fantasies. In Rome a king had to think and feel *romanamente*, and it is not difficult to envision where his sentiments would have lain had he survived into the 1880s to witness the dawn of Italian imperialism in Africa.

A very different sort of man took over as king in January 1878. Umberto I (not IV, as he should have been in the chronology of the Piedmontese crown) was almost thirty-four when he succeeded his father. Queen Victoria had sniffed of Vittorio Emanuele. "He is startling in the extreme in appearance and manner."[4] Indeed, his bristling mustachioes and swaggering air left a vivid impression on all who recorded their recollections of him. The son impressed people in a quite different way: he was quiet, reserved, even cold, and decidedly ordinary looking. A mighty public relations effort was put into motion to inflate Umberto's claims on the affections of his countrymen. He had been trained as a soldier, and much was made of his bravery on the field during the defeats of 1866. The newspapers did their part in supporting him, and, in the tradition of the time, they always remained unctuously respectful. Nevertheless, nearly everyone soon perceived that Umberto could neither duplicate his father's appeal as a symbol of national unity nor dominate the country's political life in quite the same manner.

In his first public statement as king, on the day after Vittorio Emanuele's death, Umberto vowed to continue the sacred task of his *"Augusto Genitore . . .* to make Italy one and united."[5] One week later, on 17 January 1878, the dead king's body was transported from the Quirinale to the Pantheon through immense crowds of grief-stricken subjects. On the following Saturday, the 19th, Umberto formally ascended the throne before a joint meeting of the senators and deputies in Montecitorio. There, flanked on his right by Prince Amadeo, Duke of Aosta, and on his left by the Prince of Carignano, Umberto read a discourse which had been prepared for him by the council of ministers, presided over at that time by Agostino Depretis. Before the assembled nobility and political dignitaries of the country he began: "In the presence of God I swear to observe loyally the Constitution; not to exercise royal authority except in accordance with the laws and in conformity with these; to render to everyone according to his merits full and exact justice, and to conduct myself in everything with the interests, the prosperity and the honor of the nation in view." [6] From that point on, applause punctuated nearly every sentence as the king promised to allow "Parliament, the interpreter of the national will, to guide me in the first steps of my reign."

That Umberto spoke these words did not in itself constitute a major change in Italian political life, but that he was constrained to live by them did. It is ironic that, in 1876, the Italian people had spoken expectantly of a "parliamentary revolution" when the old left succeeded the old right in power; actually, a much more significant political change occurred with the death of Vittorio Emanuele two years later. From the outset of Umberto's reign the balance of power tipped decidedly toward Parliament—really toward Depretis, who, followed by Francesco Crispi, would reassert a Cavourian sense of parliamentary power. Obviously, such a sweeping change in the character of Italian politics could not come about solely as a result of one king's personality. Even had Vittorio Emanuele lived another twenty years, it is doubtful that he could have checkmated the growing power of Parliament, much less have ignored what that growth represented in the rapidly changing circumstances of Italy's social and economic life.

Nevertheless, in this case personalities are of the highest importance. No one questioned the new king's earnestness, but he was totally lacking in charisma.

Even the plodding Depretis seemed to outshine him in the 1880s, and during the next decade Crispi completely eclipsed Umberto in the public eye. Although the monarchy did not suffer anything like emasculation during Umberto's reign, the truly virile days of Vittorio Emanuele were gone forever. In retrospect, we can see that Vittorio Emanuele's position of towering eminence in Italian political life was largely a personal triumph, depending on the public's perception of him as the "Re galantuomo," the *pater patriae*, and "the most clear-cut personification of the valor, of the will, of the unity of our country."[7] Against these Olympian achievements, Umberto only could offer his all-too-human deeds as a young cavalry officer in a losing war. He simply lacked the tremendous personal prestige of his father, and after 1878, Italy settled into something more like a true constitutional monarchy than any of the post-Cavour governments in the masterful Vittorio Emanuele's time.

Thus the Umbertian era began on a note of diminished royal authority, with Depretis, a shrewd and resourceful parliamentarian, skillfully asserting his own personal authority in a manner reminiscent of Cavour and anticipatory of those other liberal parliamentary "dictators", Crispi and Giolitti. Umberto himself seems to have chafed very little under the restrictions of a constitutional monarchy—far less, in fact, than his strong-willed and aggressively anti-parliamentary wife, Queen Margherita. For one thing, politics was a weak third on his list of passions, far behind hunting and very far behind women. Like his father, he had an eye for the ladies, and his numerous though unpublicized affairs—particularly with the Duchess Litta, who was practically a second wife to him—absorbed much time and energy.

Beyond these qualities of temperament, the king lacked the qualities of mind to play an effective role in politics. Even in the lightweight scales especially reserved by historians for the weighing of modern monarchs, he rests very lightly indeed. One disillusioned senator complained: "At one time I used to go often to the king in order to inform him about things and to express with full and free confidence my opinion. But I had to stop doing that because in no time at all he would blab everything that I had said, giving my name, my surname, my quarterings, and my ancestral home."[8] Nothing became Umberto in life like his leaving of it, and there was a brief flash of apotheosis at the end, occasioned by his assassination on 29 July 1900. The fallen king was given a martyr's burial in the Pantheon. However, until the anarchist's bullet cut him down at Monza, Umberto played a nineteenth-century version of Louis XVI to his wife's Marie Antoinette. Queen Margherita upstaged him completely, except on the parade ground, where from a distance he was said to have cut a handsome figure. Only the royal biographers have ever tried to claim more for him. Thus, as a symbol of the Italian *fin de siècle*, Umberto seemed made to order for the intellectuals: the embodiment of a bland, colorless Italy content to maintain an uninspiring status quo.

The low self-image of the Umbertian generation has been a problem for historians ever since. The Umbertian age was neither the best nor the worst of times in Italian history. Perhaps for this very reason we usually think of the years from 1878 to 1900 as a postscript to the more glamorous Risorgimento period, or as a prelude to World War I and the phenomenon of fascism. The Italian *fin de siècle* was both of those things, just as every age is a consequence of what lies immediately behind and a beginning of what looms immediately ahead. Yet there is something peculiar about our perception of the Umbertian period as a uniquely derivative age, as a relatively uninteresting parenthesis between two vastly more compelling epochs. The really odd thing about the pall covering the Italian historical stage of the 1880s and 1890s is readily discernible. We are not talking about an image created by succeeding generations of smug or superior historians, in the way that American scholars until quite recently dealt with colonial Puritans by making fun of them. The prosaic quality of Umbertian life was first suggested and fretted over by the men and women who actually lived in those times. The sense of loss, of decadence, of failure in living up to the country's highest ideals was ubiquitous. This unsparing self-critical assessment, which eventually resulted in a quixotic nostalgia for the vanished heroism of Italy's Risorgimento and classical past, became the distinguishing characteristic of the Umbertian mind, or at least of most Umbertian intellectuals and artists who have left us their impressions of the period.

In the face of so much unanimous contemporary testimony and subsequent historical documentation, it would be useless to contradict the by now invincibly and universally held opinions about the Umbertian age. It may be that historians have accepted the self-assessment of the Umbertian generation a little too closely at face value; even so, it is easy to understand why Umbertian Italy is seldom discussed on a level of importance equal with that of late Victorian England, or Wilhelmine Germany, or France in the banquet years. This epoch witnessed the climacteric of British imperialism and industrial might, the perilous drive of the Germans for power and recognition of their own imperial claims, and the magnificently prolific finale of French dominance in the arts. The achievements of Umbertian Italy look minuscule by comparison. Bismarck's biting witticism, that Italy was the greatest of the weak powers and the weakest of the great powers, seemed to strike just the right note, both for his contemporaries and for historians ever since. Italy is mentioned with a wink and a smile, as in preparation for the telling of a good-natured joke. Her dismal showing in the scramble for African colonies provides a shade of comic relief in the bloody saga of European imperialism; a spicy anecdote touching upon D'Annunzio's lecheries is always good for a laugh; and the generally hysterical character of Italian politics from Crispi on throughout the 1890s is in keeping with the rest of the Umbertian story. On the whole, the only Italians who mingle as personages of equal stature with the English, the French, and the Germans have been the infamous anarchist assassins.[9] The murderers of the French president Sadi Carnot (1894), of Spain's Antonio Canovas (1897), of Empress Elizabeth of Austria (1898), and of Umberto I (1900) were, in order of their grisly appearances, Sante Caserio, Michele Angiolillo, Luigi Luccheni, and Gaetano Bresci. Theirs was an ignominious fame, but on the international stage Italian historians of the *fin de siècle* have had little else to write about.

Except for D'Annunzio. In a vague way, he provides some balance in the Italian picture—as a political countersymbol to the anarchists, with the same capacity, unusual for an Italian of this period, to influence European history beyond the borders of Italy. I started out to write this book as an attempt to clarify that vagueness, to formulate the meaning of D'Annunzianism in the political life of Italy and in the cultural life of Europe generally. I wanted to begin at the beginning. Where did D'Annunzianism come from? Like all intellectuals, D'Annunzio was the product of a certain intellectual tradition, and it soon became clear that he had commenced his career as an enthusiastic Carduccian. This intelligence merely raised other questions. Who was Giosuè Carducci? What did he represent in Italian culture and politics? Those two questions marked the turning point of my book, changing it from an inquiry into the mind of one man to a history of an ideology, what I call the politics of nostalgia.

Actually, the despair of the nostalgic right made a symbiotic pair with the desperation of the anarchist left; but, since the anarchists have received their due from practically everybody who has written on the period, I have confined my investigation to the as yet untold story concerning the politics of nostalgia in Umbertian Italy.[10] The theme of nineteenth-century politics and culture has inspired some excellent work in the historiography of other European countries, notably Fritz Stern's *Politics of Cultural Despair* and George L. Mosse's *The Crisis of German Ideology* for Germany, César Graña's *Modernity and Its Discontents* for France, and William J. McGrath's *Dionysian Art and Populist Politics in Austria*: but nothing in a reasonably similar vein has been attempted for Umbertian Italy. John Thayer's *Italy and the Great War* provides a useful compendium of ideas and political movements for the period, but the book's title suggests that he was looking at Umbertian Italy for what it could tell us about a later period, whereas my research began and ended as an attempt to throw a direct light on the 1880s and 1890s.

Although it was not my intention to write a book of "Lives" about disgruntled Italian intellectuals of the right, some combination of biographical description and social analysis seemed to be the best approach to the subject. The careers of Carducci and the so-called *bizantini* writers, particularly D'Annunzio, richly illustrate the growth of an "ideology of resentment" on the Italian right during the 1880s and 1890s, a phenomenon which found similar contemporary expression in all the principal countries of Europe.[11] Moreover, these men were conspicuous for their mutual association as influential members of the Casa Editrice Sommaruga, the most important publishing house in Italy from 1881 to 1885. In the history of post-Risorgimento culture and politics, Carducci stands out as the archetypal *poeta vate*, or poet-prophet, a role which D'Annunzio eventually inherited and monopolized for himself. The collaboration of both writers on the staff of Angelo Sommaruga's legendary *Cronaca bizantina* affords us the hitherto unexploited opportunity to trace the development and spread of a political ideology in the socioeconomic context of the Italian publishing industry.

In Italy, journalism traditionally has served as a bridge between politics and culture. However, the activities of Carducci and the *bizantini* amounted to something less than an authentic movement, in either a political or a cultural sense. With the Sommaruga publishing house we are not entering an Italian version of the Viennese "Pernerstorfer Circle."[12] The *bizantini* struck an attitude, but they provided no definite direction; indeed, the failure of the esthetes to formulate a practical program ultimately led to their political decline around the turn of the century. Still, the state of mind itself was, from Carducci on, a pervasive force in Italian intellectual life. Carducci's dolorous message derived its principal historical significance from the vivid impression that it made on the minds of Italian intellectuals belonging to D'Annunzio's generation: liberal industrializing Italy meant hostility toward culture and ideals. For these esthetes, post-Risorgimento came to signify anti-Risorgimento, and they looked back nostalgically to 1860 and beyond, when Mazzinian visions of a Third Rome inspired a generation of heroes to transform the dream of Dante and Machiavelli into a living reality.

Carducci, D'Annunzio, and the other *bizantini* all had intensely personal visions of the heroic past, and each contributed to the intellectual tradition of right-wing nostalgia in Umbertian politics, a tradition which Enrico Corradini, the founder of nationalism, would absorb before discovering his nationalist voice. Nowadays the word "nationalism" is verbal quicksilver; it can assume almost any shape and be made to fit a bewildering variety of historical developments, from the French Revolution to the present day. I use the term here to signify, in Luigi Federzoni's words, that "political group which had as its recognized chief, Enrico Corradini."[13] If the esthetes represented nothing more than an intellectual stream in the backwater of Umbertian culture, they would hardly require serious treatment; however, the political impact of their esthetic theory was an outstanding feature of the age, and one with ramifications for the future, as the early career of Corradini amply documents. While it is no doubt true that all literature is political, if only by implication, some novelists, poets, and playwrights are explicitly political, writing works "in which political ideas play a dominant role and in which the political milieu is the dominant setting."[14] When, as in the careers of Carducci, D'Annunzio, and Corradini, the purely literary achievements of writers interested in politics are supplemented by actual and influential political experiences, then the materials for a historical study of literature and politics may be said to exist in unusual abundance. *Byzantium for Rome* is such a study.

Nor is the line of intellectual descent between the politically nostalgic writers on Sommaruga's *Cronaca bizantina* and Corradini's nationalism the whole story either. The combined importance of both these traditions in the history of fascist ideology is well known. Mussolini himself acknowledged the social and political critiques of writers like Carducci and D'Annunzio as an essential part of fascist ideology when he de-

clared that postwar fascism originated in the decadent
consciousness of the previous generation; and Corradini was often singled out by the *duce* as a fascist of
the "very first (*primissima*) hour."[15]

Yet I think that it would be a mistake to consider
these writers merely as precursors of fascism. Certainly the fascists thought about them that way, but the
true historical significance of Carducci and the *bizantini* pertains to the nineteenth century, for in their
careers we may discover how Italian politics became
modernized. The period from 1860 to 1890 was the
golden age of transformism, when an amorphous liberal center made up of the historic left and right dominated the government. This epoch drew to a close with
the emergence of an organized Socialist party, an
event which opened up an entirely new chapter in the
history of the ideological left. The Nationalist party
which appeared in 1911 may be understood as the organized response of the extreme right to socialism, as
fascism eventually became in the postwar period.
Therein lies the vital historic link between Corradini
and Mussolini. But where did nationalism come from?
What caused the young Corradini to become dissatisfied with the ideological options open to him, and to
formulate a new, nationalist option?

These questions raise a still larger question: how do
ideologies come into existence? Given the constant
movement in society, caused by pressures from within
and without, from above and below, historical analysis
is so complex that no solution, however brilliant, is
completely satisfying for all time. But by looking
closely at the politics of nostalgia—its genesis, its ascent to a position of eminence in the intellectual community of Umbertian Italy, and its *fin de siècle* crisis
—we may find an answer to this larger question, even
though it can never be the only or the final answer.

BYZANTIUM FOR ROME

CHAPTER ONE

THE POLITICS OF NOSTALGIA

IN POST-RISORGIMENTO ITALY:

GIOSUÈ CARDUCCI (1835–1907)

"Italy before all, Italy above all."
—Giosuè Carducci

In 1906, the year before he died, Giosuè Carducci became the first Italian to win the Nobel Prize for literature. The honor was at once typical and surprising: typical because, as Giovanni Papini later remarked, Carducci had the easiest and most successful of lives, both materially and artistically.[1] Secure financially as a result of an academic appointment at the University of Bologna in 1860 while still in his twenties, Carducci achieved immediate recognition from faithful friends and fellow artists as a writer of major stature. From there the path to the Nobel Prize was straight, with none of the usual detours that delay the careers of even the most favored artists. Carducci's fame seemed to radiate in ever-widening circles during the 1870s and 1880s; by the 1890s he was the acknowledged oracle of Italian literature, with all Italians hailing him as their greatest living poet.

However, outside Italy Carducci made scarcely any impression, and for this reason the award of the Nobel Prize came as a surprise to many, as it has numerous times since. In the 1890s a French critic noted that Carducci's poetry was like a good local Italian wine which, regrettably, would not travel well.[2] The almost complete lack of international recognition for Italy's foremost poet tells us something about the continued decline of Italian cultural prestige in Europe, a process that had been going on for a long time and had made the country a literary graveyard. Yet the case of Carducci tells us something more: his parochial obsession with Italian political life helped cut him off from a larger continental audience. Although this was bad for the European reputation of Italian literature, for students of Italian politics in this period Carducci's career holds a special fascination and meaning because in his writings, the esthetic tradition of political nostalgia first took shape.

It is hardly an exaggeration to say that Carducci grew up looking backward. His father, Michele (b. 1808), belonged to a generation that had been weaned on the romantic musings of Ugo Foscolo. Manzoni's *I promessi sposi* was for the elder Carducci a sacred text immune to criticism, a bronze tablet containing all the wisdom and passion to which man at his most sublime might aspire.

Giosuè reacted against his father's sentimental romanticism with merciless intolerance, inspired at least in part by the deep personal antagonism that existed between the two. Michele, a Carbonarist during his student days at the University of Pisa, had been involved in the abortive revolutions of 1830. On 14 March 1831 he was arrested, then kept in prison for a month, and finally banished for a year to Volterra, where he met and married Giosuè's mother. Thereafter he led a nomadic existence, settling at last in the wilds of Tuscany's Maremma. Giosuè was born in 1835. Through these vicissitudes Michele scarcely managed to provide his family with an adequate living from an ever dwindling medical practice. The poet later remembered that his father developed an unconquerable persecution complex; and the wine bottle became his only refuge from a fate that had condemned him "to live in one of the most obscure villages in the Maremma."[3] Unending frustration and a vivid sense of failure turned him into a brooding misanthrope. Impotent in the world, Michele became an overbearing tyrant at home, and before long he and his high-spirited son were engaging almost routinely in ugly domestic scenes. The most devastating of these occurred one night after Giosuè's Latin lessons with his father had gone rather badly. The young boy returned home to find his pet hawk strangled. When this show of patriarchal displeasure failed to have the desired effect, a wolf cub that Giosuè had been keeping was sold.[4] The heartbroken scholar eventually memorized his declensions, but he never forgave his father—or, by association, it seems, Manzoni and Foscolo.

In opposition to these Romantic Moderns, the teenaged Carducci ostentatiously harked back to the Classic Ancients. Homer, Virgil, Horace, and Cicero made the most gifted of the Moderns look inept and confused, he asserted. Goethe had expressed the matter to perfection: "Classicism is health, Romanticism is disease." Here was a faith that Carducci would never abjure, and in 1853 he added a political corollary to Goethe's axiom: "I am one of those who believe that the romantics are traitors to the country."[5] In other words, Italian patriots had to take their bearings from the country's ancient past, which was purely Italian, not from "the accursed and infamous century in which we were born," not from contemporary Italy which was "disgraceful, stupid, drunken, base, small, womanly . . . and anything but Italian."[6]

Personal pique alone would not account for the young poet's development in the 1850s, but these powerful psychological factors help explain Carducci's inspired response to Giuseppe Mazzini's call for a

Third Rome. In keeping with the mental atmosphere of mid-nineteenth-century Italian cultural life, with its dense Mazzinianism, Carducci's earliest verses—those written while he was a student in Pisa and Florence—reflect his obsession with the idea of Rome. *Rime di San Miniato* appeared in 1857. Carducci wrote a polemical introduction to this book in which he rejected modern poetry in favor of the classics and condemned "poetry that was Christian, popular, intimate, social, humanitarian, cosmopolitan and universal."[7] His publisher withheld the introduction, and it remained hidden from public view for many years; but the twenty-five sonnets and thirteen songs of *Rime* left no doubt about Carducci's contempt for Manzoni's esthetic mixture of romanticism and Christianity, a formula that had dominated Italian literature for more than thirty years. The enemy would never change. In his youth and in his dotage, Carducci always blamed the Church for the decadence of Italian society and for the softness of the Italian national character. Italy had taken a disastrously wrong turn in ancient times when she exchanged "virile paganism and patriotism" for passive Christianity and universalism.[8] As a young man the poet resolved not only to celebrate Italy's Roman past, but to make the Italians so nostalgic for it that they would settle for nothing less than a new Rome, the Rome envisioned by Giuseppe Mazzini.

This youthful enthusiasm for "classical things" appeared at first to be an academic affectation. Carducci and his student friends in Florence—Giuseppe Torquato Gargani, Giuseppe Chiarini, and Enrico Nencioni—established literary clubs, such as "Gli amici di Firenze" and "Gli amici pedanti," in which they discussed esthetic questions and shared a common faith in the ideal of Rome. However, the extinguishing shadow of war fell across these activities. The Second War

of the Risorgimento broke out in April 1859, just as
Carducci and the "pedants" were launching a literary
journal, *Il poliziano*, which they devoted to an exposi-
tion of their cherished classical principles; but the
guns of Magenta and Solferino killed their enterprise.
After just six issues Carducci queried his readers,
"During the supreme moments in which the people
of Italy must ask themselves whether or not they are
Italian, who can write of philosophy or who wants to
read articles on philology?" [9]

The momentous hour had struck for Italy. Influenced decisively by the Third Rome rhetoric of
Mazzini, who for thirty years had labored indefati-
gably to ignite a revolutionary explosion in the country, Carducci's circle now joyously waited for the
wages of that heroic labor to be paid. They were confident as Mazzini was confident. The diplomatic
machinations of Cavour and of Louis Napoleon—the
contemporary incarnations of Mazzini's ancient antagonist, Prince Metternich—would be sufficient to
initiate the revolutionary process, but not to contain it.
Events proved Mazzini right, up to a point. After the
Villafranca armistice, Cavour did lose control of the
war, and, despite appearances to the contrary, he never
fully regained it. The 1859 plebiscites in central Italy
and the expedition of Garibaldi's Thousand to Sicily
in May 1860 threw the prime minister's elaborate diplomatic strategy into confusion. Mazzini's dream of
social revolution now became Cavour's nightmare.
But the specter passed quickly. Ironically, the republicans themselves played the crucial role in its passing.
First, Garibaldi "surrendered" his southern conquests
to Vittorio Emanuele II; then, in a melancholy moment, Francesco Crispi turned the phrase which served
as a rationalization for the massive desertion of moderate republicans from Mazzini's standard: "The
monarchy unites us, the republic divides us." This

from a much-loved apostle of the master. Bitter, disillusioned, and increasingly isolated even on the republican left, Mazzini retired again into exile. In his
youth he had been prince Solomon singing the song
of Israel, but in the winter of his discontented life he
became the prophet Hosea, spewing forth curses and
evil auguries: "I have seen an horrible thing in the
house of Israel: there is the whoredom of Ephraim,
Israel is defiled."

Carducci was one of the moderates, and not only in
1861. While some of his friends among the *pedanti*
went off to war in 1859, he stayed home, working on
critical editions of Politian and Petrarch for the Barbèra publishing house. Early in 1860 he married Elvira Menicucci. Then, in November of that year he
took up his duties as a professor of literature at the
University of Bologna, where he would teach until
1904. Of shot and shell during the Second War of
Liberation, Carducci knew nothing. Later he described
the years 1859 to 1861 as time spent "in tranquil and
anonymous solitude amidst my studies and my family."[10] Marriage undoubtedly steadied Carducci. He
had suffered a tragic loss in 1857 when his brother,
Dante, committed suicide. In the following year his
father also died, apparently of grief. After these events
Carducci withdrew from the world into a vale of his
own melancholy. Elvira terminated that withdrawal,
and then the Bologna appointment gave him a fresh
start in a new career.[11]

Among the poet's many biographers, Papini has
been the loudest in lamenting that Carducci was proof
against "the mad passion of adventure that made
other poets leave behind far more than a wife or a
lectern."[12] Writing in 1918, Papini had before him the
example of D'Annunzio's participation in World War
I. On the other hand, few of Carducci's contemporaries
found anything odd in his decision to take a wife and

sit out the war in the quiet of his study. The civic re-
sponsibilities of poets have changed a good deal in the
twentieth century. Yet Carducci often expressed mis-
givings about his conduct during the war, and there
was an element of psychic compensation in his poetry
of the 1860s. How he wanted to be the Italian Aeschy-
lus, fighting at his country's Marathon, "but you
know," he wrote to his friend Torquato Gargani, a
poet who did fight, "of the great and noble things
fortune has granted me only the sentiment."[13] Unquestionably, he could take comfort in the knowledge
that Italy required his services as a live poet, rather
than as a dead soldier. After all, Alfieri was right
when he remarked, "To say lofty things loftily is in
great part to do them."[14] Carducci could agree that
his conduct was prudent, understandable, and respectable; but it was not heroic. All the more reason, then,
for the unmobilized poet to sing the praises of the
fighting heroes who "died beautifully amidst arms
and songs / for sacred liberty." Their achievement was
sacred, and Carducci envisioned his part as a singer of
hymns to "il valor latino."[15]

The dominant note in this poetry was Carducci's
appeal to nostalgia. "The Poet of the Third Rome"
proclaimed 1860 a year of heroes and gods aglow with
pride of race and country, but their ideals did not long
survive the political consummation of the Risorgimento. In the poems eventually collected in *Levia
gravia* (1868) and in *Giambi ed epodi* (1871) Carducci, drawing inspiration from the political poetry
of Auguste Barbier in *Iambes* and of Victor Hugo in
Chatiments, bewailed the impotence and confusion of
Italy's governments. The House of Savoy itself embodied Italy's tragedy during the 1860s. Had not Vittorio Emanuele proclaimed the end of the age of
poetry while announcing the age of prose? Had not
his government, led by that soulless bureaucrat Ca-

vour, contaminated the country's most sublime ideals with the base cession of Nice and Savoy at Plombières? The betrayals, the calumnies, the disasters of the post-Risorgimento decade all flowed through a straight channel from this primordial corruption. Mazzini had been horribly right about the Piedmontese after all, and Carducci did not delay in reverting to republican-ism.

If the pagan Carducci had been able to think about the Risorgimento as a morality play, then the Christ figure in the drama—the man crucified by a Sanhe-drin of Cavourian pharisees—would have been Gari-baldi, "the Hero of Two Continents." As it was, the poetry that he wrote about Aspromonte, Sarnico, and Mentana crackled with righteous indignation. Was it conceivable that an Italian government would un-leash a fratricidal attack on the country's bravest and most noble sons? The *garibaldini* were the flower of the nation; yet these upholders of the Risorgimento ideal were bloodily prevented from taking Rome by the king's army, in collusion with French and papal forces. Rome was the heart of Italy; without it, the country could not live. Carducci understood this need as Garibaldi did, according to the mystical insight of Mazzini. However, for Garibaldi, knowledge was only the spur to action; he acted on the truth, acted as an Italian hero should have. It was left for Carducci to consecrate the "beautiful gestures" of the "magnani-mous Rebel," described in poems like "Dopo Aspro-monte" as glorious aspirations toward the Ideal that were brought to grief by the craven ministers of the Piedmontese king.[16]

Sadly, the betrayals of Garibaldi merely foresha-dowed far greater calamities. Lacking an ideal, the Italian government was condemned to play an op-portunist's hand. With a political and diplomatic mastermind like Cavour in charge, Italy could expect to win some impressive triumphs in such a game, but after 1861 his successors as prime minister were at best time-serving mediocrities and at worst criminal incompetents. The stage was set for "the disgraces of 1866," when prime minister Alfonso Lamarmora, thinking that Italy might win the Trentino and the Veneto by adopting a bellicose policy, spurned Austria's offer for generous territorial concessions in the Veneto alone. Disastrous defeats at Lissa and Custoza followed instead. Thanks to the success of Italy's Prussian ally at Königgrätz, the Italians did receive Venice in Carducci's sarcastic phrase, "by gift of Napoleon III."[17] However, Lissa and Custoza broke the country's spirit, condemning the Italians "to return to the shadows, to despair forever."[18]

The conquest of Rome in 1870 might have restored the national honor, had the Italians acquitted themselves honorably. Alas, they had not. "Oh, the entry into Rome," Carducci recalled with undiminished bitterness in 1883. Clearly, the 20 September breach in the walls at Porta Pia was not the Roman victory for which all Italian patriots had yearned since 1860, and Carducci wrote accusingly, "The government of Italy went up the triumphal path as though it were the *santa scala*, on its knees with a rope around its neck, crossing its arms and shouting 'Excuse me—I cannot help doing this—they have shoved me from behind!' "[19] Carducci, a fierce anticlerical, fumed as the government worked slavishly to calm the rage of Pius IX while at the same time playing down the significance of *Roma capitale*. The Italians had a government of fear: the king's ministers were terrified lest the priests stir up the Catholic faithful, lest the French return. Carducci was sickened to think that the moment of magnificence had passed for the Italians. When the glorious mantle of imperial Rome settled on a united Italian nation, it should have been an occa-

sion for thanksgiving and celebration from the Alps
to the Straits of Messina. An age-old prophecy had
come to pass. The vision of Italy's *vati*, or poet-
prophets, from Dante to Alfieri was now an accomplished fact, but one accomplished in a manner so em-
barrassingly prosaic as to compel every sensitive and
thoughtful Italian patriot to hide his face in shame.[20]

Mazzini's death in 1872 gave Carducci an occasion
to denounce the new Italy in a public address. Carducci's romantic appearance, complete with long
wavy hair and flowing tie, belied his *gravitas* on the
afternoon of 12 March as he rose before a capacity
audience in Bologna's Teatro Communale to eulogize
the dead hero. Blessed with "the heart of Dante and
the thought of Gracchus," Mazzini had been the no-
blest Roman of them all. His *romanità* had been tested
in the fire of war and revolution for nearly five decades. Now he lay dead. "Mazzini dead?" Carducci
asked. "Is it possible that Mazzini is dead and that
Italy still lives?" Typical of prophets at other times in
history, he had been without honor in his own land;
but who could doubt Mazzini's greatness now? While
others had scoffed and jeered, he had commanded the
corpse of Italy to rise up and walk. The Risorgimento
was Mazzini's miracle, his gift to the nation that had
rejected him. Woe to the Italians, Carducci warned in
his peroration, for they had been found wanting:

> But this Italy that was born of transactions, this
> Italy that recognizes nothing but success, this Italy
> that adores accomplished facts, this Italy that has
> neither principles nor ideas nor thoughts, this Italy
> that lurches along day by day on expedients, this
> Italy that does not believe in anything, not even in
> itself, this Italy that is afraid of everything, this
> Italy whose history is the daily chronicle of thefts,
> this Italy that believes in nothing but gold, that has

no other ideal but material pleasures, this Italy that is governed by the Bank . . . this is not the Italy of Giuseppe Mazzini.[21]

If the ideal of Italy yet survived in the hearts and minds of a few patriots, the reality of "questa Italia" was a pathetic caricature of that ideal, thanks to "the thievish bastards among Italy's leaders." Carducci continued to believe in Italy as a spiritual model of past and potential perfection; it was the present that filled him with dread. The Italy of Dante and Mazzini remained inviolate, but Rattazzi and Depretis led a country that was "vile." It could not be otherwise, Carducci warned, when the principal characteristics of the country were "Machiavellianism in politics, Jesuitism in religion, and Arcadian academicism, as well as bourgeois practicality, in literature."[22]

Increasingly, Carducci sought escape from the invincible vulgarity of contemporary Italian life. In *Nuove poesie* (1873), for example, the personal, intimate, and confessional elements in his poetry predominated over the political preachments that the country had come to expect from him. Tragedies in his personal life had much to do with this change of emphasis. His mother and his son, Dante, died within the span of a few months in 1870. Moreover, his marriage had been in the best Italian tradition, respectable but without passion, and beginning in 1871 he became entangled in a tempestuous affair with Carolina Cristofori-Piva, the wife of a *garibaldino* officer.[23] Throughout most of the 1870s Carducci's heart belonged to "Lidia" of "Lunghi le tombe" and of "Avanti! Avanti!," love poems, published in *Nuove poesie*. This collection was the point of departure for Carducci's later poetry on the themes of nature, love, and history. His interest in politics remained keen, but it was no longer the sole, or even the most important impulse in his poetry.

By the 1870s, politics had become a painful subject for Carducci. The pain resulted from the tension in his mind about what he really believed. Everything had been so clear in 1860—"L'Italia avanti tutto, l'Italia soprattutto." But what did those words mean now? Perhaps his confusion had begun over the reception of "Inno a Satana," the poem which, more than any other, fixed his reputation as the *enfant terrible* of Italian literature. Although Carducci wrote the poem "really from the heart" in 1863, it was not published until 1865, and then only in a newspaper of secondary importance.[24] When "Inno a Satana" reappeared on 8 December 1869 in Bologna's *Il popolo*, it immediately became the subject of a spirited political debate. Carducci was no stranger to controversy. He had built an indestructible reputation as a radical, and not just of the parlor variety. He had put his ideals on the line, repeatedly risking dismissal from the University of Bologna and actually suffering three months' suspension without pay as a result of his bitter attacks against the government's treatment of Garibaldi. For a while the firebrand professor even resorted to a pseudonym, and it was under the name Enotrio Romano that he wrote "Inno a Satana." However, on this occasion the gadfly poet was shocked to find that the most severe criticism of his work came from the left, from the republican and democratic circles in which he had always felt most at home.

One of Carducci's closest friends and a fellow republican, Quirico Filopanti (whose real name was Giuseppe Barilli), led the attack. He assailed the "Hymn" as a snare and a delusion, replete with every heresy against the faith of the people: "It is anti-democratic in form, while the usage is hardly intelligible to those who have had a complete university education; the people will not understand one-tenth of it. It is even more antidemocratic in substance because it betrays rather than supports the people, glorifying as it does the principle of evil."[25] Then, with prophetic accuracy, Filopanti warned Carducci that to abandon Mazzini's principle of "God and People" would be the beginning of the end for his art: "You will become a reactionary or a dilettante. No other choice is possible."

Carducci responded to this unexpected criticism like a maddened bull. "Inno a Satana," he charged, was personal. It had nothing to do with politics, except that the central figure, Satan, embodied Carducci's moral protest against "the centralized and unitary despotism of Jehovah in the desert of creation. He [Satan] is defeated, but I am in sympathy with the vanquished."[26] Carducci's point was well made: Milton, not Baudelaire, had inspired him to write "Inno a Satana." Although he easily won the argument over the literary origins of his own poem, Carducci remained blind to the heart of the matter. He did not address himself to Filopanti's major criticism—that "Inno a Satana" was an intellectual orgy which, by implication, broadcast an antidemocratic message. Carducci was on the horns of a dilemma, between the conflicting forces of elitism and a Mazzinian faith in the people; but he did not yet know it.

Filopanti's prophecy concerning Carducci's drift toward reaction or dilettantism did not come to pass immediately, but the poet did move steadily toward the right. By degrees the Jacobin became a Girondin. Still, Carducci's attitude toward the monarchy remained far from friendly. In 1876 he accepted the republican candidacy for Parliament from the Collegio di Lugo. He won the election but did not take his seat because of a procedural technicality. More important, in 1878 he refused the prestigious Savoy Cross, with its munificent economic advantages. Clearly, his sympathies were still with the left.

By this time, though, Carducci's true feelings about the people stood in sharp contrast to the official platitudes he was compelled to observe as a Mazzinian republican. Already these two irreconcilable extremes had put him under unbearable mental stress. There was something grotesquely incongruous about a poet with a reputation for democratic and republican convictions who at the same time perceived in the *vil maggioranza* a mortal threat to everything most precious in Italian culture. In the 1860s only "Inno a Satana" suggested to any of Carducci's contemporaries that his radicalism contained the seeds of a reactionary political philosophy, but by the end of the 1870s the secret was out for all to see.

It is a commentary on the drastically changing political conditions in Italy during the last half of the nineteenth century that Carducci, ever a pagan patriot, began his public career as a writer of the radical left and ended it as a spokesman for extremely conservative principles. He never changed, but Italy did. With hindsight, we can now see that Carducci was always a profoundly conservative, even reactionary man, looking back to the social ideals of the eighteenth century rather than ahead to the twentieth. When the backward and provincial Italy of his youth began to assume some aspects of a modern industrial state, with all the problems of intensified class conflict, he became disenchanted and looked to the past with increasing nostalgia.

Again, Carducci's poetry of the 1870s provides the key to understanding his political evolution. Repelled by the deplorable conditions of contemporary Italy, he retreated further and further into the mists of history. The Risorgimento itself was now a subject excessively charged with emotion to be suitable for the kind of detached poetry he wanted to write. To his friend and later his biographer, Giuseppe Chiarini, he expressed at this time the desire to create "pure art." [27] In *Canzone di Legnano* (1878) he still wrote as the supremely patriotic poet; however, the inspiration for his patriotism no longer came from the recent past, as it had in the days of the Risorgimento, when he wrote paeans to Garibaldi, Mazzini, and the other leaders of those stirring times. Instead, the Italian heroes and traditions of the distant past were served up in a poetic confection reminiscent of Longfellow and the other Schoolroom Poets. Moreover, the shrillness and alarums of the earlier works were replaced by a sense of historical inevitability. In *Canzone di Legnano* Carducci wanted not to dispute the past, but to idealize it, "to render in a small way the sublime ideals of our race." [28] He had long fancied himself the *frusta*, or whip, of Italy; but with advancing age came maturity and a sense of propriety. A grandfather now, he was no longer really believable as an *enfant terrible*.

If a single event stands out as a watershed in Carducci's political life, it is the visit of King Umberto I and Queen Margherita to Bologna in November 1878. Vittorio Emanuele II had died in January, and in August the young royal pair set out on a goodwill tour of the country. They stood in dire need of good will at this particular moment, for the political position of the Savoys was more precarious than it had been in thirty years. With the old king dead, Duchess Maria Vittoria of Aosta busily promoted the ambitions of her own cadet branch of the Savoy family. At the same time, antimonarchist activity surged dramatically forward in republican, radical, socialist, and anarchist circles. The royal house had begun to lose its mystical and sacred appeal even in the lower orders of society. It was on this good will trip, for example, that in Naples an unemployed cook, Giovanni Passanante,

tried to stab the king, but succeeded only in wounding
the prime minister, Benedetto Cairoli. Even then, in
1878, it was obvious that Umberto himself could not
be counted upon to rehabilitate the family's political
fortunes. The king revealed only the slenderest talent
for leadership, and his lack of imagination, so typical
of his house, dismayed all who wished the monarchy
well. The people of Rome soon decided that they had
a *"capicione"* on their hands, and they mockingly derided him as "Umberto the Good, nothing but good." [29]

Margherita was the real star of the tour and of monarchical politics in Italy for the next fifty years. Italy
might have been dubious about its cold and inarticulate king, but from the first Margherita appeared to be
an enchanting throwback to the aristocracy's golden
age. Before long her popularity with the masses became an immense asset for the Savoys, particularly in
Naples and Sicily, where the Piedmontese monarchy
had been regarded as a foreign regime. Peasants began
to bless themselves at the mention of her name, and it
was a popular convention in Umbertian Italy that a
book-pressed daisy (*margherita* in Italian) meant
good luck. During the 1880s and 1890s thousands of
women read a weekly fashion magazine called *Margherita*, giving it unrivaled popularity among publications of its kind. In Rome the queen presided over a
circle of adoring court poets and intellectuals who
spread far and wide the certainly deceptive legend
of Margherita, *la regina colta*, a larger-than-life
nineteenth-century Elizabetta Gonzaga. This reactionary proclerical group, pining away for the vanished
beauties of a medieval social order, held up the queen
as a votive figure, a countersymbol to parliamentary,
progressive Italy, where education was ruining the
minds and democracy the hearts of the Italian people.
Nowhere in Europe was court etiquette so rigidly
maintained as in the Quirinale, and from this place

Margherita would give unstinting support to every
reactionary figure in Italian politics, from Crispi to
Mussolini.

In 1878 Margherita was twenty-seven and quite
beautiful, although as one memoir of the time has it
"she knew how to appear to be more beautiful than
she really was."[30] Carducci submitted to her charm
without a struggle. During their first meeting in Bologna the queen generously fed his insatiable vanity
and convinced him that she had committed all of
Nuove poesie to memory. On that November night he
wrote to his mistress, Lidia, about the queen's cultivated mind, her "simple elegance," her graciousness.
Overnight, it seems, Margherita became for Carducci
the personification of Goethe's meaning in *Faust*, that
"The Eternal Feminine/Lures to perfection." A few
years later Carducci wrote a memoir article, "Eterno femminino regale," recounting his meeting with
Queen Margherita; by then he was describing himself
as "Your Majesty's most obedient subject."

The republicans were incredulous: "A tribute to
the Queen written by Enotrio Romano?" They recalled
Quirico Filopanti's prophecy, but took small pleasure
in seeing his words come to pass. Carducci's relations
with many of his republican friends, long strained
over the "Inno a Satana" imbroglio, now disintegrated
completely. On 22 August 1880 he delivered a public
address in Venice's Teatro Malibran, declaring that
the left had to be consistent on the issue of popular
sovereignty: "But if popular sovereignty proclaims the
monarchy, who will not bow before the king?"[31] The
party tried to hold its poet, and in 1882 made a last
effort to extend the olive branch by offering him a republican candidacy for Parliament. He refused the
offer with the statement, "I do not feel accord with
any sect."[32] The republicans had lost him, he later
wrote, not so much because of a beguiling queen with

a memory for verse, but because "the small republican faction was threatening to ruin, to destroy the national unity that was and is the love, the faith, and the religion of my life."[33] In 1886, after accepting the liberal parliamentary candidacy for Pisa, he announced what everyone had known for a long time: "I do not hesitate to declare myself obedient to the Italian monarchy. The monarchy is today the legitimate depository of popular sovereignty."[34] Carducci lost the election, but he gained a king. For the rest of his life he defended the monarchy as Italy's only hope against the ills of modernity.

For Carducci, "modernity" was a word weighted with the most unpleasant connotations. In his mind's eye he saw the forces of modern society united in an unholy alliance against all the beautiful ideals to which cultivated men should be pledged. What troubled him most was the ugliness of modern Italy:

> Hideous buildings, the ugliest that the land of the Pantheon and of Orcagna's *loggia* has ever seen, grow and press in on us like so many nightmarish prisons. . . . It is a veritable pandemonium of apparitions, refugees from a horrible dream. . . .
>
> Oh, God! the reign of Italy ushered in the age of ugliness. Ugly are the caps and overcoats of the soldiers, ugly the state's coat of arms, ugly the postage stamps. There is about us a jaundice of ugliness.[35]

Ideals, Beauty, and Art were under attack from this Italy where the vulgar reign of "plebeian intemperance" soiled everything it touched. "*Volgarità!*" was Carducci's war cry. Vulgarity, he warned, had risen in Italy like an undulating tide: "It has invaded art, thought, politics, life—from the Palace of Finance in Rome vulgarity dominates, the only god."[36]

From the lower orders little could be expected, save

continued adherence to superstitious Catholicism or, worse, a call for socialist revolution. Carducci had a Mazzinian horror of Bakuninism and Marxism, the two variants of socialism which vied for the political allegiance of Italy's ideological left in the 1870s and 1880s. He painted these exponents of class warfare with the same brush, as "dolts of the piazza" and "drunken monkeys."

The bourgeoisie was better educated but still lacked any real "artistic heredity," still was deficient in the taste and training essential for an appreciation of Art. Carducci maintained that the rise of the bourgeoisie after 1860 completed the emasculation of Italian culture which had begun in the sixteenth century with the Spanish Domination and the Catholic Counter-Reformation. What was best in Italian Renaissance culture had been crushed under the combined weight of the Roman Curia and the soldiers of Charles V. Thus, Italy had entered the nineteenth century as a failed nation with a derivative culture. The Risorgimento promised revolution, but the post-Risorgimento denied that promise. Far from "resurging," Italian culture had been stillborn in 1860. By 1883 Italy was still incapable of producing an original culture, and Carducci wrote: "Today we are too French, too English, too German, too American; we are individualists, socialists, authoritarians—everything except Italians."[37] In other words, nearly twenty-five years after the Risorgimento the problem for Italy was still the problem of national identity. Italy had been made in 1860, but in 1883 where were the Italians?

By this time only the aristocracy seemed to offer any hope for national salvation. In 1878, as Carducci moved toward a formal renunciation of republicanism, he declared: "I am an aristocrat in art." How could he be anything else when art itself was " a thing sublimely and perfectly aristocratic"?[38] Carducci found his true political course via art, and he followed it to the end, into an alliance with the House of Savoy. Hence his politics of nostalgia were based on esthetic considerations. These notions were by no means original with Carducci. Indeed, an ideology of resentment was spreading among European intellectuals and artists in the last quarter of the nineteenth century as a reaction against what they perceived to be the distress of modern life. Gustave Flaubert in France and Paul de Lagarde in Germany, to mention two archetypal examples, advanced aristocratic conceptions of art. However, it was left for the next generation to develop some of the practical implications of their doctrine, mainly in the careers of Charles Maurras and Maurice Barrès for the French and Julius Langbehn and Arthur Moeller van den Bruck for the Germans. The same pattern unfolded in Italy. In a political sense, Carducci was the Italian Flaubert and Lagarde. First he articulated the political discontents of the intelligentsia in Italy, and then he served as an inspiration for younger esthetes like D'Annunzio, who successfully injected the politics of nostalgia into parliamentary life during the 1890s.

Carducci embraced the monarchy as a symbol of his esthetic elitism—but only as a symbol. The symbolic nature of his gesture was important, because it pointed toward a central fact of life in the right-wing intellectual politics of Umbertian Italy: i.e., the monarchy would play an indirect and even ambivalent role. Moreover, when the revolution of the radical right did occur, between 1924 and 1927, with the piecemeal establishment of the fascist dictatorship, the monarchy was conspicuous by its absence from the visible political scene. Certainly, Carducci thought well of the king, and he genuinely admired the queen. However, it is equally certain that he had a higher regard for

Crispi, the Sicilian Pentarch whose career gave some focus to Carducci's fuzzy and often contradictory political views.

It is always difficult to make confident judgments about why men do what they do, but Carducci seems to have had a persistent need to engage in hero worship. The failures and the frustrations that he experienced in relating to his father may have created a problem here. In any case, his entire political life was a restless search for a *pater patriae* who would conform to the ancient Roman ideals of perfect stewardship and sober discipline. Mazzini always held his ground as a paragon of disinterested patriotism for Carducci, but with changing conditions in Italian society Crispi, himself an ex-Mazzinian, seemed to offer the right mixture of change and tradition as an antidote to Depretis and to *trasformismo*, which the poet once described as an ugly word for an even uglier thing. With what cutting disdain did he pronounce the word "prosaic" in ridiculing the reputed good sense of Depretis.[39] On the other hand, for Crispi, eighteen years older than Carducci, no praise was too extravagant. Even after the debacle at Adua in 1896, which brought down Crispi's last ministry, Carducci proudly wrote :"I was, am, and will be unto death devoted to Francesco Crispi, because this statesman has the highest and strongest conception of Italian unity, which is the love, the faith, and the religion of my life."[40]

Born in 1819, Crispi early rebelled against the oppressive social and political institutions of his native Sicily. He began his political career as a Sicilian separatist in opposition to the Neapolitan Bourbons, but after the failure of the 1848 revolution separatism no longer appealed to him. A period of intense suffering followed as the exiled Crispi wandered through Europe, barely surviving on his earnings as a journalist and a translator of trashy French novels. Like so many

Italian exiles during those days, Crispi turned up in London; there he met Mazzini, whose visions of a Third Rome became the Sicilian's own. He worked tirelessly for the next ten years as Mazzini's most trusted agent. If anything, Crispi was even more of a republican than the master. It was Crispi who objected to the *guerra regia* when war between Piedmont and Austria erupted in 1859, and it was Crispi who maintained the deepest reservations about a motto which Mazzini himself urged on his followers in 1860: "L'Italia e Vittorio Emanuele."[41] Part of Crispi's resentment grew out of a bitter personal experience in 1853, when the Piedmontese government imprisoned him as a suspect in the Milan revolution. He never fully overcame his mistrust of the Savoys; and even during the expedition of the Thousand, in which he became known—pejoratively, to his enemies—as the "Cashier" for his logistical work, Crispi connived to checkmate Piedmontese ambitions in the South.

Crispi's attitudes toward the monarchy underwent a profound transformation in 1860, when it became obvious that the political necessities of Italian life made a republic impossible. At forty-one he had known hardly a respite from the harsh life of a revolutionary conspirator, and now there could be no question of returning again to those grim uncertainties. Crispi settled in Palermo and, inveterate journalist that he was, established a newspaper, *Il precursore*. On 6 January 1861 he made his change of heart public in an editorial: "Plots, demonstrations, insurrections are legitimate under a despotism, *but they are wrong in times of liberty*."[42]

The prospect of a legitimate political career now stretched pleasingly before him. Defeated in a parliamentary election for a seat representing Palermo, Crispi ran successfully in nearby Castelvetrano; on 18 February 1861 he entered Parliament as a member of the extreme left. There he began to lament vociferously the many failures of Italy's government, a complaint echoed and amplified from afar by the still-exiled Mazzini. For both men, Aspromonte struck as a thoroughly disillusioning experience; but whereas Mazzini called for revolution against the Piedmontese "usurper," Crispi called for understanding. Frayed and besmirched though the standard of Piedmont might be, it remained "the only flag that can be raised over all of Italy." This was the true sense of Crispi's famous remark, "The monarchy unites us, the republic divides us." For the good of Italy, all patriots had to be monarchists, no matter what their private disappointments might be. The king, for better or for worse, was the only "power of cohesion" in the country.[43]

Mazzini struck back at his erstwhile disciple with charges of "deserter" and "traitor," but Crispi defended himself with his usual energy. In a pamphlet published on 18 March 1865, Crispi maintained, "We are no longer talking about a republic or a monarchy, but of national survival—to be or not to be."[44] It had been an honor for him to be a follower of Mazzini; however, to remain a Mazzinian could only mean withdrawal from the main arena of Italian political life. The country lay writhing in a frightful mess. Austria and France wanted to see Italian unity undone, Crispi believed, while at the same time the government faced the most grave financial and political crises. How were these mortal threats to be overcome if bitter factionalism persisted? The preservation of unity had to take precedence over all other considerations, including the political abstractions of Mazzini.[45] This, incidentally, was why Crispi welcomed the war of 1866 with Austria. Yes, Italy could reasonably expect to gain the unredeemed lands from Austria; but, more than that, "Italy has need of a baptism by blood." There, in his mind, at least, lay the real advantages of a foreign war; it would augment the strength of national unity and sharpen the definition of national character. Thirty years later Crispi would still be thinking along these lines, in his fruitless search for glory on the field of Adua.

There can be no doubt that Carducci followed Crispi through every twist and turn of his political career. This primary loyalty provides a rarely failing insight into the seeming contradictions of Carduccian politics. With nearly every shift in Crispi's ideology from 1860 to 1895, a similar shift occurred in Carducci's thinking as well. Crispi, a radical Mazzini republican during the Risorgimento, accepted the monarchy immediately afterward as the only feasible alternative to a fatal civil war; and Carducci, while formally remaining a republican, concurred in that judgment. During the 1860s Crispi remained loyal to the monarchy, though he became increasingly restive over the government's performance, particularly after Aspromonte and Mentana. Carducci had an identical apprehension and wrote *Giambi ed epodi* to articulate his discontent. With the fall of the right in 1876, Crispi found a brand-new career opening up before him; he became, by turns, a minister in the Depretis government, a left-wing opponent to Depretis as a member of the *Pentarchia*, and finally, Depretis's successor as prime minister. Through all of these events, Carducci admired Crispi to a degree that fell just short of fanaticism.

The two men became friends through their mutual contacts in the country's Masonic lodges, where anticlericalism functioned as a bond of unity in an otherwise badly divided organization.[46] The power struggles between and within the lodges had nothing to do with dogma or class, for virtually all Masons were liberal and middle class. Rather, the point at issue invariably involved personal political loyalties. In the years following the Risorgimento, the national political ambitions of men like Crispi found a parallel in Masonic politics.[47] Since nearly all of Italy's principal political leaders were Masons, these divisions in the lodges reflected the factionalism that characterized Italian national politics, and, to hear Carducci tell it, he supported Crispi in every great political and Masonic battle of the day. In either arena, Carducci was always Crispi's man.

He was his own man in poetry, though. If his politics were derivative, his art was supremely original, or so it seemed to his contemporaries. It is interesting to recall that his Nobel Prize citation read "not only in consideration of his deep learning and critical research, but above all as a tribute to the creative energy, freshness of style, and lyrical force which characterize his poetic masterpieces."[48] The committee's praise notwithstanding, Carducci's genius escapes us. His poetry is a byword for the provincial quality of Italian literature in the waning years of the nineteenth century. It is unlikely that such poetry will stage a comeback in the foreseeable future. Carducci belongs to his age, but not to the ages. He spoke so directly to his own time and people that his literature, as literature, appears dated to us; indeed, even his contemporaries outside Italy thought him an old-fashioned writer. By 1906 the Nobel had already been awarded five times, and apparently it was Italy's turn. What makes Carducci a compelling figure to us now is the very strength of his local appeal in the 1880s and 1890s: the poetry, as history, is our best source of information for understanding the politics of nostalgia in *fin de siècle* Italy.

Although Carducci exerted a pervasive influence on Umbertian culture after 1881, it is a little surprising to learn that, until then, his reputation had been comparatively modest. *Nuove poesie*, for example, had been published in 1873 by subscription only among his friends and admirers in an edition of just a few hundred copies. *Odi barbare*, the collection for which he was most renowned in the nineteenth century, became his first work to enjoy even modest commercial success. Three small editions were published from 1877 to 1880, with Carducci making changes in the book each time. It was his masterpiece, and Benedetto Croce later declared that with *Odi barbare* Carducci clearly established himself as Italy's premier poet.[49] However, firsthand knowledge of his work did not transcend a relatively small circle of readers. As his disciple, Luigi Lodi, explained many years later: "The rude multitude knew only one thing about him, that he had written poetry for the Devil."[50] Outside Italy he enjoyed more popularity than any other Italian poet of the day, but in Italy itself several other poets, notably Felice Cavallotti and Giovanni Prati, had greater popular followings during the 1870s.

In 1881, when Carducci was forty-six and at the height of his creative powers, he decided to change publishers, hoping to acquire the large readership that a great writer deserved. Carducci had, by his own definition, fallen between two stools. He was not performing either function of a writer of genius: writing for an elect group of initiates, as Baudelaire had done; or reaching a large public, in the manner of Homer and Dante. Carducci had acquitted himself too well as a writer's writer, for success on that level had won him enough popularity by 1881 to make him a poet of some prominence. He was just visible enough, he complained, to be a perfect mediocrity. A large part of the problem lay with his primary publisher, Zanichelli of Bologna, who was honest but unenterprising. In a letter to the sculptor Adriano Cecioni, Carducci wrote on 19 February 1881, "From Zanichelli you get nothing but glory, which is worse than annoying."[51] At this moment Angelo Sommaruga came into Carducci's life. Perhaps the brash young publisher from Milan—the one people were already calling "the American"—could market his poetry more successfully. In the same letter, Carducci advised the sculptor to submit any writing he might do to Sommaruga, because the new publishing house in Rome would at least offer the prospect of "a little profit for you." It seems reasonable to conclude that Carducci was entertaining no less a hope for his own work, and, by acting on that hope, he changed the course of Italian literature for the next five years.

CHAPTER TWO

THE MAKING OF A

PUBLISHER IN UMBERTIAN

ITALY: ANGELO SOMMARUGA

(1857–1941)

"Carducci was our god . . .
and we were his strength."
—Angelo Sommaruga

F ollowing the collapse of his editorial empire
in 1885, Angelo Sommaruga, then twenty-
seven, passed the rest of his long life in exile,
mostly in Latin America and France, finally
returning to Italy to die in 1941. As Rome's most emi-
nent publisher from 1881 to 1885, Sommaruga
brought forth more than 130 books, and his newspaper-
journal holdings included five titles. Then disaster
struck. The Depretis government, long the object of
vilification in one of Sommaruga's newspapers, retaliated by shutting down the entire house and bringing
the publisher himself to trial. Within a few months all
was lost, and a banished Sommaruga took up his trav-
els, first to Paris and then to London, where he waited, vainly hoping that the Depretis government would
fall. Depretis had a knack approaching genius for dis-
appointing men imbued with that hope. Death finally
claimed the prime minister in the summer of 1887,
but by that time Sommaruga had long since taken up
residence in Argentina, where a new publishing career and, ultimately, new disappointments awaited

him. In 1893 Italian newspapers were filled with reports of his bankruptcy in Buenos Aires,[1] and for the
next fifteen years he disappeared almost completely
from view.

Sommaruga was destined to be haunted by failure
—a destiny which gradually wore him down and produced in his mind an invincible cynicism. That was
clearly his mood on a spring day in 1910 when C. G.
Sarti, a reporter for Rome's *Tribuna*, encountered him
in Paris where the former publisher operated an antique furniture business, purchasing merchandise in
the French capital and then selling it in Buenos Aires.
The ensuing interview, most of which took place at a
sidewalk cafe, was Sommaruga's idea. Sarti had approached him earlier, requesting an interview, but
Sommaruga refused with a curt, "My friend, I do not
have time."[2] Then, on 27 March, an article by Diego
Angeli had appeared in *Il giornale d'Italia*, claiming
that Sommaruga had been "dead for some years."
That would have been insult enough, but Angeli also
referred to Sommaruga as an "equivocal Lombard
businessman" and an "affarista."[3] The piece enraged
Sommaruga. In 1885, the year of his trial by the government, he had vowed to divorce himself utterly from
the Italian publishing world. For twenty-five years he
had remained as good as his word, but the bilious Angeli article had torn open all the old wounds. The
anguish was more than Sommaruga could bear. "Ah,
this is too much," he hissed to Sarti. The time had
come for a new generation to hear the truth about the
Sommaruga period in Italian literature.[4]

"Now I am dead," Sommaruga told Sarti, "but
once . . ." Here his voice trailed off. Yes, Sommaruga
had his memories. To have been young in Rome at the
dawn of the Umbertian age was memory enough for
any man, but to have passed that golden time in the

company of Carducci, D'Annunzio, Matilde Serao,
Luigi Capuana, and the other *bizantini* amounted to
an experience of such richness and fulfillment that it
hardly mattered what came afterward. From these
glory years in the publishing business Sommaruga
preserved no souvenirs, no mementos, save the fifty-
odd letters that Carducci had written him from the
late 1870s to 1903. "Here I have found my greatest
solace," he confided to Sarti, after the two men had
left the bustle and clatter of the sidewalk café to continue their interview in Sommaruga's rooms in the
Montparnasse quarter, on rue Boisonnade.[5] A photo-
graph of Carducci, inscribed "to his dear little Angel,"
hung on a wall otherwise covered with contemporary
artworks.[6] "What difference does it make to me, after
all, that there are those who defame me, when these
letters prove that Carducci always thought highly of
me until his last years, always regarded me with
benevolence."[7]

Indeed, Carducci's friendship was the essential precondition of the young man's success in Rome during
the early 1880s, but his career as a publisher had
begun several years earlier, in Sardinia. The son of a
Milanese merchant, Sommaruga left Milan in 1876,
at the age of eighteen, to take a job in Cagliari with a
mining company. Tall, thin, and with a complexion of
almost spectral sallowness, Sommaruga made an immediate impression in the Sardinian capital. The
young northerner was already a man of affairs, full of
schemes and stratagems on how to make his fortune.
The mining company job was a small matter, and it
absorbed only a fraction of what some contemporaries
remembered as Sommaruga's "demonic" energy. Soon
after his arrival he began to look for something else to
do. However, Cagliari was no Milan. Business opportunities were not as plentiful there as on the mainland.
Nevertheless, in Sommaruga's case boredom became

the mother of invention, and the provincial torpor of life in Cagliari forced him, he later wrote, "to distract myself from daily labor and to put moments of idleness to use."[8] It was in this mood that, on 27 February 1876, Sommaruga launched a literary journal called *La farfalla*.

As a business decision, *La farfalla* seemed to make no sense at all. Sommaruga himself was not an intellectual, and even his friends thought him a man of little culture. Lacking a taste for literature, what could have possessed him to strike out in this direction? Actually, Sommaruga transformed an apparent disadvantage into a real asset. Because he lacked a driving literary ambition, he was free to deal with writers purely as a businessman. That this would prove to be a source of prosperity for Sommaruga did not occur to his contemporaries. Although a common enough practice now, most Italians then perceived the commercial distribution of literature in the cultural marketplace as a shocking departure from traditional practice. Sommaruga had no point of view in *La farfalla*, no esthetic doctrine, save whatever would sell magazines. When Luigi Lodi, a prominent newspaperman and editor of the Umbertian period, claimed that Sommaruga had wrought a publishing revolution, this is what he meant: that *La farfalla* "was perhaps the first attempt to apply literature to commerce, to produce a literary periodical with the idea of procuring the greatest number of customers and subscribers."[9] If the idea was not new, certainly the open admission of it as a *raison d'être* was.

Sommaruga was one of those rare individuals who discover very early in life their greatest talent and how to exploit it. He enjoyed remarkable success with *La farfalla*. The young editor wheedled and cajoled several mainland and Sicilian writers into contributing stories, poems, and articles: Francesco Giarelli from

Milan, Cesario Testa (Papiliunculus) from Rome, Enrico Onufrio and Girolamo Ragusa Moleti from Palermo. The literature was very uneven, but Sommaruga cared less for erudition or style than for lively and spicy writing. *La farfalla* soon acquired a reputation as "a literary dish seasoned with the piquant sauce of erotic poetry"—a public image which did wonders for the subscription rate.[10]

Inspired by his success, Sommaruga moved back to the mainland in 1877, and on 30 September the hitherto irregularly published *Farfalla* of Cagliari became the weekly *Farfalla* of Milan. There he enjoyed an even greater success than before in attracting major Italian writers to *La farfalla*—Felice Cavallotti, Giosuè Carducci, and Lorenzo Stecchetti—as sales climbed to 4,000 copies per issue.

At the same time, Sommaruga drew the remnants of the once-powerful *scapigliatura* movement into the service of the journal. For a while the picturesque and disheveled *scapigliati* poets even used the Milan offices of *La farfalla* as their headquarters, but Sommaruga had arrived on the literary scene too late to take effective advantage of the *scapigliatura*. Cletto Arrighi's influential novel, *La scapigliatura e il 6 febbraio*, appeared in 1861, giving rise in northern Italian literature to what became known as the *scapigliatura* fashion.[11] The essential characteristics of this fashion lay in a Murgerian celebration of *la vie de bohème* and a corresponding rejection of middle-class morality. More talented *scapigliati* writers emerged after Arrighi, notably Emilio Praga (1839–75), Iginio Ugo Tarchetti (1841–69), Arrigo Boito (1842–1918), Giovanni Camerana (1845–1905), and Carlo Dossi (1849–1910).[12] Despite a passion for romantic individualism, they functioned for several years as a fairly cohesive group, meeting often to talk about literature in the subsequently famous Osteria della Noce and the Caffè Martini. Located in what was then suburban Milan, these restaurants subsequently acquired a legendary glow as the cradles of *scapigliatura* theorizing.

The books of the *scapigliati* enjoyed a wild notoriety from the mid-1860s to the early 1870s, and the career of Praga, who is the most famous of these writers today, sheds much light on the causes of the movement's reputation for shocking bourgeois sensibilities. The critics adored Praga's first two books, *Tavolozza* (1862) and *Penombre* (1864), and he immediately became the darling of Milan's literary society. A fatal decline set in not long thereafter, although the quality of the poetry in *Fiabe e leggende* (1867) and *Trasparenze* (1868) remained higher than anything the other *scapigliati* would produce. His fall was a depressing variation on a monotonous theme in modern literary history: Praga became the prisoner, and then the sacrificial victim, of his own successful image. Glorifying sickness, physical exhaustion, delirium, alcohol, sexual excess, and death, Praga began to live his hallucinations and to act out his fantasies. Whatever his shortcomings, the young man was tragically sincere. At thirty he was a desperate physical wreck, suffering from malnutrition and nervous exhaustion. He died of alcoholism at thirty-six. Praga has been called "the Italian Rimbaud," but in his boozy gutter death he more nearly resembled a Milanese precursor of Alfred Jarry.

Early death was typical in the group; so was loss of creative inspiration. Tarchetti had not yet reached his twenty-ninth birthday when he died. Camerana, though an antique by *scapigliati* standards, ended his days as a suicide. Others stopped writing early. The most bountifully talented of the group, Carlo Dossi, wrote virtually nothing after forty. Boito, following an impressive start in poetry with *Ré Orso* (1864), survives in the public memory as Verdi's librettist for

Otello and *Falstaff*—an occupation which, in Umbertian Italy, carried about the same status as that of a television series writer today.

Through Praga, who was a painter as well as a poet, *scapigliati* esthetic ideals entered the world of art; and through Boito, the composer of *Mefistofele* (1868), they entered the world of music.[13] Still, the *scapigliatura* remained essentially a literary phenomenon; and on the whole the *scapigliati* writers may be said to have translated mid-nineteenth-century French literature, principally the books of Baudelaire, Gérard de Nerval, Alfred de Musset, Théophile Gautier, and Rimbaud—and, through them Poe—into the Italian idiom.

The theories of these imitation French bohemians were a minor consideration in Sommaruga's mind. The young publisher had a greater interest in the public image of the *scapigliatura* as a decadent movement, for he quickly observed that decadence made good copy. However, he suffered the misfortune of hitching his wagon to the *scapigliatura* star just as it began to fade. Always recklessly audacious, he simultaneously launched two other publications, the *Brougham* and the *Rivista paglierina*. Both were complete failures and brought his fortunes low. In 1879, financial necessity compelled him to relinquish his interest in *La farfalla* and to accept a job with his old company in Sardinia.

A born gambler, Sommaruga always played his hunches. On the way back to Sardinia, he decided on impulse to visit Bologna in the hope of meeting Carducci, then forty-four and impatient for the national recognition he felt was his due. Doubtless, the side trip to Bologna was connected with a latent ambition to establish another literary journal, but in his memoirs Sommaruga wrote simply, "I wanted to know Carducci."[14] Whatever his original objectives, the meeting between the two men was a turning point in both of their lives, as well as in the history of Italian literature during the 1880s.

Sommaruga remained in the city for some weeks, talking with Carducci and with members of the poet's circle: Camillo Alvisi, Severino Ferrari, Giovanni Pascoli, and Luigi Lodi. He made a favorable impression on them all, especially on Carducci, who became his friend for life. Sommaruga appeared not just as another disciple in the religion of art; his talent belonged to an entirely different order. He was brash, but Carducci liked brash young men. He was a dreamer, but Carducci became fascinated by his dreams, particularly the one in which the right kind of publisher would rescue Italy's greatest poet from society's long neglect. For the moment, it was all talk over wine. Still, the ardent youth spoke so well and so earnestly on the business of publishing that perhaps something would come of it one day. Only time would tell, but meanwhile he had Carducci's blessing and moral support. When at last Sommaruga resumed his journey to Sardinia, he had a completely new outlook. His desire to meet Carducci had been gratified, but this gratification had inspired yet another yearning: to work with the poet, to publish him, and in so doing to make himself rich and famous.

Sommaruga stayed on in Sardinia for two more years, until 1881, all the while dreaming his dreams and working on the intractable problems of finance. It was easy to dream, and he wrote long letters to Carducci and the others in Bologna about his vision of the Casa Editrice Sommaruga. The flagship in his proposed publishing venture would be a literary journal, and the scene of his operations would be Rome. To Carducci he confided that his ambition was "to make Rome the most important literary center in Italy, the meeting place of various literary and artistic tenden-

cies."[15] Carducci and his friends encouraged Sommaruga and promised him their help. Writing in Carducci's name, Luigi Lodi explained to Sommaruga: "He
is very happy that you are going to Rome in order to
establish a publishing house, so happy that he will as-
sist you as much as he can, and you know that is very
much."[16] The maestro himself wrote to Sommaruga
on 24 June 1880: "If you break the ice and become a
publisher in Rome, we will arrange something."[17] His
immediate problems of finance being what they were,
Sommaruga would have preferred the "something" to
have an immediately realizable cash value; but, as
things turned out, Carducci's name alone was worth
more to him than a bank loan in any amount. Within
a year he was in Rome with enough material and letters of introduction from Carducci to get the *Cronaca
bizantina* off the ground, on a flight that would carry
him to the pinnacle of the Italian publishing world.

Roma caput mundi—once described by Metternich
as "a splendid theater, but with terrible actors"—was
now the capital of a united Italy. Sommaruga arrived
in Rome at a time when the city was bursting through
its medieval shell. Vast changes had already occurred;
vaster ones still were being contemplated. The city's
architectural transformation was only the outward
manifestation of profound social changes; and Sommaruga's arrival itself stands out as a representative example of this process. Certainly the Roman literary
renaissance of the 1880s, spearheaded by his publishing house, would have been impossible without prior
social change. Therefore, it becomes necessary to describe the social structure of the city Sommaruga had
come to conquer.

The decisive date in the modern history of Rome is
20 September 1870, when the battle of Porta Pia, won
by the army of King Vittorio Emanuele II against the

overwhelmingly outnumbered papal troops, brought the Risorgimento to a successful close.[18] At one stroke, the victory realized the age-old dream of Rome as the capital of a united Italy. From a strictly military point of view, however, Porta Pia hardly qualified as a serious engagement. The pope's soldiers put up only a token defense of the city, and casualties were light. Destruction of property was minimal.

The real battle of Rome began following the arrival of the new Italian government, when the city underwent a rapid and radical transformation. Adequate housing and office facilities had to be built for the thousands of incoming government and military personnel who, with added thousands of dependents, descended on the capital after 1870. Although for centuries Rome had been the temporary place of residence for religious pilgrims and grand tourists, the Piedmontese invasion was unlike anything the Romans had seen before. The housing shortage immediately became critical: the government calculated that 40,180 rooms would be required for state employees by mid-1871, but the mayor of Rome responded that only 500 would be available.[19] Shortages of office space and government buildings were even more severe. The ameliorative effects of emergency measures were only temporary. A law of 3 February 1871 provided for the expropriation of some convents, and soon afterward the government bought the Palazzo Montecitorio for the use of Parliament. Nevertheless, from the outset it was clear that a massive construction program would have to be undertaken.

The price of this program was high, both financially and esthetically, since it involved the virtual destruction of old Rome. Most of the magnificent suburban villas went first—the Patrizi, the Sciarra, the Massimo, the Lucernari, the Miraflori, the Wolkonsky, the Giustiniani, the Torlonia, the Campana, the San Faustino—and then their beautiful vineyards were hacked down as a period of febrile building speculation began. The city adopted a master plan in 1873, but it remained a dead letter while developers transformed much of what had been most lovely about old Rome into whole neighborhoods of urban blight. It was the first frightful age of *sventramenti*. The *fin de siècle* esthetes later looked back in horror at these disembowelings, shaking their heads sorrowfully at the new plaster "imitation Renaissance" façades, but even worse were the crowded rows of unsanitary apartment blocks that the façades concealed.

The boom created thousands of jobs and hundreds of speculative opportunities for the city's new immigrants. It also caused land prices and building costs to rise sharply, thereby creating an inflationary spiral that brought ruin to many banking houses, contracting companies, and private investors. Nevertheless, the boom continued by fits and starts throughout the 1870s and 1880s, as periods of breakneck construction alternated with periods of relative stagnation. At no time during these years did building activity halt, and even in the worst recessions, of which there were several, the city's physical transformation was only slowed, not stopped.

The Romans changed along with their city. At the top of the old, rigidly structured social pyramid stood the high clergy and the Roman aristocracy. No one questioned the prerogatives of these two groups, who shared rather than fought for power, and who profited from Rome's position as the spiritual capital of the Catholic world. The long-established noble families, like the Colonna and the Orsini, had produced many popes; and the popes had, in their turn, created many princes. Antagonism between the Church and the thirty or so families inscribed in the Golden Book of the Patriciate had long since become a historical impossibility. A small middle class of tradesmen and professional people flourished in papal Rome as well. The Church, the aristocratic families, and the ever-present tourists provided the service-oriented middle class with a secure livelihood. Social distinctions between the *borghesia ricca* and the *borghesia minuta* were scrupulously observed, reflecting the snobbishness that permeated Roman society. An impoverished agricultural and urban proletariat lived in and around the city, but Church alms relieved the worst miseries of these poor. With the one exception of 1848, the *popolo minuto* was content to keep things in Rome as they were; and Roman apathy toward the Risorgimento from 1859 to 1870 scandalized all patriotic Italians.[20]

Porta Pia, or rather the political and economic consequences of Porta Pia, quickly put an end to these traditional social relationships. The arrival of the new inhabitants, the *buzzuri* (government administrators, military officers, and businessmen from the north) and the *cafoni* (laborers, office-seekers, and adventurers from the south), added new elements to the Roman population. In a short time they became the city's dominant elements. Rome, a city of 226,000 at the end of 1870, had a population of 244,484 on 31 December 1871 and 282,214 on 31 December 1877.[21] By 1881 there were over 300,000 people in the city, and the wave of immigrants showed no sign of ebbing.

The massive influx of newcomers to Rome after 1870 created an unprecedented publishing market in the city. Prior to 1870, two publications met the principal newspaper needs of the Romans: *Il giornale di Roma*, the official sheet of the pontifical government; and *L'osservatore romano*, edited by the godson of Pius IX, Augusto Baviera. Perhaps nothing in the city changed as much after Porta Pia as the practice of journalism. Edoardo Arbib arrived in Rome on the heels of General Cadorna's Italian soldiers and immediately began to publish the *Gazzetta del popolo*, a moderately liberal newspaper which shortly afterward changed its name to *La libertà*. More radical and anti-clerical was Raffaele Sonzogno's *La capitale*, the second newspaper to appear after Porta Pia. Many others came and went in rapid succession during the 1870s. *Il tempo*, *Il tribuno*, *Il miglioramento*, *Il colosseo*, *Il campodoglio*, *L'aquila romana*, *L'eco del tevere*, *Roma libera*, *20 Settembre*, and *Il pungolo* were some of the more memorable titles to appear in the boom-and-bust atmosphere of the decade.

Only a few newspapers became important publications, for illiteracy weighted the odds against the publishers in their struggle for survival. Statistics are a cold and uncertain means of portraying the tragedy of Italian illiteracy, but the most conservative estimates indicate that, in 1861, 78 percent of Italy's total population was illiterate. By 1871 the figure had declined slightly, to 72 percent, and by 1881 to 62 percent. However, on this issue as on so many others, the North and South were worlds apart. Such progress toward literacy as Italy achieved from 1861 to 1881 took place almost exclusively in the North. For instance, in 1871, when the figure for national illiteracy stood at 72 percent, the figure for the South was 90 percent. In Calabria, a relatively progressive southern province, 79 percent of all males over six and 94 percent of all females the same age could not read.[22]

The appalling consequences of illiteracy severely hampered the development of a national press in the post-Risorgimento period. Still, Rome was not Calabria; the problem of illiteracy was much less serious for Romans than for Calabrians or other southern peoples. In fact, relative to *all* the other Italian states before the Risorgimento, the pontifical government had a highly commendable record in the area of popular

education. There were more literate people in Rome
than in most other regions of Italy at the time of unification.[23] The problems facing the new breed of publishers in Rome came from a quite different source:
the absence of a Roman journalistic tradition diminished the potential readership that any publisher
might aspire to capture. Rome was a city of churches,
not of coffee houses and reading rooms. The *dolce far
niente* attitudes of native Romans, whatever their level
of cultivation, was the bane of all publishers who tried
to crack the city's tough market. Hence, in the absence
of a Roman newspaper-reading tradition, the new publications had to rely for support on immigrants, primarily the *buzzuri*, i.e., that middle-class segment of
government officialdom and businessmen who could,
and would, read.

Newspapers with close ties to the government might
hope for success. This solution was hit upon by Giacomo Dina, whose *Opinione*, founded on 9 August
1871, soon became the city's most respected political
newspaper. It was never a popular sheet, but Dina's
connections with influential political leaders, especially Giovanni Lanza and Quintino Sella, marked him as
a man of consequence. People read *L'opinione* to find
out which way the wind was blowing from Montecitorio. Indeed, rare were the newspapers that survived
without some kind of political affiliation; almost from
the beginning of *Roma capitale*, they functioned as the
mouthpieces of political factions. In such an environ-
ment, experience as a journalist became almost indispensable for a political career; the presence of so many
former journalists at the highest levels of Italian public life during the Umbertian period resulted from this
fact. Although politics and journalism united in a
marriage of convenience, the relationship was not a
caprice of Italy's historic evolution; rather, it was an
inevitable outcome in a society where journalism

could not survive on an independent course. To make up for a crucial deficiency in readership, Italian newspapers had to find financial support elsewhere. These conditions became accentuated in Rome. The government, its lobbying supplicants, and the crowd of political factions opposed to it all moved into the vacuum and imbued Roman journalism with an obsessively political quality.[24]

Another kind of newspaper managed to survive in the rough-and-tumble world of Roman publishing during the late 1870s. This was the Sunday literary newspaper, the prototype of which, *Il fanfulla della domenica*, Ferdinando Martini founded in 1879.[25] For years Martini had written very popular articles on literature for the daily *Fanfulla*, leading Ernesto Obleight, the newspaper's publisher, to finance a Sunday literary supplement on an experimental basis. The experiment succeeded brilliantly, and within three years *Il fanfulla della domenica* was selling 23,000 copies per week.[26] As usual in the literary world, success prompted imitators, and before long many of the major Roman dailies were putting out Sunday supplements.

Inspired by Martini's major breakthrough, Luigi Arnaldo Vassallo established *Il capitan fracassa*. In 1878 Vassallo had collaborated in the founding of the still extant *Messaggero*, but two years later, financed by a small syndicate of bankers, he decided to strike out in a completely new direction. Martini's success gave him his clue—but why not combine the *Fanfulla della domenica* and the *Fanfulla* into one daily newspaper? This was the question Vassallo posed to his backers in the *Capitan fracassa* enterprise. He hoped with this newspaper both to provide journalistic commentary on the events of the day, and to publish creative literary pieces along with articles on criticism. In its literary ambitions *Fracassa* became commercially

popular and historically significant, for, although its
reportorial corps was staffed by some of the best newspapermen of the day—Giustino Ferri, Ugo Fleres, Ernesto Mezzabotta, and Aristide Morini—they were
eclipsed in the public eye by the paper's literary contributors, who formed a galaxy of the country's most
scintillating talent. Matilde Serao, Gabriele D'Annunzio, Edoardo Scarfoglio, Edmondo De Amicis, Enrico
Onufrio, E. Navarro della Miraglia, and Cesare Pascarella either began to build their national reputations
in the pages of *Fracassa*, or used the publication to add
new luster to fame already won.

The successes of Martini and Vassallo gave Sommaruga two possible models for his own publishing designs, and he visited both men shortly after his arrival
in Rome. Martini was pleased to see him; indeed, the
young man could not have come more highly recommended. On 29 May 1881 Carducci had written to the
editor of *Il fanfulla della domenica*: "I present Signor
Angelo Sommaruga to you . . . who has nothing less
than the burning ambition to take away all of your
collaborators and you yourself."[27] Carducci wrote this
in jest—but, as things turned out, his letter was stun-
ningly prophetic.

In another part of town, Sommaruga's reception
was less jovial. He sought out Vassallo in *Il capitan
fracassa*'s editorial offices, modestly situated above the
Morteo beer hall on via del Corso. Carducci had not
smoothed his way here. Only Sommaruga's reputation
had preceded him in this place, and Vassallo did not
like what he had heard or read. He remembered *La
farfalla* as "an embattled sheet whose collaborators
pretended to be in a bitter and most ferocious struggle
against nonexistent adversaries, against imaginary
classicists, against invisible romantics, against impal-
pable Philistines."[28] On the whole, it had not been a
very edifying performance. This recollection plus one

look at Sommaruga's "mongoloid eyes" and "very pro-
truding teeth," convinced Vassallo that the man could
not be trusted. He later even claimed to have said to
Sommaruga in the *Fracassa* offices, "Do you know that
you have the look of a criminal?" While Sommaruga
may have laughed at this, we can be sure that, at the
same time, he drew the measure of his man.

On 15 June 1881 the first issue of the *Cronaca bizantina* appeared. We know now that the journal was
funded on a shoestring, and that Sommaruga never
had adequate financial backing for this publication,
let alone for the large publishing house that he eventually put together.[29] He did it all with mirrors: a little capital, a lot of publicity, no small amount of publishing genius—this was his formula. In the end, it
did not work. Sommaruga was a twentieth-century
public relations man trapped in the nineteenth century; worse, trapped in a city suspended between its
medieval past and its unknown future. In 1881 the
publisher bet heavily on the jackpot possibilities of the
future, but in the long run no amount of individual
force or talent could counteract the backward-looking
tendencies of the writers he sought to manage.

Sommaruga embodied the entrepreneurial spirit
that had seized Rome in the midst of the building
boom. He also embodied another development that
had long been in progress across western Europe: the
commercialization of literature. As the traditional
aristocratic sponsor class for writers and artists disappeared, the old system of patronage was replaced by
a new system that reflected changing economic realities.[30] Some vestiges of the past remained. The salon
and the *cénacle* did not die out completely, and in
some ways they flourished as never before. Moreover,
in Ludwig II of Bavaria, Wagner had a royal patron
in the traditional grand manner. Nevertheless, vastly

more important in the nineteenth-century organization of intellectual and artistic activity was the decisive appearance of the mass public in cultural life. Holland in the seventeenth century, England in the eighteenth, and France in the age of Louis Philippe pointed the way toward the future for high culture. Most writers and artists no longer worked in a tradition of cultural continuity, as art and literature increasingly became subjected to the conditions of the marketplace. The change was not uniformly beneficent for the artists and writers themselves. The triumph of laissez-faire capitalism opened up new possibilities of expression for them, but they lost in security what they gained in freedom. The marketplace could be cruel, and the miserable fate of Rembrandt symbolized for artists the plight of genius neglected by an uncomprehending society of Philistines. Thus was the myth of Bohemia born.

Despite his reputation, Sommaruga was not Prometheus bringing the flame of commerce to Italian literature. Numerous other literary entrepreneurs had preceded him in the search for great profits. In 1871, for example, Baldassare Avanzini bought a one-third share of *Fanfulla* for 300 lire. Several years later, after the paper had been transferred from Florence to Rome, he sold his share for 80,000 lire.[31] Such a windfall was highly unusual in the publishing business—as it still is, even in wealthy and literate countries. Yet the dream was realized in Italy just often enough to keep men hoping. Sommaruga arrived in Rome full of optimism. More important, he arrived with ideas on how to merchandise literature, and with the energy to execute them. He had a design for a literary empire, and in the process of building it he carried the revolution in publishing far beyond anything achieved by his predecessors or competitors. In 1881 the transition between the old book printer and the modern publisher was only partially completed. Because he thought of himself as a businessman and an investment gambler, better able than others to sense the demands of the marketplace and to judge bestseller possibilities, Sommaruga was in a position to complete that historic transition in the Italian publishing industry.

The first issue of the *Cronaca bizantina* was a masterpiece of public relations. All the up-and-coming young writers of the day were listed on the first page as collaborators. Not all of the names are remembered today. Indeed, most *bizantini* were forgotten after the 1880s. However, a few, like Matilde Serao and Gabriele D'Annunzio, could look back to the *Bizantina* as the springtime of their long and fruitful careers. How did Sommaruga attract the young stars of the Roman literary world into his orbit? The first page of the journal's maiden issue provides the answer: Carducci. On the masthead appeared a Carducci strophe from "Per Vincenzo Caldesi" in *Giambi ed epodi*: "Italy the unready called for Rome/ Byzantium they have given her." A poem by Carducci, "Ragioni metriche," was featured in the center of the page, against the background of a red oval medallion. The rhetoric of the editorials was vintage Carducci. "Art is the only sacred mission," the *Cronaca bizantina* proclaimed; a little farther down in the same column, readers learned that "the soul of art is a horror of the common."[32]

Sommaruga understood that Carducci would be the key to the *Bizantina*'s success. The poet's collaboration exerted a magnetic force, attracting the younger generation of writers then beginning their public careers, especially those dissatisfied with humdrum bourgeois society. The staff members of the *Bizantina* were united in their admiration of Carducci:

> We love Giosuè Carducci. Because his word
> warms us, and his brilliant eyes make us tremble.

Because his verse ... is worthy of Aristophanes. ...
Because Rome when it hosts Carducci is more
Roman and Italy more Italian. Because the poet of
Italy is there. Because his smile is sweet and his
heart is great. That is why we love Giosuè Carducci;
we who are lost, we who are without genius, but
uncorrupted and believers still in the Ideal.[33]

So much adulation at first pleased Carducci, but after
a short time he confessed to Sommaruga that perhaps
the *bizantini* "love me a little too much." [34]

Sommaruga employed novel advertising techniques
to exploit this love. One of his favorite gambits was
the front-page "Declaration." On 30 September 1881
he announced:

The best of all possible news!
    Beginning with the next number, our readers—
male and female (and why not? these last have
plenty of spirit!) will always find in the *Cronaca*'s
place of honor a number of lines by GIOSUE CAR-
DUCCI.
    Enough said? [35]

As events proved, it was. The *Cronaca bizantina* did
not become an overnight sensation, but by early 1882
sales had reached 8,000 copies per number. One year
later the journal passed the 12,000 mark. By comparison, a rival publication, Giuseppe Chiarini's *Domenica
alla fracassa*, limped along with less than 6,000.[36]
Many years later Chiarini complained that this difference was due entirely to Carducci's massive support of
the *Cronaca bizantina*.[37]

In the beginning, Carducci struggled against such
an extensive commitment. He responded to Sommaruga's bogus declaration in a letter of 24 February
1882:

And now that the *Confessioni e battaglie* are finished, how will you maintain your promise to the
readers of the *Bizantina* that one of my pieces will
appear in every number? How can I write [so
many] articles and poems per year? That would be
too much even for the readers. I will try to accommodate you for a little while. I will prepare a sonnet, another short poem, and I will finish a translation of Heine's *Don Chisciotte*. But then? [38]

However, Sommaruga never relaxed his pressure on
Carducci, and the poet nearly always reacted by sending a poem or article for each bimonthly issue of the
Cronaca bizantina. Indeed, he ended up giving Sommaruga nearly his entire literary output from 1881 to
1885, including twenty-three poems, twenty-one articles, all of the *Confessioni e battaglie, Conversazioni
critiche*, and *Ça ira*. As Sarti racily explained in 1910
for the readers of *La tribuna*, "the publisher was insatiable and the poet untiring." [39]

"Carducci was our god . . . and we were his
strength," the momentarily nostalgic Sommaruga
confided to Sarti toward the end of their café interview. Sarti was enchanted. In a light moment he
asked, "Have you ever thought of making a comeback
in the publishing business?" The question brought
Sommaruga back to earth:

Sommaruga: "It wouldn't be worth it, believe me."
Sarti: "And why not?"
Sommaruga: "But don't you know that you must
   sell 3,000 copies of a book in order to make 1,000
   lire?"
Sarti: "Well?"
Sommaruga: "Well, if you buy here [in Paris] a
   piece of antique furniture at the public auction,

you can sell it in America fifteen days later and earn the same amount."[40]

With regret, the crestfallen Sarti informed his readers: "The man who has these ideas was responsible for making Carducci popular and D'Annunzio known. What a shame!"

Actually, Sommaruga's ideas had not changed between 1881 and 1910. The same vaulting ambition to seize the main chance had led him into publishing, and then out of it, eventually into the antique furniture business. Sommaruga always prided himself on being a man of affairs. As a publisher, he was adept at spotting writers with popular appeal, at cajoling them to create a product, and at marketing that product efficiently. Profit and power were his objectives; to attain them, he fully indulged his vivid imagination for the sensational. That imagination was to be his undoing in the end. Nevertheless, in building the Casa Editrice Sommaruga into a "gigantic publicity machine," he injected the element of modernity into the Italian publishing industry.[41]

CHAPTER THREE

THE RISE OF THE SOMMARUGA

PUBLISHING HOUSE: *LA CRONACA*

BIZANTINA AND THE *BIZANTINI*,

1881–1882

*"In the name we have taken there is, for those who
know how to read, a protest and an augury—we call
ourselves* bizantini *to forget the disjunction between
reality and our ideal, which is Rome."*
—Giulio Salvadori

I n 1941, when Sommaruga was eighty-four years
old and close to death, he described the "most
precious ideal" of the *Cronaca bizantina* as "the
union of what was most youthful, most healthy
and progressive in Italy in one great bond (*fascio*),
under one glorious flag, to draw from the chest of the
strong and secure the cry of victory—*Avanti!*"[1] Was
this the hazy recollection of a sick old man trying to
ingratiate himself with the fascist regime? Not at all:
these words were taken from one of his 1882 editorials.
The *Cronaca bizantina* is today remembered for its
naughty verse, its light, bantering, and frivolous tone;
but it is worth repeating that the very name of the
journal was inspired by Carducci's lines, "Italy the
unready asked for Rome/ Byzantium they have given
her." The patriots of the Risorgimento had dreamed of
creating Italy in the Mazzinian image of ancient
Rome, but the political leaders of the post-Risorgimento had only succeeded in building a new Byzantium.

Poetry had given way to prose, virtue to corruption, health to decay. This was the steady drumbeat in Italy's politics of nostalgia during the 1880s and 1890s.

The *Cronaca bizantina* began as hardly more than a showcase for the poetry and prose of Carducci. The period 1881–85 was one of political drift for him, but some of the most important milestones in his peregrination toward extreme conservatism appeared in Sommaruga's journal, most notably "Eterno femminino regale" and excerpts from *Confessioni e battaglie*. From an extreme position on the Mazzinian left, Carducci had retreated steadily toward the right, and now he hovered on the point of officially embracing the monarchy. Italy had disappointed him. The Italians had disappointed him. The burden of Italy's history, with its inquisitions and foreign invasions, had been too much for the Italian people. It might be that, in the end, only a dictatorship would suffice to keep this fractious nation whole. Carducci wrote in *Confessioni e battaglie*: "To me a dictatorship certainly does not seem so abominable as the gates of hell, but I would like to see it composed of the just and the strong."[2] However, the final note in his confessions was one of fear: "I am afraid that among a people like ours neither republics nor monarchies will be founded; I am afraid that instead we have what we deserve, Machiavelli Depretis and Tacitus Chauvet; I am afraid that in the future we will have someone even worse."[3]

Carducci's feeling of missed opportunity and his premonition that the drama of the Risorgimento, so auspiciously begun, would end in far greater tragedies than those that already had befallen the country were widely shared by members of the new literary generation which was beginning to emerge publicly around 1880. They hailed the *Odi barbare* as the masterpiece of the age, and its author spoke to them as "the only living consecrated glory" in an otherwise "petty" and "filthy" Italy.[4] In his name they genuflected before two ideals: the "religion of art," and the "superior man." The political implication of these ideals was reactionary; and, like the master, the disciples gazed upon modern Italy, the hated Italy of prose, in revulsion and despair. They harked back nostalgically to the Risorgimento, and, for them, Carducci was the keeper of that sacred memory.

It is difficult, but not impossible, to speak of a cohesive *bizantina* program. The major difficulty arises out of Sommaruga's notorious *reclame*. His sensational packaging of the *Cronaca bizantina*, with erotic illustrations, highly suggestive verse, and unprecedented high-pressure sales techniques, seems to support the claim of historians like Croce that the Casa Sommaruga degenerated into "something frivolous or scarcely serious."[5] Sommaruga's boldness in these matters became legendary, but even he thought of the *reclame* as mere seasoning for the stew, not the stew itself. The men and the women of the *Bizantina* had their idea, which they got from Carducci; it is this idea which makes the journal a historical signpost in the politics of nostalgia.

Who were the *bizantini?* Only a few contributors achieved lasting fame. Indeed, most of them, never far from the margins of Italian literary life, quickly disappeared from view with the collapse of the *Cronaca bizantina*. Names like Domenico Milelli, Emma Ivon, and Contessa Lara, so popular once, are now footnotes in history. On the other hand, D'Annunzio, Capuana, Verga, Pascoli, and Boito achieved lasting fame. Dozens of writers contributed to the *Cronaca bizantina* during its four-year history, and they wrote on a bewildering variety of subjects. Not every poem was a tribute to Carducci, and not every article dealt with the politics of nostalgia. In fact, most *Bizantina* pieces had nothing to do with either subject. Why, then, do we say that the *Cronaca bizantina* was Carduccian, that it appeared as an early expression of the politics of nostalgia? These questions raise still others. How can we measure the meaning of a journal or its influence? Even insofar as the historian can hope to be scientific, the last question is an imponderable; but the meaning of a journal, its central point of view, may be found in the writings of its major regular contributors. The major regular contributors to the *Cronaca bizantina* were Cesario Testa, Gabriele D'Annunzio, Edoardo Scarfoglio, and Giulio Salvadori. These four writers exerted an especially powerful influence because they, unlike Carducci, lived in Rome and became directly involved in the day-to-day planning and editing of the *Bizantina*. We must look now at the role each played as a member of the journal's "Roman staff."

Cesario Testa (1852–1922)

The most prolific of the *bizantini* was Cesario Testa. In his memoirs Sommaruga remembered him as "my right arm," and, indeed, under various pseudonyms (e.g., I. L'Angelo, Costantino Duca, and especially Papiliunculus), Testa contributed poetry, criticism, and articles of general interest to nearly every issue of the *Cronaca bizantina*.[6] In addition, he wrote "Ciò che si dice," the journal's gossip column which gained notoriety for its scandalous chitchat. His services to the *Cronaca bizantina* went far beyond these literary contributions, however. Although Testa never took the title of editor-in-chief, he acted in that capacity from the first, coordinating the activities of his younger fellow editors, D'Annunzio, Scarfoglio, Salvadori, and, of course, Sommaruga.

Short, slight, and extremely near-sighted, Testa grew up in Turin and early came under the influence of the *scapigliatura* theories that characterized literary circles in northern Italy during the 1860s and 1870s. The bohemian qualities of that literature left a permanent imprint on Testa's mind, and his reputation as a *refractaire* dates from this initial contact with the writings of the *scapigliati* poets. Their delight in baiting the bourgeoisie, particularly on the subject of religion, was highly contagious in Testa's case, and he remained a dogmatic atheist for the rest of his life.

Testa began his literary career in Turin as a journalist on the notorious anticlerical periodical *L'anticristo*. He signed these articles of his youth "Belial," and daringly denounced God as "an immense decrepit idiot." [7] Later in life, Testa translated the Latin verses of Pope Leo XIII; but, as he explained, it took an act of the will in conjunction with a love of Latin for him to undertake the project. By then (the 1890s) the flaming indignations of his youth had more or less subsided, although he always retained the mannerisms of a village atheist.

The *scapigliati* poets had appealed to Testa's antireligious biases through his imagination; Darwin appealed to them through his mind. The history of Darwinism in Italy is a fascinating though neglected topic. The key figure promoting Darwinian ideas among Italian thinkers was Roberto Ardigò, whose books and articles had an enormous impact on the minds of Italian university students and intellectuals during the 1870s. Testa had educated himself in the modes of Comte's positivism, but exposure to Spencerian ideas on social Darwinism through Ardigò's work gave the young poet a system. With Andrew Carnegie, Testa could say, after absorbing Darwinism, "At last, all is clear to me." His atheism now buttressed by the most advanced philosophical ideas of the day, Testa was prepared to express these views in something more demanding than the newspaper column.

He became acquainted with Sommaruga through the *Farfalla* enterprise in 1876. Testa's early poetry appeared in this journal, and Sommaruga oversaw the publishing of the poet's first book, *Primi ed ultimi versi* (1880). Sommaruga, still in Sardinia at this time, used his contacts with Tipografia del Commercio in Cagliari to get Testa's poetry published. A grateful author wrote the following inscription on the book's frontispiece: "To Angelo Sommaruga, My Friend." *Primi ed ultimi versi* was not a success, but the friendship was. When Sommaruga arrived in Rome, where Testa had been working as a minor government official, the poet unreservedly threw in his lot with the *Cronaca bizantina*.

Testa was the ideal man for an editorial job on the *Bizantina*. Though a published poet, a classicist, and a linguist, Testa put his own ambitions aside in the interest of promoting the journal. His loyalty to Sommaruga seems to have been primary at this time. Furthermore, Testa had two other qualities in his favor: first, he was a starry-eyed Carduccian, drawn to the maestro by a shared contempt for the Church and for religion; second, he had a clear view of his own limitations as a creative writer. Later, he described the *Cronaca bizantina* as "a masterpiece . . . whose material in prose and in verse (except for mine) was never surpassed for originality and innovation of enthusiasm and interest."[8] D'Annunzio, Scarfoglio, and Salvadori—all about ten years younger than Testa—were more origi-

nal writers, and he knew it. This knowledge made it
easier for him to play the role for which he was ideally
suited, that of coordinating editor.

Testa's personality cast a giant shadow across the
pages of the *Cronaca bizantina*. He wrote all of the
journal's program statements. The first (15 June
1881) was cited in Chapter II (see page 00). In a second program statement (1 January 1882), he described the *bizantina* faith in greater detail:

> . . . the truth—the grand and immutable truth; the
> truth that reposes in nature, that guides the instinct,
> that inspires human reason. This is what we want,
> this is the course that we are running in our tourna-
> ment of intelligence. For us, then, the new year does
> not signify a new life—as the old and vulgar adage
> has it. We will search to improve ourselves because
> thus has decreed the universal law of progress; to
> correct ourselves where we have erred, because we
> are not infallible and it is human to err; to harden
> ourselves because to win is the calling of the strong.

These were the sentiments and the language of social
Darwinism, a theme which combined perfectly in Testa's mind with atheistic anticlericalism.

Testa's own contributions to the *Cronaca bizantina*
were not always ferociously anticlerical or implacably
Darwinian. Much of his writing for the journal had a
playfully sophomoric tone. Actually, this is what the
Umbertian reading public wanted and expected from
him. When he attempted to become serious, the applause was noticeably less enthusiastic. Adept at con-
triving pleasant rhymes, Testa was out of his depth
the moment his overtures to the Muse became earnest.
The failure of *Primi ed ultimi versi* should have made
this clear to him; nevertheless, he went on producing
quantities of deplorable verse for the *Bizantina*. His

"Song of the Atheist" is representative of his efforts in this genre:

Nature is my book, my Bible
Woman is my angel
Science is my cult. Here is my heaven:
The Beautiful, the True and Love![9]

Noble sentiments perhaps—but expressed in verse which posterity only remembers for a laugh.

Testa's mind was of the mid-nineteenth-century positivist type so mercilessly satirized by Flaubert. He saw history moving inexorably toward a utopian destination. We no longer need religion, he often proclaimed, because we have a better, surer faith with which to replace it: Science. Darwin had shown the way in his *Origin of Species*; then Spencer in England and Ardigò in Italy had drawn the necessary social conclusions from scientific evolution. Men could now put away the things of children, and first to go should be the outmoded superstitions of Christianity. For Italians, this meant rejecting the papacy, an institution which Testa believed would better serve mankind "in a river or in a sewer."[10] What man of intelligence or sensibility could tolerate even for a moment the absurdities of Catholicism? Nothing saddened Testa more than the sight of a young boy on his way to one of Rome's multitudinous seminaries. His heart broke every time he saw these *pretini*, doomed as they all were to an unnatural life of celibacy and denial. The worst of it was that, in their own tormented frustration, they would grow up to impose the same twisted values on yet another generation of Italians. Precisely for this reason, Testa concluded, Italy did not possess "in their entirety, the fundamental qualities of the potent northern peoples, discipline, duty, and even character."[11]

What a bracing contrast to this "priestly cretinism" was young Gabriele D'Annunzio, in the eyes of his older colleague. Testa adored D'Annunzio, dedicating a number of his *Bizantina* poems to "the beautiful son of the sea." Here he found youth, beauty, talent, genius. D'Annunzio was more than the "Napoleon of Italian literature," as his admirers had begun to style the eighteen-year-old poet; he was, for Testa, the new Italy: "I, older and already tired, in you salute/our beautiful ideal." [12]

Gabriele D'Annunzio (1863–1938)

The youthful D'Annunzio arrived in Rome at the end of 1881, but his reputation had preceded him by more than a year. *Primo vere*, his first book of poems, appeared in the summer of 1879, when he was just sixteen. The volume was unabashedly Carduccian in tone, but even so unfriendly a critic as Benedetto Croce later remarked: "An adolescent Italian could not have removed himself from the influence of writers like Carducci, Stecchetti, Verga, and Capuana; and D'Annunzio did not remove himself [from that influence] in *Primo vere*. . . . But it is a notable work of assimilation." [13] A second edition of *Primo vere*, much changed from the first, appeared the following year, inspiring Giuseppe Chiarini's now-famous review, "A proposito di un nuovo poeta," in the 2 May 1880 issue of *Fanfulla della domenica*. It began: "My new poet is a young man of sixteen years, who is now finishing his secondary school studies in the Collegio Cicognini of Prato; his name is Gabriele D'Annunzio, and he is presenting the public with nothing less than an entire volume of *odi barbare*." [14] Coming from Chiarini, Carducci's best friend and most ardent supporter, this was extravagant praise. At one stroke he baptized D'Annunzio into the Carduccian faith and made him a prince in the hierarchy.[15]

Lonely, contentious, and homesick for his native Pescara, D'Annunzio had turned to poetry as an escape from the quiescence of boarding-school life. However, what had begun as a mere distraction soon turned into an all-consuming vocation, and the object of his enthusiasm was Carducci. In March 1879 the "vain and presumptuous boy" as D'Annunzio described himself, summoned the courage to write the maestro a letter, announcing his ambition "to fight by your side, o Poet!"[16] He expressed the same sentiments in a letter to Chiarini the following year. Both men were touched by the youth's impetuous enthusiasm and impressed by his precocious talent.

Chiarini's review of *Primo vere* was a spectacular breakthrough for D'Annunzio, who quickly followed up his success with another book, *In memoriam*, dedicated to his recently deceased grandmother. Disappointed by the inferior workmanship of this piece, Chiarini had no compunction about taking D'Annunzio to task in print. D'Annunzio, the critic reasoned, must not be lulled into a false sense of security, into thinking that talent alone would give him literary *carte blanche*. The *In memoriam* review was harsh, with none of the mitigating reservations that might have removed the sting from Chiarini's main critique: "After this, we say it frankly, it is to be doubted that D'Annunzio has the high conception of art without which it is impossible to raise oneself above the level of mediocrity."[17] This scathing criticism turned the poet's triumph of the previous year into ashes. Out of spite and wounded pride, he took his revenge by circulating the rumor that a young *Abruzzese* poet named Gabriele D'Annunzio had died tragically in a riding accident. When the newspapers picked up the story, D'Annunzio had his laugh. Just as a shocked and

grieving literary world grew accustomed to the calam-
itous loss of so young a bard, D'Annunzio merrily reappeared. The prank had the happy effect of giving
him enormous publicity at just the right moment. In
December 1880 the *Fanfulla della domenica* began to
publish his poetry on a regular basis. Already he was
a distinct national celebrity, if not yet a writer of national importance.

D'Annunzio's meteoric rise in the Roman literary
firmament was assisted by several influential artists
and writers from his home province in the Abruzzi.
Alerted by Chiarini's enthusiastic review of *Primo
vere*, they were already disposed to help him when he
arrived in the city. The painter Francesco Paolo Michetti took him up first and introduced the young man
to the *Abruzzesi* celebrities then residing in Rome.
The most famous of these were the sculptor Costantino
Barbella, the musician Francesco Paolo Tosti, and the
writer Edoardo Scarfoglio. D'Annunzio charmed them
all, and Scarfoglio remembered:

> . . . at the first sight of that curly-headed boy with
> the sweetly feminine eyes, I felt strangely struck.
> . . . Gabriele immediately appeared to us all as the
> incarnation of the ideal romantic poet: adolescent,
> courteous, handsome—nothing, in short, prevented
> him from representing for us the sublime youth
> hailed by every romantic writer from Chateau-
> briand to Victor Hugo. And with familiarity, our
> admiration for him grew. In the winter and spring
> of 1882, Gabriele was for all of us the chief subject
> of discussion, almost the object of an incredible cult.
> He was so meek and so affable and so modest, and
> supported the weight of his growing glory with
> such grace, that all ran to him in a spontaneous ac-
> tion of friendship, as to a sweet miracle that in the
> vulgarity of literary life one does not often find.[18]

Through his contacts in the *Abruzzese* circle, D'Annunzio met Sommaruga, and the poet rapidly became a star contributor to the *Cronaca bizantina*. D'Annunzio had come to Rome with thoughts of pursuing a law degree at the university, but that ambition was soon forgotten as one literary triumph followed another. Life in Umbertian Rome carried D'Annunzio along in a rush of excitement. To "Lalla" (Giselda Zucconi), the girl he had left behind in the provinces, he wrote: "Here in Rome all is a great ferment . . . of literary and political life. I have much to do from morning to night, I travel here and there, I listen to proposals, I give opinions, I discuss, I even fight alongside my small phalanx of friends and followers."[19]

Lalla herself was jettisoned early in the poet's swift ascent of Mount Parnassus. D'Annunzio left her and his provincial past behind, moving, on the strength of his poetry, into the loftiest social circles—as his marriage in 1883 to the noble Maria di Gallese attests. From 1882 to 1884 the bulk of his poetry appeared in the *Cronaca bizantina* and, later, in books issued by the Casa Editrice Sommaruga. Moreover, as time passed, D'Annunzio played an increasingly important role on the editorial staff of the journal. Although Carducci never lost his hold on the affections of the *bizantini*, by 1883 D'Annunzio was seen by many of his colleagues as the true embodiment of the *Bizantina*'s spirit. It is not difficult to understand why this gradual shift toward D'Annunzio occurred. Carducci's contributions to the journal came from distant Bologna, whereas D'Annunzio resided in Rome, helping to make the *Bizantina*'s policy decisions and acting as coeditor. Beyond that, Professor Carducci, a grandfather now, and increasingly drawn toward monarchist politics, was perhaps too old and too respectable to serve all the intellectual and artistic needs of the more ardent *bizantini*. The new generation of writers needed a new iconoclast, and D'Annunzio seemed to fit their requirements perfectly. Whereas Carducci was held in awe by the *bizantini* as the incarnation of what was best in the Italian past, D'Annunzio represented youth and the future.

Edoardo Scarfoglio (1860–1917)

When he wrote his first glowingly benevolent reviews of D'Annunzio's poetry, Scarfoglio was presiding as the unofficially acknowledged leader of the *scuola abruzzese*, a group of artists and writers from the Abruzzi who had settled in Rome around 1880. In that year Carabba di Lanciano published his first book, *Papaveri*, which the critics contemptuously dismissed as bad Carducci. "Ugly, even most ugly [*brutissimi*] verses" was the twentieth-century judgment of Pietro Pancrazi, who admired Scarfoglio the newspaperman and happily noted that Scarfoglio "the *poetino*" never uttered another serious note after the *Papaveri* disaster.[20] Like many a failed poet before and after him, Scarfoglio turned to criticism. By 1882 he had risen in those ranks to become the *Cronaca bizantina*'s chief literary critic.

A fervent Carduccian, Scarfoglio modeled his criticism and his own work after that of the master. Although criticism, like poetry, was only a passing phase in Scarfoglio's career, Carduccianism was not. In 1885 he formally gave up criticism in order to concentrate on political journalism, where he found his true voice. From 1885 until his death in 1917, Scarfoglio built a reputation as one of the outstanding newspapermen and editors of the period. If his forte in this field were politics, his faith was always and intransigently Crispian—that is to say, authoritarian, expansionist, imperialist, and antisocialist. More than Testa and much more than D'Annunzio in the 1880s, Scarfoglio took his Carduccianism whole, and that meant imbibing a strong dose of Crispi's politics. All of this was evident in Scarfoglio's earliest *Cronaca bizantina* writings. Moreover, there was hardly even a pause, much less a break, as he switched from criticism to political commentary. Here Carducci had shown him the way: literature was politics, and politics, literature.

In a series of *Cronaca bizantina* articles written from 1882 to 1884, Scarfoglio developed the argument that the health of Italian letters was linked to the political, economic, and social well-being of the Italian state. He professed to see some hopeful signs in the work of a few contemporary writers. The short story in particular had benefited from a renaissance, dating back to Treves's 1866 publication of Caterina Percato's tales of life in Friuli. New literary talent had come along continuously since then, and it was the pride of the *Cronaca bizantina* to publish the contemporary masters of the short story, principally Giovanni Verga, Luigi Capuana, and Matilde Serao. Still, Scarfoglio complained, the "problem of ignorance" continued to impede Italian literature in two ways. First, no present-day writer could boast the erudition of a Petrarch or a Boccaccio; this defect was, in itself, a measure of the past's superiority over the present. Second, the Italian reading public, what there was of it, suffered from the "most abysmal ignorance in the world." How else to explain Carducci's lack of popularity, except to admit that putting good books into the hands of Italians was like "casting pearls before swine"?[21]

Like Carducci, Scarfoglio regarded Italy with seeming ambivalence, for he appeared simultaneously to attack and to defend it. However, his attacks were inspired, *à la* Carducci, by what both men designated as the modern threat to the country's true traditions, i.e., to the Two Romes of Mazzinian rhetoric. The contrast between those heroic epochs in Italian history and the tawdry present was more than Scarfoglio could bear: "Are we not a people of clowns?" he asked in 1883:

> We do not understand anything anymore, we do not know how to do anything, we are like monkeys, without grace and without intelligence. We have art academies, which ignore even the most elementary principles of art, we have a government which supports literary congresses that are presided over by ignoramuses who know nothing of grammar . . .; we have a crowd of painters and art historians who only know how to lose themselves in arid academic discussions; we have a multitude of magazine writers who present to us as news the most absurd clichés . . . who deserve only the whip; we have a regiment of orators who put the public to sleep with their ridiculous declamations.[22]

The Third Rome and the people who lived in it were unworthy of their past. Mournful and dismayed by "the sad spectacle of Umbertian Italy," Scarfoglio turned from the present and cast a lingering look back to the country's *chanson de geste*, the Risorgimento. With Carducci he asked, Why are the Italians unworthy of their Risorgimento heritage? Why is there such a sickening disjunction between the promise of 1860 and the reality of 1883? And, with Carducci, he answered that ineffable grandeur had been followed by grotesque mediocrity for essentially historical reasons. In other words, the Risorgimento was, to use Croce's phrase about fascism, a parenthesis in Italian history. As Carducci had recognized, the source of the present Italian tragedy lay in the Counter-Reformation and in the period of Spanish domination. The middle of the sixteenth century was the great divide in Italian history, the cutoff point between the magnificent culture of the Renaissance and the country's collapsing fortunes down to modern times. The whole of Italian history after 1550 was but a melancholy postscript to the Golden Age. Beginning with the Catholic Counter-Reformation, "Italy was afflicted by the Spaniards, by the Holy See, and by the saddest curses that ever poisoned or embittered the spirit of a nation."[23] True Italian patriots had to get on with restoring the national character to its former state of exuberant health and sublime creativity. Only then would the Italians be able to throw off their cultural "vassalage" to the French.[24] Only then would the precondition for the realization of Mazzini's Third Rome vision be present.

Giulio Salvadori (1862–1928)

Unlike the other *bizantini maggiori* who had been drawn to Rome in hopes of launching their careers, Giulio Salvadori arrived in the city with his family at the age of twelve. Born on 14 September 1862 in Arezzo, Salvadori had graduated from a Roman *liceo* in 1880 and was enrolled as a student of literature at the university when, like D'Annunzio, he abandoned his original design in favor of a career in literary journalism. Even in his *liceo* days Salvadori had published some poetry. Characteristically for this entire generation of young Italian writers, he dedicated his best-known early piece, "A Gesù Cristo" (1879), to Carducci. There is a strong note of irony in the anticlerical paganism of his youthful writings: Salvadori eventually became a devout Roman Catholic, a teacher in Milan's Catholic University of the Sacred Heart, and, after his death, a candidate for beatification in the Church.[25]

In retrospect, the *Cronaca bizantina* chapter in his life struck Salvadori as a childish delusion, yet his seriousness of purpose was always beyond question. Even in his earliest youth he was a disciple in search of a faith. For a while he thought literature alone would be sufficient to all his needs; however, in 1883 he confided to his novelist friend, Antonio Fogazzaro,

> You live apart from militant literature . . . but if you knew what thorns are strewn along the way here where one feels more strongly the whirl of all the ambitions, of all the desires, of all the febrile life that destroys our generation. . . . I for my shame live right in the highest and fastest circle of the whirl, and also for my shame I have inside of myself a force which carries me higher against my will and makes me raise my eyes to still higher levels.[26]

With what relief did he finally surrender to Holy Mother Church in the lonely fastness of Ascoli-Piceno, following his separation from the *Cronaca bizantina* in 1884. Like St. Augustine, he seemed to arrive at the true faith as a result of succeeding disillusionments. Salvadori's moral earnestness led him restlessly on, from Parnassus to Science to Carducci to spiritualism and, finally, to Christ.[27] This was not the usual progression of the *bizantini*, but Salvadori was an unusual man.

Salvadori had come to Sommaruga for the same reason that had motivated his colleagues on the *Bizantina*. They all wrote for the various journals and literary newspapers then flourishing in the city, but from Sommaruga's initial appearance in Rome the *Bizantina* had stood out against its competitors because of Carducci's well-publicized collaboration. Carducci's name had a magnetic power, drawing all these young men into Sommaruga's service. This was of course less true for Testa, whose relations with Sommaruga went back to 1876 and had long since deepened into friendship; but even Papiliunculus revered Carduccianism as an article of faith. For the younger *bizantini* (D'Annunzio, Scarfoglio, and Salvadori), Carduccianism was religion itself. In their eyes, Sommaruga appeared to be just another publisher. He was younger and less stuffy than others of his breed, but a publisher and therefore an enemy nonetheless. Sommaruga did not make his way in Rome by offering more money to these writers; on the contrary, he occasionally paid for their sonnets in kind, with cookies and flowers.[28] Rather, he won them over by playing his only trump card—Carducci—with consummate skill.

To Carducci's call for the coming generation of Italians to complete the hallowed task of the Risorgimento by making Italy great and respected in the world, Salvadori responded with rapturous abandon. The challenge seemed aimed directly at him. D'Annunzio and Scarfoglio had similar feelings, and all three of these young writers used the *Cronaca bizantina* to work out the meaning of Carduccianism in their own lives. For D'Annunzio, Carducci embodied the celebration of pagan virtues. Scarfoglio explored the political implications of the master's work. Salvadori strove to understand the moral basis of the Carduccian protest. What, exactly, was the underlying significance of the *Bizantina* motto, "Italy the unready called for Rome / Byzantium they have given her"? A glance at Carducci's strophe on the masthead should have disposed of the critics' charge that the journal was merely a gossip sheet of scandal and nonsense. "In the name we have taken," Salvadori wrote, "there is, for those who know how to read, a protest and an augury—we call ourselves '*bizantini*' to forget the disjunction between reality and our ideal, which is Rome."[29] Here the *bizantini* thought they had pinpointed the Italian tragedy of modern times. "To the voice of Rome we are more deaf than ever," Salvadori lamented.[30] It was the lament of his generation.

Umbertian society was "putrid and vain."[31] Only Carducci remained pure. His poetry alone escaped the contagion of mediocrity, and mediocrity was the modern disease, especially in art. As an editor of the *Cronaca bizantina*, Salvadori defended the "ideal world of Carduccianism" with puritanical zeal; not for him the erotic poetry and suggestive *reclame* which Sommaruga employed to enlarge the readership. These things were, at best, necessary evils and, as time passed, unnecessary evils—to be avoided and condemned. The potential for conflict between Salvadori and Sommaruga was present from the beginning, because the poet wanted to launch a righteous crusade on behalf of his hero, whereas the publisher primarily cared about putting the *Cronaca bizantina* on a paying basis. Sommaruga was supple and swayed easily in the changing winds of literary fashion. Salvadori possessed very different character traits: he moved with extreme difficulty from the straight-and-narrow path that his conscience charted. Theirs was a confrontation between two classic personality types, the pragmatic opportunist and the true believer.[32]

Salvadori had a sparklingly clear idea of what the *Cronaca bizantina* should be: a mirror image of Carducci's poetry which was patriotic, inspirational, didactic, and beautiful: "It will be, I want to believe and hope, the first link in the chain of gold that will rejoin indissolubly art with life."[33] He grew increasingly restive as the inevitable hack writers, "glorifying this small bourgeois life" with their cheap and silly romanticism, began to infest the *Cronaca bizantina* offices.[34] These were the money-changers in the temple; to their doctrine, "art for art's sake," he responded, "Art for art's sake, it is said, but the subject matter must be *true*; art for art's sake, but the truth must be palpable."[35] Truth—that was the concern of art; and to the question, how can we know the truth, Salvadori answered by borrowing a leaf from the book of his colleague Cesario Testa:

> Now the concept of life, thanks to science, is re-established, healthy and entire. That which the Greeks felt naturally and the Italians of the Renaissance intuited, now, after long peregrinations, after innumerable disturbances in the human conscience, *it is known*. Because of modern science many risky hypotheses, many hazy syntheses, many conclusions deduced from insecure theories are falling or will fall. But the concept of life, which is the most glorious conquest of august science, will not fall. And from this concept derives or will derive, perhaps not the formula, but the new direction of art.[36]

In other words, the artist should not be "a sick dreamer"; instead, "we desire and we hope that he will be a man who lives, who knows how to live and who understands life in a healthy way."[37] A few years later the serious young man would be writing just as seriously about "the battle for Christian art" in *Canzoniere civile* (1889). However, in 1882–83 Salvadori was the perfect Carduccian acolyte, whose militancy made him an exemplar for the other *bizantini*.

Salvadori espoused an idea that Sommaruga had the good business sense to reject as the guiding editorial principle of the *Cronaca bizantina*. The publisher tried to strike a delicate balance on the question of Carduccianism, taking second place to no man in his admiration and respect for Carducci, but at the same time realizing that to turn the journal into a catechism of the true Carduccian faith would be too restrictive. It would have prevented him from achieving the grand objective of his strategy: to create a major publishing house engaged in the production of books, journals, and newspapers of all kinds. Sommaruga saw the *Cronaca bizantina* as only the initial stage in the execution of his total design. With this journal he hoped to establish his reputation as a reliable, efficient, and honest publisher. Above all, he wanted writers to know that, "in sending me their articles, they did not have to obey any program imposed by the editors, and that they did not run the risk of having to cut and modify this or that passage." Thus, Sommaruga concluded, "they were enticed into publishing their pages in a journal on which the most renowned authors in Italy collaborated, even if one of them professed ideas different from those of another."[38] The main thing in the publishing business was "to know how to sell." Sommaruga did not care to determine the ideological content of literature; rather, he hoped to reach the maximum sales potential of the material that the house agreed to publish. Although this was another of Sommaruga's ideas which his contemporaries put down as *"americanescamente strepitosa,"* it allowed him to build his publishing business on a much broader base than Salvadori's notions would have allowed.[39]

More than any of his writers, Sommaruga realized that the crucial question for the *Cronaca bizantina* would be economic. This knowledge enabled him— actually, forced him—to become a pioneer in the Italian publishing industry. The subsequent history of that industry has brought into high relief the paradox of Sommaruga's place among the *bizantini*. The literary idealists who guided the *Cronaca bizantina* barely tolerated, and eventually despised, the businessman-publisher; yet Sommaruga was the only true revolutionary on the *Bizantina* staff. Salvadori's vision of the journal as an "augury" came true in a way that he clearly did not wish—for Sommaruga's insistence on running the journal as a business operation, rather than as a *cénacle*, proved decisive in the publishing industry, although only in the long run.

The most important facts in the history of the Casa Editrice Sommaruga are these: the publisher began his career with little capital, and without backers. Others had started out with similar handicaps, but no Roman publisher had ever overcome them. Sommaruga did. He survived and flourished, by using his special relationship with Carducci to attract writers who became the *bizantini maggiori*. Next, he used his success with them as an entering wedge into the larger world of Italian literature and scholarship. The official Carduccians, holding forth in their favorite meeting place, the Caffè d'Aragno, dominated for a while, as the master's Bologna disciples (Lodi, Pascoli, and Alvisi) joined the swelling *Bizantina* staff of collaborators. Because of this repetitiveness, Sommaruga called for, and received, a balancing eclecticism. The young socialist from Milan, Filippo Turati, sent poetry. Soon Sommaruga made bigger catches. Giovanni Verga and Luigi Capuana, Italy's foremost realists, contributed short stories, and Verga's *Cavalleria rusticana* was first published in the *Cronaca bizantina*. Then came a spectacular coup: Emile Zola, perceiving the *Bizantina* as a vehicle of Italian naturalism, sent support and material from Paris. Success generated success. Matilde Serao, a disciple of Verga, became a regular contributor and established a national reputation under the pseudonym Riccardo Joanna, writing a satirical society column entitled "Salotti Romani." The eccentric vagabond writer Cesare Pascarella wrote Romanesque poetry for the *Bizantina* whenever he stayed in town long enough to collect his thoughts and attend to his Muse. Many others bustled in and out of the crowded *Bizantina* offices in the Palazzo Ruspoli on Via Due Macelli; so many, in fact, that Sommaruga felt obliged to take a larger suite of rooms on Via dell'Umiltà. The move was symbolic of yet another decision by the ambitious publisher: to expand his operations by proceeding with the second stage of his design for literary empire.

CHAPTER FOUR

THE SOMMARUGA PUBLISHING

HOUSE AT ITS ZENITH,

1882–1884

*"In argument I feel that I am always
a little of my opponent's opinion."*
—Ernest Renan (masthead quotation on *Nabab*)

The memoirs of Angelo Sommaruga, *Cronaca bizantina (1881–1885): noti e ricordi*, are filled with expressions of pained regret. In this book the story of his own fall is made to appear all the more tragic because of the heights he reached as Rome's foremost publisher in the early 1880s. While the *Cronaca bizantina* was not an overnight success, after six months it had the largest readership for any Italian journal of its kind. Moreover, with the first profits from that enterprise Sommaruga was able to begin publishing books. He launched this part of his career with what was, for him, considerable caution. He had acquired some experience in book publishing during the previous year, in connection with his efforts to get Testa's *Primi ed ultimi versi* accepted by Tipografia del Commercio of Cagliari. When the book proved a commercial failure, Sommaruga received a quick, painful lesson on how easy it was to lose money in publishing. Late in 1881 he published a small edition of G. O. Annichini's *Intermezzo*, and one of *Bozzetti sardi* by his old friend from *Farfalla* days, Ottone Baccaredda. Neither book created a stir in the Italian literary world. Sommaruga

apparently lost money on both ventures, and early in
1882 we hear of him publishing a book at the author's
expense.[1] With this foray into vanity publishing, Sommaruga momentarily touched the bottom of an otherwise brilliant if brief career.

A turning point in the early history of the Casa
Editrice Sommaruga came in 1882. Clearly, the writers were with him; Carducci had seen to that. In that
year alone Sommaruga published *Eterno femminino
regale* and *Confessioni e battaglie* by Carducci, *Canto
novo* and *Terra vergine* by D'Annunzio, an edition of
Cesare Pascarella's romanesque poetry, *Er morto de
campagna*, and a collection of Giacomo Leopardi's
poetry edited and introduced by Ruggiero Bonghi.
The next year was even better. First came new editions of D'Annunzio's previously published works. In
rapid succession Sommaruga published Luigi Capuana's *Storia fosca*, Matilde Serao's *Piccole anime*, another edition of *Confessioni e battaglie*, and Carducci's
long dramatic poem, *Ça ira*. Then came the *annus
mirabilis*, 1884. Verga, D'Annunzio, and Carducci
submitted new material; and the great Zola, in what
might have developed into an international breakthrough, gave Sommaruga *Voluttà della vita*. However, by that time the Casa Editrice Sommaruga was
on the edge of a precipice. In 1885 it slipped over the
edge, to its destruction—but not before bringing forth
a new edition of Count Stefano Jacini's sociological
masterpiece, *I risultati dell'inchièsta agraria*.

No matter how successful or respectable he became,
Sommaruga was always denied the adequate financial
backing that he craved.[2] Part of the problem was the
city itself. Rome never had played a significant role in
the Italian publishing industry; by trying to change
that situation, Sommaruga challenged the industry's
traditions and vested interests. Publishers in Milan
and Turin viewed the Casa Editrice Sommaruga with

hostility and alarm. On 1 September 1882 the *Cronaca bizantina* announced, "Rome is imposing itself. Rome is winning the literary prize."[3] To some extent, the statement was true; at least, no other publishing house could match Sommaruga's impressive record for that year. Yet, at the same time, the very truth of his boast caused resentment, jealousy, and antagonism. The old charge that Sommaruga owed his success to shady dealings grew to the proportions of an indestructible legend. He himself did not help matters by proclaiming in the *Cronaca bizantina* on 16 January 1884, "I nourish myself on *reclame!*"[4] He was being perfectly honest: Sommaruga had to stoke public interest with scandalous materials in order to survive.

It has been said that, for a society to have high culture, it must have low culture. Sommaruga had an instinctive grasp of this point, although he would have added that, in addition to high and low culture, society needed all the cultural gradations in between. His understanding was born of the need to solve what contemporary publishers describe as the "cash flow problem." Sommaruga was rarely ahead of the bills, and nearly always behind on them. He took pride in publishing poetry by Leopardi, Carducci, and D'Annunzio, but, in order to offset the small profits and even the losses that resulted from these serious publications, big profits had to come in from the potboilers. And so, at the same time that he published Carducci's *Confessioni e battaglie*, P. Valera's *Amori bestiali* was rushed into print; likewise, Verga's *Drammi intimi* was followed by Rocco De Zerbi's *L'avvelanetrice* in the 1884 catalogue. Just before the Casa crashed early in 1885, Jacini's monumental pioneering study of the southern problem appeared in an odd pairing with *L'arte della bellezza nella donna: segreti della toletta* by Lola Montez. The "collezione Sommaruga" was a peculiar assortment of high- and lowbrow offerings, quite in keeping with the twentieth-century publishing practices of many reputable houses, but highly irregular and even disturbing for Sommaruga's contemporaries.

What most disturbed his competitors were Sommaruga's promotional campaigns. Those for his potboilers gained special notoriety; of the 135 books that he published from 1881 to 1885, a large number dealt with sexual themes, particularly adultery. He enjoyed enormous commercial success in 1883 with such confessional books as *Versi: intimità* by Contessa Lara (Evelina Cattermole Mancini) and *Quattro milioni* by Emma Ivon. These women were already infamous: the first as an adulteress and a bohemian poet; the second as an actress and as King Vittorio Emanuele's favorite mistress. Sommaruga was at his most cunning when he had possibilities like these to exploit. Contessa Lara's lovesick rhymes met with such a favorable public response that the publisher had one of his writers on the *Bizantina* staff, Domenico Milelli, adopt the pseudonym Conte di Lara for yet another Sommaruga publication, *Rime*.[5] Sommaruga worked tirelessly to draw the last drop of blood from his bestsellers. If a book could be successful once, then why not twice, under a slightly different title and format? Although Sommaruga did not invent the idea of the spinoff, he made more use of it than anyone before him. There was no law against it—and, after all, as he once wrote to a friend, "I'm not in this business for the glory alone."[6]

The main vehicle of Sommaruga's publicity operation was the *Cronaca bizantina*. Early on, that journal served a triple purpose in the Casa Editrice Sommaruga: first, to give D'Annunzio, Scarfoglio, and Salvadori an opportunity to act as Carducci's votaries while simultaneously advancing their own careers; second, to attract the most talented writers in the country, regardless of their ideological positions; and, third, to run Sommaruga's book advertisements in a publication with a high readership. The journal's success on all three counts transcended even the most sanguine expectations of its founder. Once more, Sommaruga ran true to form: if one journal brought him such acclaim and support, what might a second bring? Or a third? What was to prevent him from bringing his unique style of publishing into the daily newspaper field? These were the challenges and opportunities that faced the twenty-five-year-old publisher in the autumn of 1882. He responded with characteristic flamboyance, by embarking on an expansionist policy which ultimately brought him control of the *Domenica letteraria*, the *Messaggero illustrato*, *Nabab*, and the *Forche caudine*, as well as the *Cronaca bizantina*. We must now turn our attention toward these later publications, to examine their roles in the rise and fall of Angelo Sommaruga.

The Domenica letteraria

Lack of capital forced Sommaruga to initiate his expansionist policy with moderation. His first step was to buy an interest in Ferdinando Martini's *Domenica letteraria*. Martini (1841–1928), once a passionate Mazzinian and always an admirer of Carducci, was another of the many journalists in Rome who managed to combine literary and political ambitions. For years a regular contributor to *Il fanfulla*, Martini collected his best early articles on theater and literature, publishing them under the title *Fra un sigaro e un altro* (1876). He founded *Il fanfulla della domenica* in 1878, but broke with his publisher, Obleight, in 1882 over strong political differences. Soon afterward he established the *Domenica letteraria*. Meanwhile, Martini's political career, begun in 1874, progressed rapidly. Always intensely nationalistic, this future imperial governor in Eritrea (1897–1900) and senator of the realm under fascism (1923) was made secretary general in the ministry of public instruction by Depretis in 1884. With this appointment Martini's political and editorial duties at last became incompatible, and he gave up the *Domenica letteraria* completely. However, many months earlier Sommaruga had eclipsed his influence on the journal.[7]

Despite Martini's literary abilities and his staff's professionalism, the publication never enjoyed much popularity under his direction. Yet Sommaruga took over the foundering *Domenica*, supremely confident that his administrative skills would turn failure into success "because," he wrote in his memoirs, "for a periodical to prosper it is not enough for it to be well staffed, it must be well administered, too."[8] Martini had been too much an intellectual and statesman, Sommaruga reasoned, to operate a journal successfully under modern conditions. Sommaruga himself was happily free of both handicaps. Moreover, he possessed a formula that had produced the most gratifying results in the *Cronaca bizantina*, and he anticipated even greater success with the *Domenica letteraria*.

Failure followed instead—ironically, brought about by what Carducci described as "too much of the same old thing."[9] Carducci had attempted to dissuade Sommaruga from acquiring the *Domenica letteraria*; when his appeals proved unavailing, the poet wrote, "O unhappy Angelino, co-proprietor now also of the *Domenica letteraria*. I do not have enough tears to shed for your unhappiness."[10] Carducci believed there were already too many literary journals, and that only a few should be permitted to survive. In Carducci's view the *Domenica* was not worthy of salvation, and he persistently badgered Sommaruga to give it up. In January 1883, for example, he complained about the

"Salvadorian and Scarfoglian uniformity" of Sommaruga's new review. Then, on 10 November of that year, he wrote Sommaruga: "The last number of the *Bizantina* is well done. Very well done! But I don't like the last *Domenica letteraria*."[11] Less than three weeks later Carducci informed the publisher: "I am warning you now that I will no longer send anything for publication in the *Domenica letteraria*. It is a sheet designed for the least intelligent and the most ridiculous class of Italian readers."[12]

Why did Carducci denounce the *Domenica letteraria* with such vehement scorn? At first glance, it seems that he should have approved of the journal for the same reasons he gave when supporting the *Cronaca bizantina*. Sommaruga's new review was staffed by loyal Carduccians who believed that they were opening another front in the war for Beauty and Art. Yet the disciples were growing restive, and the *Domenica letteraria* reflected changing attitudes toward the master. For example, it printed Scarfoglio's famous "geriatric" remark about Carducci, who, though still the premier poet of the day, "is by now a grandfather and a member of the Superior Council and too burdened with examinations: public life has in large part changed him and the *Cronaca bizantina* has in large part absorbed him."[13] The implication was that Carducci had already enjoyed his most creative moments as a poet. The coming generation could look to him for inspiration, but a younger bard was needed. More and more Scarfoglio and the other *bizantini*, now writing for the *Domenica letteraria* as well, turned to D'Annunzio as the light of the future.

Sommaruga moved quickly to mend his fences with Carducci—not that they ever had tumbled down very far. The two maintained a cordial and even affectionate correspondence despite all the tension over the *Domenica letteraria*. On 18 February 1883 Carducci

wrote Sommaruga concerning Luigi Lodi (1857–
1933), one of the poet's foremost Bologna disciples: "I
need to set up Lodi in Rome . . . . Lodi needs to make a
living, and he merits it more than most."[14] Sommaruga was only too glad to oblige, and later that year
he offered Lodi the editor's job on the *Domenica letteraria*, thereby granting Carducci's request and giving him a personal reason to support the journal again.
This would have been a clever strategy, had Carducci
been less adamant about the pressing need to limit the
number of literary periodicals: quality, not quantity,
should be the goal. Carducci wished "Gigi" well, but
at the same time felt sure that the *Domenica letteraria*
job was a mistake for his protégé.[15]

The poet called it exactly. Lodi was destined to become an institution among Rome's newspapermen and
editors. He eventually wrote for all the city's major
publications, and in the 1890s founded several newspapers—most notably *Il giorno*, a much-written-about
experiment in literary-political journalism.[16] None of
this later success was foreshadowed in the *Domenica
letteraria*, where Lodi's problem was essentially the
one that had plagued his predecessor. Although Martini had tried to create an independent personality for
the *Domenica letteraria*, his journal never overcame
the appearance of being a poor relative of the well-
established *Fanfulla della domenica*. He had stressed
the importance of nationalism and the need for civic
and cultural revival. He even had tried to give the
journal a look of social awareness by publishing an
impressive two-part series on Italian illiteracy, but
sales still remained low.[17]

Like Martini, Lodi struggled in vain to chart an independent course for the review, employing numerous
expedients to revitalize the flagging journal. Nothing
seemed to work. In the end, it was plain that Lodi
could offer his readers little more than variations on

the Carduccian theme that the early *Cronaca bizantina* had made its own. Lodi's own articles drew praise for their style and eloquence, but even a moderately attentive *Cronaca bizantina* reader would have heard it all before. Like everyone within the original *bizantini* circle, Lodi had been initiated into the rites and dogmas of Carduccianism. Even more than the others, Lodi could lay claim to a special grace for having received the word directly from the Master. Certainly he succeeded where Salvadori had failed, and the *Domenica letteraria* became a missionary tract. Sommaruga no longer had time to oversee all of his publications with the thoroughness that he had lavished on the *Cronaca bizantina*. Under Lodi, the new journal seemed to pick up where the earliest issues of the *Cronaca bizantina* left off, as a newsletter for a club whose members were all Carduccians. The gospel according to Lodi stressed verities made familiar by the *bizantini maggiori*; e.g., "It is in this fusion of critic, of lyricist, and of politician that Carducci's power and superiority originate. . . . He is the greatest, after Dante, of Italian political writers who have turned their thought and art to the greatness and to the future of the country."[18] Like so many other literary-minded members of his generation, Lodi looked about Italy and saw a wasteland of mediocrity—save for Carducci, whose "books sounded like the mystical trumpets of the Bible; they transport us to a higher plane of awareness."[19]

Stirring as all of this rhetoric might have been to the Carducci faithful, it did not increase sales. At the same time, Lodi's worshipful articles failed to change Carducci's mind about the *Domenica letteraria*, and by 1884 the poet's correspondence was filled with expressions of disappointment over the immoderate expansion of the Casa Sommaruga.[20] By then it was clear that the Lodi appointment had achieved neither of its main objectives: to boost *Domenica letteraria* sales, and to bind Carducci more firmly to Sommaruga. In desperation, the young publisher attempted to salvage the *Domenica letteraria* early in 1885 by replacing Lodi with Antonio Giulio Barrili (1836–1908). Under different circumstances, Barrili's appointment might have produced the miracle that Sommaruga needed. From 1865 to about 1890, Barrili was one of the two or three most popular writers in Italy; only the books of Edmondo De Amicis consistently enjoyed slightly higher sales. Barrili had the best-selling author's primary gift: he wrote easily on topics with popular appeal. In twenty-five years he tossed off more than sixty novels, all stressing heroic love, the spirit of sacrifice, and domestic virtues. The Italian reading public could not get enough of this literary formula, and the Barrili novel became an annual (indeed, usually semi-annual) event in the publishing business. The biggest successes were *Capitan Droderò* (1865), *Santa Cecilia* (1866), *Val d'Olivi* (1873), *Come un sogno* (1875), *Cuor di ferro e cuor d'oro* and *L'olmo e l'erdere* (1877), *Il bianco spino* (1882), and *La montanara* (1886). None survives today as a book to be read seriously. When they are mentioned at all, it is with a laugh at their stereotyped characters—chivalrous heroes saving spotless heroines from dastardly villains in situations of relentless melodrama. This fiction survived just long enough to make Barrili a wealthy man, and to earn him a place in the history books as one of the age's "representative" writers.[21]

Barrili had lived his most famous books. Born in Savona, he studied law at the University of Genoa and at the same time began to write for some of the city's newspapers. In 1859 he enlisted in the Piedmontese army and saw action against the Austrians. The following year he took part in Garibaldi's invasion of Sicily, an experience that transformed the young man and made him a Garibaldian for life. At war's end, Barrili resumed writing for Genoese newspapers; however, Garibaldi's call to arms always sounded like Roland's horn to him. In 1867 he fought at Mentana, where he suffered a serious wound. Mentana disillusioned Barrili with the new Italy, and his subsequent three-year term in Parliament transformed that disillusionment into hopeless disgust.[22] The realities of Italian political life were so appalling that, as a man of sensibility, he could only find surcease in literature and art. That was a familiar escape route, but few made such a good living along the way as Barrili.

While Sommaruga's inner ear could detect the hum of success at miraculous distances, even a deaf man might have heard Barrili's splash in the Italian literary world. The publisher certainly thought he had scored a decisive coup in January 1885, when Barrili agreed to run the *Domenica letteraria*. The novelist enthusiastically assumed his new position with a program of Garibaldian succinctness: "Beauty with a virile thought—that is the art I love."[23] However, it was already too late for the *Domenica letteraria*. The journal suspended publication less than three months after Barrili's appointment, a victim of the catastrophe that overtook the Sommaruga publishing empire in March 1885.

The Messaggero illustrato and Nabab

Meanwhile, from April to December 1884, Sommaruga had expanded his publishing house to its maximum dimensions, by either acquiring or founding three publications: the *Messaggero illustrato*, *Nabab*, and the *Forche caudine*. He began with the *Messaggero illustrato* as he had begun with the *Domenica letteraria*, by taking over an established journal. However, "established" is somewhat misleading here; the first issue of the *Messaggero illustrato* had appeared only on 2 March 1884. Sommaruga took it over on 24 April, hoping to cash in on the burgeoning market for illustrated weeklies. This was strictly an investment tactic. He seems even to have been self-conscious about what the vulgar *Messaggero illustrato* might do to his image, and the sheet, "as though ashamed of itself," was operated apart from the other Sommaruga publications.[24] Nevertheless, Sommaruga's vanity as a businessman ultimately suffered the most acute embarrassment, as the *Messaggero illustrato* continued to lose money. Since a quick profit was the publisher's sole motive, his enthusiasm waned once the journal's financial prospects became clear. Sommaruga experienced the most dismal failure of his mature publishing career with the *Messaggero*, and he was looking for a way to bury his mistake when a rash of disasters brought down the entire house.

If Sommaruga regretted the *Messaggero* as an unfortunate indiscretion, he always remembered *Nabab* as his pride and joy.[25] *Nabab* was Sommaruga's most ambitious foray into the field of daily journalism, and his choice of Enrico Panzacchi (1840–1904) was inspired. A man of renowned erudition, Panzacchi had earned degrees in philosophy at Bologna and in literature at Pisa. At Bologna he had naturally come under the influence of Carducci, and the two men formed a close friendship, although their mutual romantic interest in signora Cristofori-Piva turned them into bitter rivals for a time during the 1870s. From the University of Bologna, Panzacchi went on to establish a reputation as one of the foremost public speakers of the day. In the 1890s he drifted back into the university world, as a professor of esthetics at Bologna, but in the 1880s he was trying to make his mark as a poet and journalist. A word from Carducci had the usual effect, and in 1884 Sommaruga made Panzacchi the director of *Nabab*.

Panzacchi described the paper's program in the maiden issue, which appeared on 21 December 1884. The spirit of *Nabab* was in the masthead motto, Ernest Renan's "In argument I feel that I am always a little of my opponent's opinion." The editor promised, "The newspaper will be a showcase in which all ideas and opinions will be displayed."[26] Such a policy statement was, in itself, news. We must remember that Italian newspapers of the 1880s were, to use the words of Luigi Lodi in his autobiographical memoir, *Giornalisti* (1930), "exclusively dedicated to an end of political propaganda."[27] Italy's illiteracy problems and the lack of a strong journalistic tradition had made it impossible for a newspaper to survive without party or pressure-group support. *Nabab* sprang into existence as a nearly monstrous exception to this rule. Panzacchi chose his staff with an eye toward providing *Nabab* with a variety of viewpoints on all the important issues of the day, and the results of his policy were extraordinary.

Of all his publications, *Nabab* most fully captured the spirit of what Sommaruga wanted and needed to do in his publishing firm. From the beginning he had hoped to build a clearinghouse for everything vital in Italian literature and thought. Rome was the capital of his operations, but the house of Sommaruga would be truly national in its appeal, attracting writers from all schools and readers of all tastes. This did not mean, as some of his critics on the *Bizantina* charged, that he had become an apostate to the Carduccian faith. Certainly, Carducci himself never thought this way about him. It simply meant that Sommaruga chose to open his doors to all, not just to singers of Carducci's song.

It so happened that, by nature and temperament, Sommaruga stood as far removed from the partisan imagination as a man could; but, in his particular case, catholicity of publishing viewpoint evolved as a matter of vital economic necessity as well. He saw almost immediately that he would have no future as the publisher of a Carducci *cénacle* alone. A market existed for this literature, but not the kind of market that would sustain a major publishing house. Although Carducci had been his salvation in the beginning, Sommaruga would have to save himself in the end. He thought he could do this only by casting his net wide.

The brief history of *Nabab* richly illustrates what Sommaruga intended by employing a strategy which, in some crucial ways, is without equal—even in twentieth-century publishing. Eclecticism has become a way of life for contemporary publishing firms, but newspapers—above all, Italian newspapers—remain intensely ideological, committed to some political point of view or party. Although this commitment is more artfully concealed in American newspapers, it is no less real for all that. What Sommaruga and Panzacchi did in *Nabab* went so far beyond normal publishing practices that there still is no professional term to describe it. "Comparative journalism," weak as it is, comes close to capturing the spirit of the paper's editorial policy; but even that term will remain an abstraction unless some examples of its meaning are given.

What were the principal issues of the day during the period of *Nabab*'s publication, from 21 December 1884 to 28 February 1885? To judge from the newspaper's sixty-eight issues, church-state relations, the railroad conventions, and anarchist terror were very prominent; but, for sheer volume of copy, the agrarian question and Africa outweighed all other concerns. Not the tone, but the structure of *Nabab*'s eclectic policy on these two issues is instructive, for in this newspaper "eclecticism" meant parallel commentary by the staff's motley members.

The agrarian question received national attention in the aftermath of Stefano Jacini's *L'inchiesta agraria*, a multi-volume work which documented, in irrefutable and depressing detail, the horrendous poverty and backwardness of Italian agriculture, particularly in the South. Belief in the natural wealth of Italy's arable land had been a major premise of Risorgimento logic; once freed from foreign domination and exploitation, this wealth would rapidly make Italy one of the most favored countries in the world, Italian patriots confidently predicted. After the publication of Jacini's findings, no one could take this myth seriously. Now the agrarian question no longer could be put off. What was to be done about the dreadful misery of Italy's peasants? In keeping with Panzacchi's program, *Nabab* presented its readers with answers running the political gamut. Jacini and his critics to the left and right were discussed and analyzed in a continuing series of articles. Panzacchi even published letters to the editor on the subject, and in these individual protests we can hear the alarums of war between the ideological right and left. The issue of agriculture joined in mortal combat the socialist left and the as-yet-unnamed right. To the socialists, who preached that the land belonged to him who worked it, conservatives retorted that the land belonged to him who owned it.[28] From that fundamental antithesis almost everything antagonistic to the politics of *trasformismo* was derived. What stands out in *Nabab* as truly remarkable is the juxtaposition of these viewpoints in the columns of one newspaper.

The same thing occurred with the fateful African question. Imperialism was an old issue in Italian politics, and during the 1870s many Italians had hoped

their country would assume the white man's burden
in Tunisia. Unfortunately for them, this was an honor
coveted by the vastly more powerful French, now
anxious to recoup the prestige they had lost in the
Franco-Prussian War. After that conflict, Bismarck
had secretly encouraged the French to undertake an
imperialist policy in Africa, as well as in the Far East
—anywhere, really, as long as he could have his way
in Europe. However, when the Congress of Berlin
(1878) recognized France's suzerainty in Tunisia, the
Italians pronounced themselves humiliated. Francesco
Crispi led a chorus of the disenchanted as he bemoaned
"the hard lesson of 1878."[29] He, more than anyone
else, understood the spirit of anguish behind Carducci's indignant denunciation of "This sad infuriated
Italy in its pigsty full of comedians, thieves and ruffi-
ans."[30] With so many Italians in a glowering mood,
the government of Cairoli—famous for its "empty but
clean hands" policy in foreign affairs—collapsed. The
subsequent Depretis administration set out in some
haste along the path leading to the Triple Alliance
with Germany and Austria.

The raucous imperialist minority now argued that,
with her northern flank protected by the Triple Alliance, Italy would be free to join the European scramble for African colonies. That such an argument
should appeal to enthusiastic imperialists is unexceptional; but that a sober liberal like Depretis, with the
responsibility of power and office, should be persuaded
by it is remarkable. At once castigated by enemies and
admired by friends for his *buon senso*, Depretis presided over the administration that launched Italy's
maiden imperialist campaign in East Africa, chosen
because it was one of the few parts of the continent
not already subjugated by other European powers, and
because of the growing Italian presence there, in the
holdings of the Rubattino Shipping Company in As-

sab.[31] It most assuredly was not the problem of "excess capital" that drove Depretis to this decision; the Marxist-Leninist interpretation of imperialism does not apply in the Italian case, as Antonio Gramsci vigorously pointed out.[32] Not only did Umbertian Italy lack capital for export; the country was also dangerously dependent upon foreign capital for its own economic requirements. At the same time, the romantic search for glory and prestige, so dear to the hearts of the imperialists, left Depretis and other establishment liberals utterly cold.[33] The prime minister was not one of those Italians who thrilled to Carducci's image of *Roma guerriera*.[34] No; for the Depretis government, the African issue served almost purely practical functions: as a distraction from the government's gloomy record of domestic failure, and as a safety valve for the growing pressure of internal agitations. In 1884 domestic and foreign policy became fatally linked, with Africa a desert mirage dancing before the eyes of leaders whose people were further away than ever from the promised land of Risorgimento rhetoric.

No specific imperialist policy was laid down right away, but the government could scarcely conceal its impatience for an opportunity to act. The chance came in 1884, when African tribesmen in Assab killed Gustavo Bianchi, an Italian scientist and explorer. A punitive expedition left Italy in December. The stage was now set for the first of many Italian tragedies in Africa.

The embarkation of the Italian expeditionary force touched off an acrimonious debate in the nation's newspapers. *Nabab* succumbed to the national hysteria, but in a unique way. Instead of presenting its readers with frenzied commentaries from the left, right, or center, *Nabab* published frenzied commentaries from all parts of the political spectrum. Understandably, the positions of the historic right and left received the most coverage. The right, traditionally cautious in foreign affairs, opposed Italian expansion—irredentist or African—on the grounds that Italy could not afford it.[35] The left, now identified with the establishment, supported government policy: Bianchi's murder had put the national honor at stake, and it was necessary to avenge him *pour encourager les autres.*[36]

Nabab's in-house debate between spokesmen for the two traditional parties was supplemented by commentaries from the ideological left and right. There were no socialists on the staff, but one Henriquez pseudonymously echoed the socialist position on the African question. That perspective was championed in Parliament by Andrea Costa, who, from his seat on the extreme left, proclaimed: "Gentlemen, the Italy that works, I dare say the real Italy, does not want a colonial policy."[37] The real Italians wanted bread and work at home, not spectacles in distant lands. One did not have to be a socialist in order to agree with Costa on this point. Henriquez began scornfully by observing that Italy, ever the poor relation of France, "is always a day and an idea late." The heart of the Assab matter was envy. Depretis and his foreign minister, Mancini, were simply bedazzled by Ferry's *tour de force* in Tunisia, Madagascar, the Congo, and the Tonkin Gulf. Now the Italians were trying to do in Assab what the French had done all over the world with such seeming ease. The government statements about Assab were lies. Not revenge, but imperialist exploitation had motivated the Italians to invade Africa.[38]

The use of pen names by *Nabab* writers gave the paper a picturesque air, but the historian is often at a loss in tracing their true identities. However, in the case of "Orao," the detective work is somewhat easier; his articles match, in style and sentiment, the im-

perialist hyperbole of Alfredo Oriani (1852–1909),
who took up the socialist challenge and simultaneously denounced the historic left and right.[39] *Superba-
mente solo*, the fascists were to say of him: superbly
alone in a wilderness of calumny and error. This was
Mussolini's epitaph for the author of *Fino a Dogali*
(1889) and *La lotta politica in Italia* (1892). In life,
Oriani was a writer of remaindered novels, ignored
history books, and unstaged plays. In death, he became the paladin of the fascist ideal: imperialism.
What the fascists liked most about Oriani's imperialist
writings was his emphasis on the spiritual qualities of
Italy's mission in Africa. This emphasis is clear in
Orao's *Nabab* articles, which are historically significant as one of the first expressions of an entirely new
tradition in Italian politics, the tradition of the radical
or ideological right. His logic on the African question
anticipated the arguments of Italian imperialists for
the next three generations:

> . . . we have need of a test, from which we must
> extract advantages that are not only material, that
> must prepare us for something different and for
> something more than a small colonial expansion.
>
> Also because the sacrifices that we will make in
> Africa will enhance our prestige and our future in
> Europe.
>
> And let us leave behind to their foraging those
> frightened rabbits who tremble at any vision of
> combat; let us leave behind those good and prac-
> tical bourgeois to their account books.[40]

Though a failed writer, Oriani enjoyed great success as a talker; his medium was not the printed page,
but the informal conversation. He would have preferred a teaching career. His great hero at the University of Bologna, Carducci, always inspired him; but

Oriani had to be satisfied with his "chair" in Bologna's Caffè S. Pietro. Here he preached the gospel of Africa to all who would listen. Among his *scolari da caffè* were the young Luigi Federzoni and Mario Missiroli, who would carry Oriani's ideas and rhetoric into the Nationalist party. From there, the path to fascism was unobstructed.

While Enrico Panzacchi tried to promote the concept of comparative journalism in *Nabab*, another Sommaruga editor, Pietro Sbarbaro, was well along in his attempt to launch the most peculiar newspaper of the decade. This was the infamous *Forche caudine* which became the largest-selling newspaper in the country, with a sales of 150,000 copies per issue in 1885.[41] The *Domenica letteraria* had been a disappointment; the *Messaggero illustrato* was a disaster; *Nabab*, though promising and gaining in sales with every issue, did not make any money for Sommaruga. The *Forche caudine* did. Huge sums came into the publishing house through the pen of Pietro Sbarbaro, whose books and articles were Sommaruga's best money-makers in 1884 and 1885. With the publication of *Re travicello o re costituzionale?* and *Regina o repubblica?*, and with the founding of the *Forche caudine*, Sommaruga reached the commercial zenith of his publishing career. It was the victory of Pyrrhus, with annihilating defeat looming on the next horizon.

The way for Sommaruga's ultimate failure had been paved even earlier by dissension within his own house. Success and expansion demanded a price. For long the original phalanx of Carduccian *bizantini* had grown estranged from Sommaruga. To them, his publishing house seemed to have developed into a symbol of the very vulgarity they wished to expose in their writings. Salvadori and Scarfoglio were particularly adamant on this point, but the publisher's confrontation with D'Annunzio finally brought matters to a crisis. Then Sbarbaro came along. For most of the *bizantini*, the *Forche caudine* was the decisive affront to their dignity as artists of the ideal. We must turn our attention now toward these two interrelated episodes in the history of the Casa Editrice Sommaruga: the *bizantina* schism, and the Sbarbaro affair.

CHAPTER FIVE

GABRIELE D'ANNUNZIO

(1863–1938) AND THE

BIZANTINA SCHISM,

1883–1884

"Don't hinder my way with your ruinous publicity!"
—D'Annunzio to Sommaruga (1884)

Sommaruga's interview with *La tribuna*'s Paris reporter, C. G. Sarti, in the spring of 1910 had unforeseen consequences. The former publisher had initially contacted Sarti in order to answer Diego Angeli's charges in the *Giornale d'Italia*. Sarti's column gave Sommaruga an opportunity to set the record straight, and to reminisce a bit about the past. Not that he would ever get back into publishing. "It wouldn't be worth it, believe me," was the way he put it, in a response which served as a benediction for the interview.

The publisher in Sommaruga had been exorcised: that much was certain and irrevocable, he claimed. Yet Sommaruga always remained alive to any potentially profitable business opportunity. Sarti's closing question about a comeback in the publishing business probably awakened in Sommaruga's mind possibilities long dormant or repressed. This is speculation, but speculation supported by a curious episode in the life of the wandering Milanese. There is a substantiated account of Sommaruga approaching Gabriele D'Annunzio in January 1912 with a "semi-editorial proposal." The account is that of Tom Antongini in *Vita segreta di Gabriele D'Annunzio*. Having served as D'Annunzio's private secretary for many years, Antongini was equipped by experience to act as the poet's Boswell. He wrote several memoirs on the life of his legendary employer, but *Vita segreta* was the best of them.[1] In it he told the strange story of this Paris meeting between D'Annunzio and Sommaruga.

D'Annunzio had retired to Paris from Florence in 1910, one step ahead of his creditors. They had swooped down on his Florentine residence, the Villa Capponcina, and had stripped the rooms bare of their fabulous art treasures. Nearly everything was sold at a public auction, and only the salvation of his library by a generous friend prevented the catastrophe from being complete. At forty-seven, D'Annunzio seemed finished in Italy; his credit exhausted, he had no place left to go. Now the poet looked beyond the Alps, to Paris, where he would start over, accumulating new debts and fresh triumphs. The French took him up, rather like a new fashion in clothes, and D'Annunzio soon became the most preferred dinner guest and lover in the city. So much favor would have broken the constitution of a different man, but D'Annunzio and Paris of the banquet years were perfectly suited for each other. He responded to the adulation with just the right mixture of enthusiasm and arrogance. Not since Napoleon had an Italian enjoyed such a thorough conquest of the city.

At the time of Sommaruga's unexpected visit, D'Annunzio had reached the peak of his Parisian notoriety. *Le martyre de Saint Sebastien* had been staged the previous year, with Ida Rubenstein in the lead. Opening night was the theatrical event of the season. All of Paris was there to be shocked, and D'Annunzio did not disappoint his audience. Titillation through the salacious juxtaposition of religion and sex had always been his strong point, but *The Martyrdom of Saint Sebastian* went past the boundary of mere erotic bold-ness, and into the realm of sacrilege. Debussy's music and Bakst's stage sets intensified the effect of D'An-nunzio's sensational script, and the play became an immediate *succès de scandale*. It had a brief run, how-ever. After the initial shock waves wore off, critics perceived that *Saint Sebastian* had little but shock to recommend it, and the tragedy closed without reaping the financial harvest that D'Annunzio and his backers had anticipated.

Now the lack of money became acutely distressing. This was nothing new in the D'Annunzio household. While still in his early twenties he had remarked, "I am a creature of luxury, and the superfluous is as necessary to me as breathing."[2] Sleek greyhounds, beautiful women, thoroughbred horses, high fashion clothing, luxurious living quarters, exotic perfumes, and costly jewelry were the objects of his connoisseur's instinct. He lusted after whatever struck his fancy, regardless of the cost. Bills were a nuisance, to be ig-nored or avoided whenever possible. Periodically they caught up with him *en masse*; on those occasions a crisis would occur, and D'Annunzio would resolve it by moving. Then the cycle would start all over again. D'Annunzio observed with some petulance that French creditors seemed to have less patience than the more accommodating Italians. His wiles were lost on the French; they wanted their money on time. He was in a quandary after the *Saint Sebastian* box-office failure, and extreme measures were being contem-plated. For D'Annunzio, that always meant flight un-der cover of darkness.

It was in these straitened circumstances that Som-maruga found him. The two men had not seen each other for more than twenty-five years, since the re-grettable incidents of 1884–85. During the interval

D'Annunzio had often sent autographed copies of his books to Sommaruga. These conciliatory gestures strengthened Sommaruga's resolve to go ahead and present his scheme. Apparently D'Annunzio customarily sent out so many complimentary copies of his books that he could not keep track of them all, because, upon hearing Sommaruga's name mentioned by the servant, he exclaimed, "Sommaruga . . . But good Heaven, is he still alive!" After reading about his own death in Angeli's article and then hearing D'Annunzio's exclamation, Sommaruga may have begun to wonder why people were in such a hurry to bury him.

Here were two middle-aged men who once had been friends, and then bitter enemies. In the warmth of D'Annunzio's rooms they could forget the enmity and remember the friendship. Antongini witnessed it all, and he wrote that, after some pleasant talk about the old days, Sommaruga eventually came around to the business that had brought him to the poet's residence just outside Paris. D'Annunzio listened intently as Sommaruga reminded him that the Giolitti government had recently suppressed certain verses in his *Canzone dei Dardanelli*. With its usual *Italietta* attitudes, the government lacked the courage to allow an authentic Italian patriot to speak his mind. Really, almost nothing had changed in Italy since the days of Carducci and "Aspromonte." Sommaruga's idea was simple and potentially very lucrative for all concerned. He had brought with him twenty volumes of *Canzone dei Dardanelli*. Would D'Annunzio have the patience to write the suppressed verses in each copy? "I am ready to pay you 500 lire a copy," Sommaruga concluded. "That makes 10,000 lire which you will have made without much effort."

D'Annunzio beamed his most ingratiating smile as he agreed to the terms. It would be done at first light the next day, he told Sommaruga on the way out. Yet the next day passed, and then another, without D'Annunzio bestirring himself. At last Antongini reminded him of his promise. "Oh, that," he answered his secretary. "You know it is such an annoyance for me to write the same thing twenty times that I don't feel like doing it. Tell [Sommaruga] that I authorize him to imitate my handwriting and that in compensation I will accept 5,000 lire."

Sommaruga listened patiently as Antongini made D'Annunzio's counterproposal. D'Annunzio had not changed, and Sommaruga may have permitted himself a knowing smile when Antongini had finished. We cannot be sure, because Antongini described the scene in only the most general terms.[3] We do know that Sommaruga refused the offer: "Tell him that for my part I thank him very much for the authorization, but seeing that once as a publisher I was wrongly put in jail on his account, if only indirectly, when I was thirty-seven years old, I do not feel like returning there at fifty-six. The pity is that I will never get my twenty volumes back. Oh well, *pazienza*!" Actually, the publisher was only twenty-seven at the time of his incarceration; but everything else that Antongini recorded here was more or less true—especially the part about Sommaruga's copies of *Canzone dei Dardanelli*. D'Annunzio never returned them.

As we have seen already, D'Annunzio entered Sommaruga's life in the early 1880s as another promising young writer. He came more highly recommended than most, for Chiarini's review of *Primo vere*, "A proposito di un nuovo poeta," served as an unofficial imprimatur. Although Chiarini did not make D'Annunzio's reputation with one column, it was a start that few sixteen-year-old writers might have expected. Scarfoglio, Michetti, and the other *Abruzzesi* residing in Rome took their cue from Chiarini and launched D'Annunzio into the world of Sommaruga publications, first on the staff of the *Cronaca bizantina* and then as a contributor to the *Domenica letteraria*. From 1882 to 1884 the Casa Sommaruga published one or two of his books annually.

Sommaruga's first concern with D'Annunzio was, of course, to discover the most effective way of marketing his work. This was not an unusual concern for a publisher in Italy or anywhere else, but to his contemporaries Sommaruga's advertising techniques appeared very "American," i.e., they suggested a high-pressure promotional image. Sommaruga differed from his competitors in that he had a total concept of the publishing process. A book was a product, like bread or cheese; but, unlike staple food products, books could not depend on a sustaining natural market. The failure of publisher after publisher in Italy was proof enough of that fact. To market his product properly, a modern publisher needed far more than the traditional skills required to produce a book: he also had to know how to advertise that book, and how to distribute it. More than that—and this rang especially true in Italy, where illiteracy was high and reading habits poor—a publisher literally might have to create a public demand for a writer's work. Sommaruga's forte lay in this kind of public relations—specifically, in creating an image for a writer, and then working to market the writer's books on the strength of that image. He was perfectly unscrupulous about distortions, exaggerations, and sensationalism. Sommaruga's boldness in these matters became the talk, and then the scandal, of Umbertian Rome; but in the beginning no one, least of all his writers, could argue with success.

In D'Annunzio's case, the image problem was solved effortlessly. Chiarini himself, in his review of

Primo vere, had given Sommaruga a clue. After comparing the book not altogether unfavorably with Carducci's *Odi barbare*, Chiarini expressed concern about one "serious imperfection" in D'Annunzio's poetry, involving

> . . . the ostentatious display of sentiments and desires that it pleases me to think are not real. The poem entitled "Ora satanica" is poetically and morally ugly. A young man of sixteen years, full of wit and heart, full of enthusiasm for beautiful things and for art, as our poet is, must desire something better than infernal turmoil with howling and insensate hoots, than the breasts of whores on which to pass the night.[4]

Such "absurd ravings" were produced by the feverishness of youth, the critic concluded, and would pass with time.

Sommaruga soon discovered that D'Annunzio's ravings were good for business—ever so much better, in fact, than the seascape poetry, the hymns to the Abruzzi, and the love sonnets to his Lalla in distant Pistoia. The sober poet of the sea, of the Abruzzi's blue skies, of young love's eternal grace sold fewer books than the poet of "insensate hoots." Of course, Sommaruga welcomed the ecstatic critical enthusiasm for D'Annunzio's early nature poetry. The sixty or so poems in *Canto novo* (1882) immediately established him as the leading young poet of the day. His images of the Adriatic "kissed by the Abruzzi's sun" seemed to delight every important figure in the country's literary establishment. Scarfoglio was awash with sentimental enthusiasm as he reviewed his friend's celebration of "the immense joy of living/ of being strong, of being young/ of tasting earthly fruits/ with voracious teeth strong and white."[5] Here was the new

Carducci. Here was one perhaps even greater than Carducci. In the same year, Sommaruga published D'Annunzio's *Terra vergine*, a collection of nine short stories inspired by the same love of nature. Again the reviewers exhausted their store of superlatives. Cesare Pascarella could only say that, with *Terra vergine*, "we are in the Abruzzi."[6] Even Verga himself was not a more skilled local colorist. Carducci and Verga: the paragons of Italian literature, and already D'Annunzio stood as their equal. What might this prodigy accomplish when he reached the fullness of his powers?

Sommaruga observed D'Annunzio's success and was pleased, but not as pleased as he would become during the next year, 1883, when the young poet wrote *Intermezzo di rime*. There is a paradox in Sommaruga's reaction to this book, for *Intermezzo di rime* was a paralyzing critical disaster. Even Scarfoglio condemned these poems as "impoverished, convoluted and foolish verses for which no other punishment would be more opportune or apt than to pass over them in silence."[7] At the time, though, few critics passed over the book silently. Not all of them despised it, but Chiarini expressed the majority view when he denounced *Intermezzo* as the handiwork of a "pig poet." We may well wonder what all the commotion was about. The following passage is an example of what so shocked Chiarini:

> We stopped. Above our heads the radiance
> rained placid and fresh; in our flesh a new languor
> stirred, almost penetrating the skin,
> softening the veins. Now a desire of acute
> voluptuousness stabbed me before that unconscious
> virgin fair—"I am very tired"—
> she said, curling her body . . .
>   O how

her throat was visible amidst the wave of her hair
and her irises were lost, flowers down in the milky
   white
circle under her eyelids! O how her round breast
poured out of her dress!
      I felt over my eyes
descend a fleecy veil; and I fell on my knees.[8]

The critics' bane was meat for the publisher, and
Sommaruga welcomed the public outcry over *Intermezzo di rime*. The 1880s were fully modern, in the
sense that notoriety outweighed merit in the Italian
literary marketplace. The age of the bestseller had begun, and that meant the triumph of public relations
over every other consideration in the publishing industry. Sommaruga's exploitation of the *Intermezzo
di rime* scandal was a pioneering example of the uses
to which all commercial publishers eventually would
put publicity. He swiftly mounted a campaign to promote the controversy swirling around D'Annunzio.
With this end in view, the *Domenica letteraria* spon-
sored a debate on the merits of *Intermezzo di rime*.
The articles by in-house writers and outside contributors seemed to touch a public nerve, and sales for the
Letteraria picked up for a while as a by-product of
Sommaruga's tactic. There was no telling where his
mind, so fertile in expedients, would stop. If the articles were that provocative, he reasoned, why not publish them as a book? And so *Alla ricerca della verecondia* saw the light.
   The *Intermezzo di rime* promotion ignited Sommaruga's campaign to push D'Annunzio's decadent
image. Anyone who takes the trouble to read his earliest work will discover that the young D'Annunzio was
a swarm of possibilities. His talent was so great that
he could produce any effect he chose. The induce-
ments for him to produce a decadent effect by writing

corrupt and immoral verse progressively increased. Almost by imperceptible stages he passed under the spell of Sommaruga's publicity campaign: D'Annunzio the dandy, D'Annunzio the esthete, D'Annunzio the *boulevardier*—a perfumed, pomaded seducer, enchanting all with his charm, wit, and elegance. These are the images that cluster about the D'Annunzian legend. How little they correspond with the picture of young Gabriele arriving in Rome at the end of 1881, a country boy just out of high school, without artifice, with nothing but good looks and a frequently remarked on lack of guile accompanying his undeniable literary talent.[9]

Where did the decadence come from then? Sommaruga did not concoct his publicity campaign out of thin air. A human being contains many different potential personalities, and circumstance favors the dominance of one. D'Annunzio might have developed in any of several directions, but the temptations and opportunities in Umbertian Rome for a gifted poet of his temperament made it unlikely that the country boy would mature into a country gentleman. The entire city entered into an unspoken conspiracy to debauch D'Annunzio, and never was there a more willing debauchee. Perhaps that was why Paris seemed not to affect him in later years: he had already been through a similar experience, and little remained to be corrupted. By 1883 Sommaruga's task as D'Annunzio's publicity agent was quite simple. D'Annunzio gave him plenty of material to work with, both in his writings and in his private life. His marriage to Maria di Gallese, who was already five months pregnant at the time of the ceremony, scandalized Rome, just when the city was also going into shock over *Intermezzo di rime*. On 12 January 1884 D'Annunzio wrote to his friend Enrico Nencioni, "With the innate temerity of my character, I have committed danger-

ous acts of madness, the last of which was a flight and
a kidnapping followed by enormous scandals. You can
imagine my enemies, the Philistines, all the mob of
moralists, in tumult. There were calumnies, slanders,
duels, lies; there was hell to pay."[10] Sommaruga was
just the businessman to exploit the commercial possibilities in all this, and in the process D'Annunzio's
decadent reputation took shape.

Yet Sommaruga had begun to overreach himself,
and the D'Annunzio promotional campaign wound up
by alienating the poet and causing a schism among
the *bizantini*. The *verecondia* controversy subjected
D'Annunzio to a degree of criticism for which he was
psychologically unprepared, and after the *Letteraria*
debate on *Intermezzo di rime* he withdrew in sullen
silence from all the *bizantini* who had not supported
him.[11]

His relations with Scarfoglio worsened almost daily
in 1883, and finally the two fought a duel. D'Annunzio sustained a light wound, but it was a trifle compared with the injuries Scarfoglio had earlier inflicted
on his vanity. In the beginning Scarfoglio had been
D'Annunzio's warmest supporter, bestowing numerous rave reviews on his earliest work, particularly the
Bizantina poems celebrating the Abruzzi.[12] Yet, like
Chiarini, Scarfoglio sensed a noxious element in this
poetry. For Chiarini, the problem with D'Annunzio
involved moral decadence; for Scarfoglio, it was decadence of style.[13] D'Annunzio's growing interest in
Oriental themes, his use of exotic imagery, and his
penchant for dandyism were all early examples of an
uncanny faculty for appropriating fashions in thought
and in deportment just before they gained widespread
acceptance. D'Annunzio nearly always had a superb
sense of timing.

Nevertheless, Scarfoglio feared that these changes

in style augured ill for his friend. Separated from the natural sources of his inspiration, D'Annunzio would degenerate into a disgusting fop. Scarfoglio lamented the transformation of his "ingenuous, modest, and sweet" friend into the new Gabriele, "clever, vain, and calculating"—the antithesis of the country boy he once knew. Worse, D'Annunzio's art underwent a similar transformation: "Farewell to the serene and pure contemplation of nature. . . . Art which earlier had been everything to him, became a childish game for the delight of those poor ladies who wanted some sonnets in their albums."[14] In the name of sacred friendship, Scarfoglio wrote the mercilessly satirical "Da parte degli amici (A Gabriele D'Annunzio)." Where was the rough-hewn poet from whose "soul haughtily/ As a beast from his lair to the assault/ The sonnet sprang impatiently"? Who was this pathetic imposter? Nature's child had become society's spoiled pet poodle:

> Now the ladies of Rome educated
> the uncivilized boy in a moment.
> And those wild curls, they combed
> into little tassels flowing in the wind.[15]

What a fall was there. The once-virile master of sea-scape poetry now looked the part of "an English groom," and in the end he would sound like "the poet Ko-Ko who speaks with magicians."[16]

Soon after their duel, D'Annunzio patched up his differences with Scarfoglio. Both men agreed that the real cause of the poet's difficulties was none other than Sommaruga; he stood revealed at last as a grasping rogue who, under a verbal patina of Carduccianism, worked to ensnare and corrupt the *bizantini*. D'Annunzio now retired to the ancestral Villa del Fuoco on the Adriatic, to escape the frantic pace of Rome—

("this most ridiculous Babylon," he called it) and to
think about the future. Clearly, Sommaruga's manage-
ment of his career displeased him. Writers traditionally mistrust agents and despise publishers. However, in
the 1880s the division of labor between publisher and
agent was still off in the future, and Sommaruga had
to carry both crosses up Mount Parnassus. The burden
proved unbearable long before he reached the top.

D'Annunzio, suspicious and disgruntled, harbored
his resentments in silence until 1884, when the Casa
Sommaruga brought out his latest collection of short
stories, *Il libro delle vergini*. In what he thought was
a master stroke for his publicity campaign on D'Annunzio's behalf, Sommaruga had a special cover made
for *The Book of the Virgins*, offering a provocative
view of several half-naked women in a variety of
erotic poses. It was nothing more than the usual Sommaruga publicity gimmick, the kind of come-on that
he customarily employed; but D'Annunzio became
furious. On 24 June he mailed a copy of the book to
Nencioni, having "ripped from the volume its infamous cover."[17] Sickened by what he called Sommaruga's "duplicity," D'Annunzio wrote his publisher a
blistering letter on the same day:

> Tacitly you want me to write another *Intermez-
> zo*! But the *Intermezzo* is the product of an in-
> firmity, of a mental weakness, of a momentary
> decadence. The inspiration for the *Intermezzo* is to
> be found in the tenor of my life during that false
> epoch. The *Intermezzo* is not a pornographic book;
> it is a human document; it is a manifestation of
> unhealthy art, in which only a few verse stanzas
> have any real merit.
>
> Now I am renewed; I no longer write verse; I
> write prose serenely; I study.

> Don't hinder my way with your ruinous publicity![18]

D'Annunzio's complaint bewildered Sommaruga, and his bewilderment becomes understandable when we consider a letter that he received only three months earlier. Concerning *Il libro delle vergini* D'Annunzio had written, "I believe that its success is assured. . . . I have juxtaposed the most audacious material with the most mild. The locale shifts back and forth between a bordello and a church, between the scent of incense and the smell of the sewer. You will see."[19] D'Annunzio added, almost parenthetically, that he would need more money than he had originally agreed to accept, and for the next several weeks the two men haggled over royalties. When Sommaruga refused to alter the original contract, D'Annunzio threatened to seek another publisher. Finally they reached a compromise, and Sommaruga published *Il libro delle vergini*, never suspecting that D'Annunzio would make a moral issue over the book's cover design. The publisher was not guiltless; he confessed in his memoirs, "I was wrong not to submit the cover design to him for his approval, and I admit that it was really ugly."[20] Three months later D'Annunzio broke with Sommaruga and signed a contract with Treves of Milan.

It was the first tremor of a great earthquake. D'Annunzio's defection set in motion a series of other defections, and on 11 October 1884 most of the *bizantini maggiori* made a public declaration of their break:

> The undersigned no longer have anything to do with signor A. Sommaruga, with any of his journals, with any product of his editorial house.
>
> G. Salvadori   G. D'Annunzio   M. Serao

G. Rovetta   E. Scarfoglio   L. Capuana
                                     Carlo Dossi[21]

Sommaruga faced this secession with Lincolnesque decisiveness. In an open letter to the *bizantini*, he promised "to put all my cards on the table." There followed a case-by-case analysis of his dealings with each detractor. Scarfoglio, for instance, had been a little childish; but he knew the literary scene well, and would be difficult to replace. D'Annunzio was simply being vindictive about money; he wanted to use the *Vergini* cover design as an excuse to get out of his contract. Sommaruga very mistakenly attributed Salvadori's defection to the poet's disappointment over a *Cronaca bizantina* decision not to run his commemoration of the deceased poet, Giovanni Prati, publishing instead one written by Carducci. In fact, Salvadori had become completely disenchanted with the Casa Sommaruga long before the D'Annunzio schism occurred, and for reasons that were much deeper than Sommaruga could comprehend.[22] Interestingly, the publisher lamented that he would miss Matilde Serao the most: "From her pen came the 'Salotti Romani' articles [signed by her pen name Riccardo Joanna] that made such an explosion in the aristocratic world, an explosion comparable to that of the *Forche caudine* in the political world."[23]

No matter, Sommaruga would carry on with new writers. He would be of good cheer as long as Carducci stood by him. D'Annunzio and Scarfoglio had already tried to turn Carducci against Sommaruga. Writing from the Villa del Fuoco, D'Annunzio depicted the schismatics' side of the controversy, essentially deploring Sommaruga's base attempt to dilute the ideological purity of the *bizantini*.[24] Scarfoglio's attack on Sommaruga, "that pirate of commerce," was even more furious. In a letter written on 8 October 1884 he explained to Carducci that "the bad faith and the villainy of Sommaruga" had driven the *bizantini* away. After making dark allusions to Sommaruga's turbulent private life, including an especially snide remark about the publisher's affair with a ravishing Roman beauty, signora Adele Mai, Scarfoglio concluded: "To prove to you that I and the others have abandoned Sommaruga for motives of pure morality, it is enough for you to know that I am left with a novel on my hands and no publisher. . . ."[25] Neither letter convinced Carducci. He put off both young men, claiming to understand nothing of the petty bickerings among the *bizantini*. Anyway, Carducci had to be above the fray. As the master of all his disciples he could be the partisan of none.

Yet in fact Carducci did choose sides. Early in October he wrote a warm letter of support to the beleaguered publisher under the salutation, "Caro Angelino." There was the usual Carducci persiflage and then this: "You know, I have always liked you quite a bit."[26] Such a brief statement, but in those words Sommaruga found balm for his soul.

Carducci's motives here reveal the complexities of the man as much as any act in his eventful life. He liked Sommaruga well enough, but there was also the question of money. As Carducci had explained to Chiarini on 5 June 1884: "You are right, Sommaruga is a monster. But I must save him; if not, he will not pay me what I am owed [8,000 lire]." Still, the money was far from the whole story. In the same letter he added, "knowing Sommaruga inside out I know that he is a good boy who has been unlucky."[27] Chiarini, who despised Sommaruga, spent a lifetime trying to talk Carducci out of this opinion, but to no avail. In 1903, when Carducci, a crippled invalid, wrote his old publisher for the last time, Sommaruga was still "Caro Angelino."

Sommaruga's comparison between the *Forche cau-dine* and the "Salotti Romani" was ironic because his relationship with Pietro Sbarbaro had caused many of the old line *bizantini* to break with him. If the *Cronaca bizantina* had not been founded with a spe-cific political or literary aim in mind, all the *bizantini* agreed that a great cultural battle had to be fought, in Carducci's name, against the Philistines. It would not have done to press any of these writers on the precise objectives of this mighty struggle, or, to demand that they explain who, exactly, the enemy might be. Such matters were assumed, rather than demonstrated. However, the pressure of affairs caused Sommaruga to lose sight of this assumption, and inevitably he lost the respect of the Scarfoglio-D'Annunzio-Salvadori wing of the *Bizantina* staff by claiming to be no more than a businessman. Then, by financing Sbarbaro's yellow journalism, Sommaruga pronounced himself a vulgar businessman at that, and the young idealists hastily dissociated themselves from him.

These intellectuals wanted an answer to D'Annun-zio's question, "Who will liberate us from the torture of the Forche?"[28] Even Carducci voiced disgust over what he called Sbarbaro's "ravings." In a letter to Sommaruga, written on 17 June 1884 he complained, "I don't know what purpose the *Forche caudine* can serve except to maintain this unhealthy literature that afflicts the century."[29] The poet counseled "modera-tion, discretion, order," but these were not words to catch the publisher's attention. In his letters to Som-maruga from June to October, Carducci rarely failed to denounce the *Forche caudine* as an "unwholesome publication" or as "a not very beautiful institution." He implored Sommaruga to break away from Sbar-baro while there was still time. It was wasted ink and paper. He might just as well have tried to prevent a meteorite from crashing into the earth.

Sommaruga did not immediately perceive the full magnitude of the *bizantina* schism, even hoping that, in the end, it would be a blessing. After all, his original base—his Carducci—remained secure. His enterprises had proliferated to include many different kinds of journalism and every level of taste in book publishing. The Casa Editrice Sommaruga was flourishing as never before. Yet he knew better than anyone else that success was contingent upon success. Sommaruga the image-maker was the most image-conscious publisher of his time. Let some disruption occur, some break in the continuity of the public's esteem or faith in a celebrity's image, and no one could say what the consequences would be. Sommaruga's image was a success image. Now that this massive defection had happened, the potential loss in profits and prestige was large. He had never really solved the cash flow problem, and with the *bizantini* gone money surely would get tighter, at least in the short run. He needed time to think, to plan; but he also needed money to keep the "publicity machine" running. If only Carducci were present to give advice. However, in his heart Sommaruga knew what that advice would have been: to sell off the surplus operations, and cut back to the *Cronaca bizantina* bone. That advice the publisher did not want to hear, and he kept his own counsels.

The schism forced Sommaruga to make a gamble which he had little chance of winning, though at the time no one could have foreseen the magnitude of his loss. As the old guard abandoned him, he looked for fresh recruits. The pickings were meagre, as anyone who reads the last six months of the *Cronaca bizantina* will observe. The condition of the Casa was much more grave than Sommaruga at first realized, because he could not replace the talent that he had lost. How his enemies savored the scandal. With what delight they contemplated his embarrassment. One clearcut success might restore him to favor, though, reestablishing the integrity of the image that he had worked so assiduously to promote.

In the fall of 1884, the question for Sommaruga was where to look for the best prospects of that clear-cut success. It did not take him long to discover that he had but one chance to remain solvent while the schism receded from the public consciousness. The only Sommaruga publication that enjoyed roaring sales after the schism was Sbarbaro's *Forche caudine*. Sommaruga hesitated briefly. True, his affiliation with Sbarbaro had gotten him into trouble with the *bizantini*; but they were the past, and there was no use worrying about them any longer. Sitting around the spacious Via dell'Umiltà offices, less crowded now than in the old days—strange to be talking about the old days at twenty-five—Sommaruga concluded that this critical moment called for desperate measures. He made a fatal miscalculation by continuing and strengthening the alliance with Sbarbaro. The *Forche caudine*, at first a weekly publication, began to come out twice a week with supplements, providing in the words of one contemporary diarist, "enough insolence for all."[30] Toward the end the *Forche caudine* appeared to be one with the Casa Sommaruga; in the public mind, the identification of newspaper and publishing house was complete. For Sommaruga this coupling proved disastrous. Step by step he walked along a path of gold to his ruin, all the time hoping that the stupendous sales of Sbarbaro's hysterical rantings would rescue him from the threat of oblivion. The *Forche caudine* did bring him profits, but at a terrible price.

It is more than likely that, on the night when Sommaruga visited D'Annunzio in France, the two at least mentioned the recent re-publication of Scarfoglio's *Il libro di Don Chisciotte*. The book had been published originally by Sommaruga in 1883. It created no stir then, but by 1911 the nostalgia value of *l'età bizantina* was already immense. Scarfoglio's *Don Chisciotte* held the distinction of being the only primary source memoir written by one of the *bizantini*, but it took a quarter-century for this fact to become important. Scarfoglio prayed conventionally at all the stations of the Carduccian cross: art was sacred, the crowd vile, Italy tragically betrayed by the false leaders of the post-Risorgimento. At the same time, it was a potpourri book. Scarfoglio threw everything into it: hitherto unpublished letters by Carducci, Chiarini, De Amicis, and many others affiliated with the Casa Sommaruga; essays old and new on the plight of Italian literature, and on the aims of the *Cronaca bizantina*. The title had a double meaning—to suggest an image of idealism ("We are the Don Quixote of Criticism"), and to remind everyone that the *bizantini* were Carduccians, for *Don Chisciotte* was the name of a Bologna newspaper closely associated with Carducci.[31] It all went for nothing at the time. What had such picturesque charm in 1911 had no appeal at all in 1883; and the book failed so completely that it reinforced the author's decision to abandon literary criticism for a new career in political journalism.

We know that Sommaruga derived intense satisfaction from Scarfoglio's new preface for the 1911 edition, "Ventisette anni dopo." This preface also served as the confession of a man whose most painful memory was his role in Sommaruga's tragedy. Scarfoglio described the annihilation of the Casa Sommaruga as a "monstrous iniquity," adding with regret and contrition: "Even the most unaware will be convinced that if his wings had not been violently torn off, this agitator of the most lazy men would have done something grand and beautiful."[32] When it came time for Sommaruga to write his own memoirs, in 1940, he simply quoted Scarfoglio's "Ventisette anni dopo" preface for that part of the story. His antagonist's confiteor was conclusive testimony that Sommaruga had been the schism's victim, not its perpetrator. What pleasure it gave Sommaruga to have the old *bizantini* come around one by one to resume their friendships with him. Scarfoglio's preface was an absolving last word which made the betrayal less painful to recall. Vindication, Sommaruga explained in *Cronaca bizantina: (1881–1885): noti e ricordi*, robbed him of all desire to launch a polemic: "I lack any polemical incentive to refute point by point, as I could, the inexactitudes, the calumnies and infamies that were said and published about me. It would take too much of an effort, and I don't feel the least need to do it."[33] Yet he could not help but wonder what "grand and beautiful" thing his publishing house might have accomplished had the schism never occurred, and had he not been forced into the fatal Sbarbaro alliance.

CHAPTER SIX

POLITICS AND CULTURE IN

THE SOMMARUGA PUBLISHING

EMPIRE: PIETRO SBARBARO

(1838–1893)

"Sempre avanti Savoia!"
—Queen Margherita (masthead quotation on the
Forche caudine)

In 1911 Benedetto Croce concluded a five-page essay on Pietro Sbarbaro with this observation: "In truth, I would have been able to write less on Sbarbaro if thirty years or so ago he had not represented an important part of Italian life, and if the opinion had not formed (which persists still among some) that he, notwithstanding the defects of his temperament, was a man of great genius and an excellent writer."[1] Croce would have none of the Sbarbaro legend. Even Sbarbaro's literary prolificacy, such a convincing proof of genius to his contemporaries, did not impress Croce, himself a graphomaniac. His was a "banal fecundity," Croce observed, accurately: today the books and articles of this apologist for the House of Savoy are mentioned with derision when they are mentioned at all.

Though unreadable now, Sbarbaro's work enjoyed an astonishing vogue in the mid-1880s. When Sommaruga wrote his memoirs, he recalled that Sbarbaro's *Regina o repubblica?* was by far his company's greatest commercial success.[2] This fact is of crucial im-

portance in the history of Sommaruga's publishing
house because of its influence on his strategy after the
Bizantina schism. Sbarbaro's appeal baffled Sommaruga. Certainly in appearance Sbarbaro was as unlikely
a best-selling author as one could imagine. Short,
obese, and almost completely bald, with a long, un-
kempt beard flowing down his chest and resting on an
immense paunch, he suffered constant ridicule from
his enemies; but his bizarre appearance only height-
ened the public's interest in him, once the contents of
his queer books became known.[3]

Sbarbaro was one of those best-selling authors whose
fame is like a comet, flashing brilliantly for a moment
and then vanishing forever. Nevertheless, as late as
the time of Croce's devastating analysis, a shimmering
haze of notoriety clung to Sbarbaro's name. This is not
surprising, for survivors from the 1880s still remembered the infamous Sbarbaro and Sommaruga trials
of 1885, which ended the *Bizantina* age. The *Forche
caudine* lived on in popular legend long after the
writhings of its last victim, Angelo Sommaruga, were
stilled.

Sbarbaro was only seventeen when he got his first
newspaper job, although even earlier he had announced his ambition to become a university professor. Actually, he seems to have pursued academic and
journalistic careers simultaneously, beginning in the
late 1850s, when he directed the *Saggiatore* of his
native Savona while still preparing for the university.
There was nothing unusual in any of this activity;
indeed, his early career reminds us in many ways of
the young Carducci's. Both men were representative
intellectuals from the provincial middle class, following the normal channels for advancement. Both also
began their public careers as the Risorgimento neared
its climax.

Sbarbaro became passionately devoted to the cause of Italian independence. Twice he interrupted his studies in jurisprudence and political economy at the University of Pisa for patriotic reasons: in 1859 to fight in the Second War of Liberation against Austria, and in 1861 to edit *Espero*, the pro-Cavour newspaper of Giuseppe La Farina's National Society. After Cavour's death, Sbarbaro returned to Pisa as the assistant to his teacher, Gian Battista Michelini, who had been the leading disciple of the early nineteenth century liberal economist, Giovanni Domenico Romagnosi. Sbarbaro took his degree in 1864.

The young scholar's ambition was to teach, but he had to wait until the following year for a regular opening in political economy at the University of Modena. Sbarbaro blamed the government for the delay, and this may have been the start of his bitter personal antagonism toward Italy's political leaders. After all, the government controlled the Italian university system, making university teaching positions (like other civil service appointments) subject to the uncertainties of changing administrations, particularly for junior faculty members.[4] In the meantime he kept busy as the director of Ancona's *Corriere delle Marche*. There is some evidence that Sbarbaro taught political economy at the University of Ancona, but if he did so it was on a part-time basis.[5] This pattern of alternately—and often simultaneously—working on newspapers and teaching was to be the chief characteristic of his professional life until the 1880s.

Sbarbaro displayed a high degree of excitability in both lines of work. An impassioned liberal, he revered Gladstone in politics and Channing in religion. The laissez-faire principles of the Manchester School he considered unassailable. Here again, Sbarbaro spoke for his class and generation. There was nothing exceptional about his liberal Christian views for an Italian university professor of this era; but from the first Sbarbaro defended them with a zeal that many thought excessive. He quickly earned a reputation as a redoubtable polemicist, both in print and behind the lectern. It was in this last capacity that Sbarbaro provoked the ire of university officials.

He had come to the University of Modena as the fair-haired boy of Italian scholarship, with a large and growing reputation based chiefly on *Sulla filosofia della ricchezza* (1864).[6] Moreover, the Modena years (1865–72) witnessed the publication of several more of his books. In quick succession Sbarbaro wrote *Da Socino a Mazzini* (1866), *Sulla università di Modena* (1867), *L'economia politica e libertà* (1868), a three-volume series entitled *Degli operai del secolo XIX* (1868–69), and *Della libertà* (1871). Neither this flurry of publications nor his record as a provocative teacher could counteract the ill effects of his volatile personality. In 1872 he was dismissed from his academic position for "political reasons."[7]

Documented information for this period in Sbarbaro's life is sketchy, but apparently his advanced views on freedom of speech resulted in frequent clashes with university and government officialdom. Giuseppe Mazza, his admiring and often careless biographer, wrote in *Sulla vita e sulle opere di Pietro Sbarbaro* (1891) that, rather than drift into the easy life of an ivory-tower academic, Sbarbaro chose to become the "professore apostolato."[8] Mazza did not disclose the precise aims of this apostolate, but other less sympathetic commentators have suggested that Sbarbaro early developed into an intellectual megalomaniac, consistently alienating his less charismatic colleagues.[9]

The prime minister, Giovanni Lanza, personally retained a kindly attitude toward Sbarbaro and encouraged him to hope for another appointment in the un-

specified future. However, no amount of benevolent
concern from a politician in distant Rome could as-
suage the young professor's distress. For the thirty-
four-year-old Sbarbaro, dismissal from the University
of Modena on what he termed "specious grounds" was
a personal misfortune from which he never fully re-
covered. Fifteen years later, after he had become famous, Sbarbaro would write about the "treachery" at
Modena as the beginning of his "Via Crucis."[10]

In 1872 Sbarbaro took advantage of his unsought
and unwanted leisure to write *Sulle opinioni di Vincenzo Gioberti intorno all'economia politica e alla
questione sociale* (1874). Already evident was the
obsessive concern for self-justification that became
such a prominent feature of his later years. For the
introduction he simply strung together a litany of
quotations from favorable reviews of his earlier books.
Especially satisfying was an article in *The English
Theological Review* on his treatise, *Della libertà:* "He
hates tyranny with a perfect hatred," wrote the English reviewer. Sbarbaro cited this judgment with
pride. His intellectual credentials and moral stature
impressed the English, but the Modenese professors
had their doubts. So much the worse for the Modenese
professors.

Sulle opinioni di Vincenzo Gioberti was a summary
book, a useful though unexceptional five-hundred-
page compilation of all Sbarbaro's liberal ideas up to
1874. Not the substance, but the style of this book was
remarkable. He began with the customary praise for
John Stuart Mill, Theodore Parker, and William
Gladstone. The book's ostensible subject, the author of
On the Moral and Civil Primacy of the Italians
(1843), appeared in a less flattering light. After all,
Gioberti had been a priest, even if a relatively en-
lightened one; and insofar as he remained faithful to
Catholicism, his thought suffered. In Sbarbaro's view,

clericalism was the dangerous rock of Scylla on one
side of Italian politics, facing the socialist whirlpool of
Charybdis on the other. Through this perilously narrow strait the liberal cause had to be guided by all
fair-minded Italians.

Sbarbaro had claimed as much in his earliest tracts
and in his speeches as a delegate to various workers'
congresses during the late 1850s and early 1860s. In
Vincenzo Gioberti he substantiated, documented, and
fleshed out these views. Against the anti-liberal attacks of the mystics and the socialists, "humanity
could find no other defense than the doctrine which
harmoniously reconciles the principles and rights of
liberty . . . in a concert of human interests."[11] Italy's
great social problem would be solved "by educating
the nation in the cult of Law and Liberty; by making
the people religious, tolerant, and hard working."[12]
These were the normal utterances of a classic nineteenth-century liberal.

However, there was a tension in Sbarbaro's prose,
an impatience often verging on frenzy that revealed
a deep disquietude of mind. All the politicians were
"vulgar knaves" working for a "state despotism."
Every socialist, victimized by the "savage theories of
communism," conspired to transform Italy into a "democratic despotism." The Mazzinians were less dangerous now, "inclined toward mitigated socialism,
illogical, inconsequential, vague and indecisive"; but
republicanism, even with Mazzini gone, remained an
enemy to be refuted and destroyed.[13] The churchmen,
save his own Unitarian heroes from Socinus to Theodore Parker, were "mystifiers" and "charlatans."
Against these errors Sbarbaro favored "true liberalism," but he did not yet know how to translate abstract liberal principles into a program of political
action. His political education during the rest of the
1870s was to suggest a way.

In the same year when *Vincenzo Gioberti* appeared, Sbarbaro received a teaching appointment at the University of Macerata, as a professor of philosophy and administrative law. Again he alienated powerful colleagues as a result of "fierce polemics," which seem to have originated over his crusades for disarmament and world peace.[14] Most of the other professors viewed Sbarbaro as a hopelessly neurotic crank whose immediate departure from the university would be a blessing for all. Their opposition gave the Depretis ministry an excuse to dismiss Sbarbaro in 1876.

He moved to Bologna, where he taught at an atheneum for a time; but two years later, with the appearance of the Cairoli ministry, Sbarbaro accepted an appointment at the University of Naples. This lecturer's position was a godsend. At forty, Sbarbaro could no longer think of himself as a young professor with the future before him. He had published nothing for several years, and had begun to fade from view in his profession. Things went better in Naples, at least temporarily, and he taught public administration in relative peace.

Sbarbaro's mature political beliefs began to crystalize in Naples. The "parliamentary revolution" of 1876, in which the conservative right lost power, filled him with dread. The sole Italian political leader in whom Sbarbaro retained faith was the right's Giovanni Lanza, and now that doughty paladin stood in opposition. Sbarbaro later published an adulatory memoir of his hero, together with selected correspondence between the two men. That book, *Medico e ministro: lettere di Giovanni Lanza* (1883), reflected Sbarbaro's dismay over the post-1876 changes in Italian politics. Although many liberals professed to see no difference between the left and the right, Sbarbaro deplored the moral vacuum in which Depretis, the "Mago di Stradella," formulated policy. Moreover, the indignant professor took an apocalyptic view of the anarchist uprisings, pitiful failures though they were, which seemed to occur with distressing frequency after the left gained power. These revolutionary events pushed Sbarbaro farther to the right, but not as far as he would eventually go.

In 1880 Sbarbaro wrote *Il partito conservatore in Italia*.[15] Here, for the first time, he recognized the need for the "clerical sect" in any future conservative coalition. This recognition marked a decisive change in Sbarbaro's thinking, because it allowed him to move well beyond the ideological confines of Risorgimento liberalism. As a Unitarian, he could not envision a philosophical accord with Catholicism, but Catholics would be indispensable in the coming political struggle with socialism. He reasoned that, if the Catholic faithful could be brought into the Italian political arena as supporters of the existing order, the socialist-anarchist threat would be met by an irresistible force. Thinkers like Jacini and Sonnino had been saying the same thing for years, but, in calling for an alliance of all Italians worried about the "excesses of the democratic principle in the social order," Sbarbaro took an important step forward in his search for an authentic political party of the right.

The fall of the second Cairoli ministry in May 1881 was a disaster for Sbarbaro. With the return to power of the Depretis government, Sbarbaro reaped the whirlwind he had sown in his intemperate attacks on the most powerful man in Italian politics. Depretis had Sbarbaro fired shortly afterward on the pretext that his "polemics" were unbecoming to a university professor. Such were the perils for an outspoken dissident in Umbertian Italy. Married and the father of a growing family, Sbarbaro was out of work once again. He had known the anxiety of the unemployed; now he felt the despair of the unemployable. Sbarbaro was now forty-three, but at any age the prospects of employment for a thrice-sacked professor would be hopeless.

Angelo Sommaruga rescued Sbarbaro from the ash heap. He published Sbarbaro's *Medico e ministro: lettere di Giovanni Lanza*, but this modest biography and anthology offered only a faint hint of what the pair's extraordinary publisher-author relationship would produce. Sbarbaro's interminable feuding with various university and government officials in 1882–83 created a sensation in the scandal-mongering Roman press, and Sommaruga moved quickly to capitalize on the free publicity. Sbarbaro, too, realized that the celebrity conferred upon him by the newspapers was a powerful weapon in his war against the men he described as "the authors of my ruin." On 5 May 1882 Sbarbaro wrote to his wife, Concetta, that he was on the way "toward the temple of glory and immortality."[16] Sommaruga publications would give him a forum where he could strike back at his antagonists, and Sbarbaro eagerly accepted the young publisher's contract.[17]

Sommaruga's hunch paid an enormous dividend with the publication of *Regina o repubblica?*, but he later recalled that the book was a mixed blessing. "It would be impossible," he wrote in his memoirs, "to enumerate the polemics and the attacks that this book inspired. And from that moment on, the most bitter criticisms were launched against me, and I was accused of bringing forth scandalous publications."[18]

In fact, *Regina o repubblica?* was the sequel to *Re travicello o re costituzionale?*, a Sbarbaro book that Sommaruga had brought out several months earlier, although the publisher claimed the two manuscripts were written as one book. In a foreshadowing of the Maxwell Perkins–Thomas Wolfe collaboration, Sommaruga had to organize and quite literally edit Sbarbaro's rambling manuscripts into books of publishable length. The story of how *Regina o repubblica?* came into existence as a spinoff from *Re travicello o re costituzionale?* is a case in point. Sommaruga remembered:

> I knew of his extraordinary prolixity when I agreed to publish his *Re travicello o re costituzionale?* so I did not wait for him to stop sending me chapters [before going to press]; seeing that with the chapters already on hand I had enough for a good-sized volume, I published the book and put it on sale without even notifying him of what I had done. And in the meantime, Sbarbaro continued to send me chapters. But when he saw the published volume, he, who had not succeeded in finding a publisher before, was so happy that he did not make the slightest protest. "That which remains," he said, "will comprise another volume."[19]

The other volume was *Regina o repubblica?*

In *Re travicello o re costituzionale?* Sbarbaro struck the note that would dominate all of his subsequent political writing: "The king reigns but does not govern! . . . I am fighting this principle because it is the root of everything that is false in public opinion. . . ."[20] How easy it was for him to see in his own personal misfortunes a microcosm of Italy's ills. Having been victimized himself by unprincipled ministers who passed in and out of power, Sbarbaro could think of no other remedy for Italian political problems than the elimination of *trasformismo* itself, which inevitably produced the reign of "vulgarity."

From his own private tragedy and pain came understanding. Everything was at last clear: only the king could save Italy from the corrupt transformist politi-

cal system, symbolized at its most deadly level by
Agostino Depretis, "the great contraband dealer from
Stradella."[21] If the ideal of every society were admittedly democracy, that ideal could never be attained under the rule of politicians like Depretis, who
only educated the people for wantonness. In its evolution toward democratic practices, a people required
time and education. The king promised to give Italy
both, as a symbol of unity opposed to the potentially
anarchic factionalism of the parties, and as an exemplar of devoted patriotism.[22]

"I send forth a cry of alarm!" Sbarbaro wrote in *Re
travicello o re costituzionale?*, the first of his jeremiads
aimed at awakening in the king a sense of the monarchy's danger; but a much more forceful statement
along these lines appeared in *Regina o repubblica?*.
Again, he preached that Italy needed a moral regeneration, only in the later book his readers learned that
the alternative to ethical rebirth was the complete collapse and destruction of the nation: "Either Margherita or death! Either Italy will conform to the model of
domestic virtues provided by the royal family, or it
must conform to the example of Lucrezia Borgia . . .
and it will fall."[23]

Sbarbaro described his doomsday vision in the lurid
introductory chapter to Part II, entitled "Decadenza e
corruzione degli ordini dello stato nell'Italia del
1893." He looked ahead to 1893 as the year when a
terrible catastrophe, far worse than that which destroyed Pompeii, would befall Rome. The pattern of
history never changed: the wage of sin was death. He
wrote scathingly of the imaginary political figures
who might be in office at that time, such as "Don
Fabrizio De Profundis," whose chief counselor "has
two daughters, one of them beautiful and the other
cross-eyed; and now he sleeps with one, now with the
other."[24] This kind of titillating copy made *Regina o*

repubblica? a best-seller and won him an immense reading audience.

Sbarbaro had found his mature literary style at last, and what made it unique was the startling mixture of biblical probity with fishwife idiom. He pushed aside obscenity charges with the egotistical claim that, if Dante and the prophets of the Bible could use colorful language in a sacred cause, so could a modern Italian patriot. In Chapter XX of *Regina o repubblica?*, for example, he related the exploits of Italy's minister of education in 1893, "Francesco dell'Utero." Knowing readers were not slow to recognize in the portrait a likeness of Francesco De Sanctis, the renowned literary historian who, while acting as minister of public instruction, had engaged Sbarbaro in several well-publicized disputes. Such men could only bring about the demise of the monarchy, and once a republic was established, Italy would be condemned to endure horrors recalling "the obscene saturnalia of the Terror and the orgies of 1793!"[25]

The highlight of Sbarbaro's terrible vision was his own imaginary trial at the hands of republican "scandalmongers, thieves, pederasts, and dope dealers."[26] Naturally, he kept all the choicest lines for himself. His courtroom testimony took the form of Ciceronian orations, and in a final long harangue he proclaimed: "I raise myself against you! And I rise as the defender of the crown that now lies fallen in the blood of civil discord, that is broken by foreign armies . . . and I do so in the name of the same humane and liberal principles that you have written on the frontispiece of the book [that describes] our new social life."[27] It was a virtuoso performance, but Sbarbaro's plea for the restoration of morality and sound political institutions went unheeded by his opponents. The predictable result was that Italy fell victim to foreign invasion.

How he savored the role of avenging angel:

"Against this cesspool of Byzantine corruption, that grows and grows daily, we fight with the name of Sella in politics and with the ideal of a virtuous queen in the social order. And he who is not with us is against us!"[28] As for the latter, Sbarbaro simply referred to them as the "Lega dei Malfattori;" and as a contrast to the pure whiteness of the ideal Italy that he loved, the dark purpose of these malefactors made a perfect target for his polemical shafts.

If *Regina o repubblica?* gave Sbarbaro fame, the *Forche caudine*, a curious mixture of newspaper and personal newsletter, gave him a pulpit.[29] Sommaruga played a vital role in both enterprises. He had no interest in Sbarbaro's mission, but he surmised that the author of two best-selling books might turn an even greater profit for the Sommaruga publishing house as a newspaper editor. "The great success enjoyed by Pietro Sbarbaro's two volumes," Sommaruga wrote in his memoirs, "gave me the unhappy idea—and this I call it because for me it was fatal—to make myself the publisher of a weekly that he would edit, the *Forche caudine*."[30]

Many of the planning sessions for the *Forche caudine* took place in Sbarbaro's jail cell. Through much of June and July in 1884 the best-selling author beat a path between the Tribunale Correzionale in the Convento dei Filippini behind the Chiesa Nuova and the Carceri Nuove in Trastevere. The first of Sbarbaro's many trials for libel occurred shortly after he spat in the face of Guido Baccelli, Depretis' minister of instruction. The "spitting trial" (*il processo per lo sputo*), as the newspapers called it, inspired one of Baccelli's best friends, the Roman poet Giggi Zanozzo, to write "Un Manifesto Contro le *Forche caudine*," which was signed, among others, by Giulio Salvadori. In this broadside Sbarbaro, introduced as "a vulgar

delinquent," was accused of writing "disgusting filth,"
of "criminal cowardice," and of "moral turpitude."
Sbarbaro's pollutions, Zanozzo charged, had made "a
bordello of the Italian capital."[31] The accused got off
lightly for his spitting offense, but young Alfredo
Baccelli, the minister's son, forgave less easily than
the court. One July afternoon he caught Sbarbaro in
the Piazza Colonna right in front of the crowded Caffè
Falchetto. The irate youth gave Sbarbaro two hard
slaps before the applauding on-lookers.

Later that same month Sbarbaro became involved in
a litigation with Augusto Pierantoni, a professor who
happened to be the son-in-law of the Italian foreign
minister, Pasquale Stanislao Mancini. Sbarbaro called
the professor "a Himalaya of ignorance" and used him
in a series of articles as an example of the nepotism
that permeated Italian politics and university life.
This time the court condemned him to eight months
in jail and ordered him to pay a fine of three hundred
lire. Sbarbaro avoided this punishment by publishing
a retraction, but within days he again took after Pierantoni in print for "monumental bestialities and
grammatical mistakes."[32] It seems that thereafter
Sbarbaro was obliged to go about Rome incognito for
a time and that the *Forche caudine* became something
of an underground newspaper, with frequent government sequestrations.

Never in the history of Italian journalism has any
semi-legal newspaper enjoyed such a phenomenal
commercial success, and the key factor in that success
was the editor's uncanny ability to exploit his own
notoriety. Sbarbaro's personal accounts of his trials
provided the people of Rome—indeed of all Italy—
with a marvelous summer entertainment. In this way
the *Forche caudine* became the direct beneficiary of
its founder's indiscretions, and Sommaruga became
the indirect beneficiary. The newspaper grew at a sen-

sational rate. The first number had appeared on 15 June 1884, but by August sales were estimated at 150,000 copies per issue, "a number that for those times was really exceptional," Sommaruga pointed out, "particularly for a paper made up of one man's personal polemics."[33]

These polemics were inspired by the phrase of Queen Margherita that Sbarbaro carried on the masthead: "Sempre avanti Savoia!" He was always devoted to the queen, and she became for him a Beatrice in the crusade to clean up Italian politics. In practical political terms this meant a reactionary reduction of Parliament's role in policy-making, and a return to the *Statuto* so that the king could resume his rightful place of authority and govern Italy.

Sbarbaro made his meaning clearer in "Per Intenderci," the lead article in the paper's maiden issue. "We are outside the Constitution!" he declared with customary shrillness. The Italians were living in the throes of anarchy, and all patriots had the duty to revive their faltering institutions. In this struggle—"the moral Risorgimento," Sbarbaro called it—his newspaper would have a role to play: "the *Forche caudine* will be the pillory, the scaffold, the torture chamber for all those who have committed political crimes, hypocrisy, and outrages . . . all of them must face the *Forche*."[34] But the just need not be afraid, for the editor would judge everyone with "serene impartiality." Only the perpetrators of "piggish" acts, those disgusting vermin who threatened to make Italy a "fornocracy" (*fornocrazia*) had cause to fear the wrath of Sbarbaro. In a companion article entitled "Tremano Tutti" he appeared almost to feel pity for his quarry: "Who can describe the dismay of those evil-doers caused by the simple announcement of my firm resolve to raise the veil of falsehood that covers the turpitude of their private lives? Who can speak of the fear caused . . . by the threat of revealing their lies?"[35]

Obviously, belated recognition as a writer had gone to Sbarbaro's head, and he interpreted the triumph of *Regina o repubblica?* as a personal vindication. Sbarbaro had always affected a superiority complex as a cover for his insecurity, but popular success had made him ludicrously bumptious. He was perfectly serious when he wrote, "The sword of General Garibaldi in 1860 will, in 1884, become the pen of Pietro Sbarbaro." Who could doubt his qualifications for this sacred mission?

> As for my character, who am I?
>
> A man who since 1854 has worked, studied, and lived uniquely for justice, for the country, and thus for the truth: a man who has fought for Unity and Independence—who has consecrated all of his being to the one and to the other and to the improvement of the working classes, without paying any mind to his own future and his own well being . . . a man who at the age of twenty-five was called to fill the university chairs of Silvio Spaventa and Francesco Trinchera in one of the most illustrious universities in the country; a man who has never mortgaged his conscience or his person to any party: who combats the arbitrariness and the abuses of all ministers, even of his own friends . . . a man who all of the most illustrious men of the Risorgimento, including Camillo Cavour, his nephew Alfieri, Tommaseo, Mazzini, Aurelio Saffi, Giuseppe La Farina, General Garibaldi, and Lorenzo Valerio—even when they did not share his opinions—have honored and continue to honor with their friendship and respect.
>
> These are *my titles* which give me the right to speak to the people of their rights, of their duties, of their grievances, and of their interests.
>
> What are the titles of my detractors?

I await the response from the pimps who mold
public opinion in order to make *money*.[36]

At forty-six, Sbarbaro intended to make full use of
his "moral authority" in the *Forche caudine*. True to
his reputation for graphomania, he wrote virtually the
entire paper himself. Nearly all of the articles dealt
with the twin themes of restoring the monarchy to its
rightful place and of exposing evil-doers in Parliament. His increasingly conservative views were not
unique, and in no sense did he act as a pioneer in
setting them forth. In fact, there is little evidence that
Sbarbaro gained any genuine ideological following
through the *Forche caudine*. His vogue depended less
on what he said than on how he said it. Although anti-
parliamentary sentiments had grown enormously
among Italian intellectuals, Sbarbaro's monarchism
was, at most, only an incidental element in his success. The triumph of the *Forche caudine* registered
primarily as a triumph of style.

More than anything, the salacious element in Sbarbaro's "mission" attracted Sommaruga and nearly
everyone else who read the *Forche*. Sbarbaro had
whetted his readers' appetites for sensational scandal
in *Regina o repubblica?*; in the *Forche caudine* he set
about to satisfy them. He was not the first newspaperman to attack the government, but no one before him
had called Depretis the head of a "moral dictatorship"
or Crispi "the bigamist of Palermo"—at least not in
such shockingly graphic terms.

The volume of his anti-administration criticism
rose in November 1884, after his arrest for violating
the country's censorship laws. In the next three weeks
the *Forche Caudine* underwent seven sequestrations.
Undaunted and only further infuriated by "barbaric
persecution," Sbarbaro returned to the fray each time
more determined to destroy the Depretis government.

The times might be decadent, Sbarbaro lamented, but Depretis could not govern "with the uterus" forever. As the sequestrations of the *Forche* mounted, Sbarbaro abandoned all restraint in his attacks, condemning Depretis as "the new Circe who transforms all around him into pigs." [37]

The *Forche*'s polemic against Crispi, too, became more vitriolic in late 1884. Crispi's private life had long been the subject of newspaper copy in Italy. During a long public career he had accumulated many enemies because of his controversial political views, and because of questionable dealings in which his government connections enabled him to profit financially, as in the tobacco monopoly scandals of the late 1860s. [38] However, the personal attacks against him became unusually severe only after 26 February 1878, when Rocco De Zerbi, the director of *Il piccolo*, accused him of bigamy. The charge, which touched off a national scandal when other newspapers picked up the story, came less than a month after his marriage to Lina Barbagallo. If this nuptial ceremony only signified that Crispi, at age sixty, was lucky enough to win a young and beautiful bride, then his fellow Italians might simply have winked at it, admiring the exuberance of an elder statesman. Alas, for Crispi it signified something more. Rejected and abandoned was Rosalia Montmasson, his wife of nearly a quarter-century, who had suffered with him through all the painful years of exile and deprivation. Crispi had met her in Turin, and she had fled with him to Malta after the suppression of the Milan uprising in 1853. They were married by a priest in Malta shortly before moving on to England the next year. Rosalia was what the novelists used to call "of low origins," but her heroic devotion to Crispi made a great impression on all who knew them. She achieved national fame as one of the three women in the Thousand, and Felice Cavallotti gave her a kind of literary immortality in a popular patriotic poem: for an entire generation, Rosalia became known as "The Angel of the Wounded."

Shortly after the close of the Risorgimento, Crispi and his wife moved back to Turin. While pursuing his parliamentary career there, he met Lina Barbagallo although their relationship did not become romantic for several years. Meanwhile, Crispi's affairs with other women (notably Luisa del Testa, by whom he had a son, Luigi), got him into boiling water at home. Then, in 1873, Lina gave birth to Crispi's daughter, Giuseppina. Unlike signora Carducci, Rosalia had no intention of resigning herself to an Italian wife's fate; instead, she retaliated by making Crispi's life as miserable as the rage of a powerful woman scorned could. Her best efforts in this direction were extremely effective, according to contemporary accounts, and it was not long before Crispi began seriously to contemplate suicide.[39] He finally decided to leave home instead, and their separation became formal in 1875. Three years later, after solemnly declaring that in conscience it was impossible for him to recognize the validity of a religious marriage, he married Lina in a civil ceremony. Crispi expected that her socially prominent family would help him advance his political ambitions at court; however, he did not count on the tremendous uproar occasioned by the De Zerbi bigamy charge. The scandal struck so hard that Crispi was forced to resign his ministry in the Depretis cabinet, and shortly afterward the entire government fell.

In 1884 it was rather late to be dredging up these events from Crispi's past, although, in defense of Sbarbaro's original cast of mind, it must be said that he did try to add to the Sicilian's disgrace. Intimating that the bigamist of Palermo might also be a "trigamist" (*trigamo*), the editor reminded *Forche caudine* readers that in his youth Crispi had been married to one

Rosina d'Angelo. Since there was no actual proof of her death, Sbarbaro, for one, would not be surprised if Crispi had three living wives. As for the question, why bring all of this up now, Sbarbaro had on hand what he imagined to be a stinging reply: the *Forche caudine* was not the place to reveal when and where a miserable woodcutter might sleep with his own daughter, but the private lives of the king's ministers and of Parliament members should be subject to public scrutiny.[40] In the case of a reprobate like Crispi, whose name had become a byword for philandering, Sbarbaro speculated that the ancient Polish punishment for adultery might be applicable, whereby "the man guilty of having seduced another man's wife would be brought to the public marketplace and there suspended by the guilty organ, with the choice of dying in that uncomfortable position or using a razor to free himself."[41] The sanctity of the family had to be preserved, at least in the private lives of Italy's political leaders; otherwise the country would degenerate into a "House of Tolerance" where "uterine terrors" and "horizontal women" held sway.

This was too much. Long derided as the "professore mattoide," Sbarbaro was now denounced by his victims as the "professore porco." On 15 February 1885 the government issued a decree shutting down the *Forche caudine*, thereby setting in motion the events which culminated in the destruction of Sommaruga's publishing house.

Croce was right: Sbarbaro's work cannot bear critical examination, and it is as difficult for us as it was for Sommaruga to understand the appeal of books like *Re travicello o re costituzionale?* and *Regina o repubblica?* One contemporary observer may have been right about the *Forche caudine* situation when he explained that the Italians were so disgusted with their

government, "Any attack, no matter how excessive
and unbalanced, against the domineering politicians
of Italy would be considered a vindication of the public conscience."[42] However, why the *bizantini* re-
coiled from Sbarbaro is much less of a mystery. Their
revulsion might seem perplexing when we read sam-
ples of his political rhetoric, which in its moral quality
had a Carduccian ring. In 1884 he asked:

> What have we done in Rome for the past four-
> teen years?
> In Rome we have not witnessed the appearance
> of any orator, tribune, or apostle who represents
> new ideas. . . . Everything is cheap and poor, every-
> thing reveals the signs of a whorehouse, not the
> city of the Third Risorgimento and of the human
> conscience that was inaugurated on 20 September
> 1870.
> Remember that and protest in silence![43]

When he wrote in that manner, Sbarbaro sounded
like an apostle for the politics of nostalgia. And that
was precisely the problem for the *bizantini*. When the
fool is heard speaking the truth, does that not make
the truth sound foolish? Sbarbaro's position appeared
to be an absurd caricature of their own; thus he made
them all look ridiculous. For men who took themselves
and their cause as seriously as the *bizantini* did,
laughter was the unkindest cut of all. D'Annunzio
spoke for the entire group when he demanded to know,
"Who will liberate us from the torture of the *Forche?*"
What a delicious irony for all concerned when the
liberator of the *bizantini* turned out to be the very
man they all had condemned as the arch nemesis of
the country's highest ideals, Agostino Depretis himself.

CHAPTER SEVEN

GIUDICATEMI!: THE FALL OF

THE SOMMARUGA PUBLISHING

HOUSE, 1885

"*Sommaruga has a good heart, a wonderfully
good heart. He has done much good for
many people.*"
—From Carducci's testimony at
Sommaruga's trial (1885)

When the Depretis government closed down the *Forche caudine*, it simultaneously ordered Sommaruga to desist from any further publishing efforts. This order sounded the death knell of his publishing house. During the next several months Sbarbaro and Sommaruga were brought to court on a number of charges, chiefly for defamation of character, violation of the censorship code, and extortion. Their trials took place consecutively in the summer of 1885, with both events receiving front-page coverage in the country's leading newspapers.

In *Cronaca bizantina (1881–1885): noti e ricordi*, Sommaruga glossed over the judicial murder of his company: "I do not want to mention here the matter of my trial. . . . My personal misadventure could not interest the reader. It is not right to stir up the memory of unhappy events; it is better to leave them in their place of silence."[1] He was more outspoken in 1885, however, in *Giudicatemi!*, an account of his ordeal at the hands of the government. All the bitter-

ness of the 1910 Sarti interview in Paris was presaged
here: "This book will be the last that I send to press.
With this I close my career as publisher."[2] Happily
for students of Umbertian Italy, Sommaruga did not
keep his word. Yet *Giudicatemi!* had the ring of a final
testament: "Books! Newspapers! Oh, I have published
many books, yes; oh, I have published many newspapers, but I don't want anything more to do with
them, never again."[3]

He attributed his downfall not to the Depretis government, but to his own refusal to link the Sommaruga
publishing house with any ideology or interest group:
"I tried to give, insofar as I was able, an impulse to
our young literature, without tying myself to any
school or party. But in this I made a mistake: for I was
without friends. If I had given myself to a party, if I
had made myself the interpreter of only the radicals
or only the moderates, or this or that group, they at
least would have commiserated with me in my fall."
What hurt him most was the refusal of his own journals to help him:

> And of my own journals, of those journals that
> after four years of assiduous work and sacrifices I
> was able to put on a paying basis, the best of them
> [*Nabab*] did not print a single word in my defense;
> and when there was talk of publishing a declaration
> on my behalf, no one had the courage to sign it;
> those were the same people who only a short time
> before had emptied bottles of champagne in my
> own house while pledging support to me.
> And after all this, you wonder if I would become
> a publisher again?
> Oh boy![4]

The eclectic nature of his publishing house was, in
fact, not the cause of Sommaruga's fall. In *Giudica-*

temi! Sommaruga asked to be judged on the basis of his overall achievement as a publisher, but his trial turned on an altogether different issue: Sbarbaro. The *Forche caudine* served as the rallying point for all of Sommaruga's enemies, and at the same time the paper's notoriety discouraged many of his friends from lending him their active support. These facts became clear in the light of the government's cases against the two defendants, beginning with the Sbarbaro trial and its aftermath.

Sbarbaro stood trial from 18 June to 10 July 1885. The courtroom crowd was enormous, and the oppressive Roman heat of summer took a heavy toll in fainting gallery onlookers. The one big surprise during the proceedings was the arrest and imprisonment on 26 June of Sbarbaro's lawyer, Tommaso Lopez, for his role in an embezzlement scheme. For several days the Lopez affair grabbed all the headlines, although Sbarbaro finally inched his way back onto page one. The replacement for Lopez was Angelo Muratori, an ex-deputy. Sbarbaro got a big laugh when the judge asked him if he were ready to proceed with his new lawyer. The defendant rose, looking straight at the judge, and exclaimed, "Sempre avanti Savoia!" This was not the last comical note in a trial that involved one hundred and forty-five separate pieces of testimony, including many depositions.

Sbarbaro himself did no laughing on the day of judgment when, as most observers expected, the verdict went in favor of the government. However, to everyone's surprise, Sbarbaro was found guilty not on the major charges pertaining to the country's press laws, but on a charge that initially appeared incidental to the prosecution's main case. The *Forche caudine* did not enter the picture at all. Instead, Sbarbaro received a two-year prison sentence for having written what the prosecution described as "menacing letters" (*lettere minatorie*) to Francesco De Sanctis, the minister of public instruction, during one of his many altercations with the government, and to other administration officials.

Ironically, the government trial, far from destroying Sbarbaro, gave his career a powerful if short-lived boost. Sympathy for him began to grow that fall, when the court of appeals added five years to his sentence. Nearly everyone outside the government thought this excessive, and Italian newspapers attacked the appeals court as a stooge for Depretis. The press was not alone in calling the court's verdict a heavy-handed attempt by the government to silence one of its most outspoken critics. In December the voters of Pavia elected Sbarbaro overwhelmingly to Parliament, and by means of a legal technicality he was freed from prison to enter the halls of Montecitorio.[5] In a symbolic gesture, the self-styled "Tribune of the People" took immediate advantage of his freedom to mount a makeshift chariot and, accompanied by noisy supporters, he rode through the streets of Trastevere to the shouts and hurrahs of the crowd.[6]

For all that, Sbarbaro's fame really passed its zenith in the summer of 1885. For example, none of his later newspapers approached the popularity of the original *Forche caudine*. At first the *Forche caudine: nuova serie* (18 June–6 August 1885) promised to do well, and Sbarbaro even boasted 500,000 readers.[7] Making allowances for this self-indulgent claim, interest in the Sbarbaro trial ran high; and the new *Forche*, which was little more than a compilation of the imprisoned editor's letters, enjoyed an early summer vogue. Sales quickly dropped, however. His *scritti incarcerarii* were supplemented by lurid articles on supposedly well authenticated homosexual and prostitution scandals in Rome, but the *élan* of the old *Forche* was missing.

Less than a month after the court handed down Sbarbaro's prison sentence, the *Forche caudine: nuova serie* disappeared.

Even his political career went badly. The opportunity to sit in Parliament promised to be the capstone of his crusade to build a truly conservative political party, but the promise was never realized. Sbarbaro took his seat on the extreme right, and he made numerous long-winded, florid speeches. His exaggerated theatrical delivery created the usual impression, and the popular press had a field day celebrating him as the Umbertian Gracchus. Nevertheless, by this time Sbarbaro had degenerated into a thoroughly *opéra bouffe* character, manifestly incompetent either to build or to direct a new political movement. Ugo Pesci, reporting on Sbarbaro's first address to his constituents in Pavia, noted: "It is not the same Sbarbaro who speaks, it is not the man whose university discourses were hailed as stupendous even by his enemies. . . . He forgets what he wants to say, he digresses, he talks about himself too much." Pesci concluded by remarking that everyone seemed to consider the occasion a good-natured joke that had turned into "a sad farce."[8] For a little while the conservative landowners and businessmen who elected him paid lip service to his pristine Manchesterian liberalism; however, they had no serious intention of forcing the government out of the economy. In their minds, government monopolies and tariffs vastly outweighed the need for theoretical consistency. Even Sbarbaro's call for a regeneration of Italian politics along monarchist lines went unanswered, and in the end he failed to parlay his *succès de scandale* into something more substantial. In 1886 his mandate was not renewed.

What happened? Again, we are fortunate to have complete runs of the various newspapers which Sbarbaro edited in 1886, and these tell the story pretty well. The year began auspiciously for the new parliamentary deputy from Pavia. His prestige had never been greater, and on 10 January 1886 he announced this new status in the first issue of *La penna di Pietro Sbarbaro: deputato al parlamento nazionale*, a newspaper that he edited for the Roman publisher Edoardo Perino, famous for his line of "pocket classics" (*classici tascabili*). Wary of the trap that had destroyed the Sommaruga publishing house, Perino freely exercised the right to delete any of Sbarbaro's articles that might be offensive or illegal. The result was a colorless *Penna di Pietro Sbarbaro*. The editor's moderate appeals for the principles of Manchesterian liberalism and Unitarianism left his readers bored. Sbarbaro's new tone was that of St. Francis preaching to the birds of the fields; but his "lay sermons" were not what the newspaper-buying public had come to expect from the "mad professor."

Indeed, this is not what Sbarbaro really wanted to give them. That he felt uncomfortable with this new image is clear from the nature of his break with Perino, on 4 April 1886. In "A Declaration" Perino explained Sbarbaro's resignation as the result of their constant bickering over what would and what would not go into *La penna di Pietro Sbarbaro*. Never a complaint employee, Sbarbaro protested repeatedly, in Perino's words, when his "violent articles . . . against respectable families, against deputies, against all the major publishers, and directors of journals" were dropped from the *Penna*.[9] A divorce between editor and publisher became inevitable.

After their split, Perino was understandably bitter toward Sbarbaro. Like his fellow publisher, Sommaruga, he had expected to make a substantial profit from Sbarbaro's writings. Instead, the *Penna* had lost money. Perino tried to recover what he could by publishing old Sbarbaro articles in *La penna: effemeride settimanale*, but this contradictory practice proved unworkable. On the one hand the publisher complained of Sbarbaro's "moral suicide" and, on the other, ran his increasingly dated newspaper pieces. The second *Penna* died out on 29 May 1886.

Meanwhile, Sbarbaro's independent *La penna d'oro di Pietro Sbarbaro: ex deputato al parlamento italiano* had appeared on 4 April. Free of Perino's restrictive hand, at last, Sbarbaro attacked his enemies in a manner reminiscent of the original *Forche caudine*. His parliamentary victory could be interpreted only as a condemnation of the "Government of the Uterus!"[10] Since his own departure from Montecitorio, the chamber was populated exclusively by "the sons of Etruscan women!"[11] Depretis's newspaper, the *Popolo romano*, was the "Hygienic Manual of the Uterine Government!"[12] No, Sbarbaro had not taught at Bologna in the nude, as his enemies claimed, "but would that have been any worse than what commonly occurred in the halls of Parliament?"[13]

Perino observed all of this and reflected on his narrow escape from the Sbarbaro involvement: "Hardly was he beyond the reach of my modest censorship when he returned to his old self, a kind of furious bull, charging blindly against people and tossing them to the left and the right."[14] Only constant vigilance had saved Perino from Sommaruga's fate. Sbarbaro himself was compelled to make a genuine escape in May, when his parliamentary immunity expired. With tongue in cheek, Perino assured the readers of *La penna: effemeride settimanale* that Sbarbaro "has promised his friends—and they certainly are not many—to send from Switzerland his prose pieces embossed with the usual obscenities against one and all, and with the usual praise for his own person."[15]

From Lugano, Switzerland, came Sbarbaro's much-muted word. The war against Depretis, symbol of "the

immense abomination that is contemporary civilization," went on; but Sbarbaro no longer expected to
defeat his implacable foe.[16] Years of struggle, both
imaginary and real, had worn him down at last. His
vindication would come, but only with the fullness of
time. For the present he was a fugitive from "uterine
justice," and with his usual melodramatic flair he
signed many of these *Penna d'oro* articles, "Anno 1 del
mio Esilio."

Defeated by his enemies, Sbarbaro felt abandoned
by his friends. Of course, neither the king nor the
queen had ever taken up his cause. While in prison
Sbarbaro had written a long poem to Queen Margherita, "Salve o regina." In it he made a supplicant's
appeal to his "incomparable model/ of human gentle-
ness," elsewhere described as "that angel of goodness,
of pulchritude, of innocence, of charity and of grace":

To you who think of the miserable
Who live for the afflicted
To you who never forget
Unknown derelicts[17]

From the first she had pegged Sbarbaro as an odious
clown who surely would harm the monarchy before
he was finished, and his pathetic doggerel only succeeded in eliciting her icy disdain. By 1886 even
Sbarbaro seemed to have gotten the royal message. A
sign of his disillusionment with the queen was the
conspicuous omission on the *Penna d'oro* masthead of
the "Sempre avanti Savoia!" motto. In a whimper of
self-pity over his inability to collect the money due
him from newspaper vendors in Italy, Sbarbaro wrote
the last issue of the *Penna d'oro* on 23 September
1886. Compelled to return to his native land, he was
imprisoned again and spent the next five years in a
Sassari jail. In 1891 Sbarbaro gained release and im-

mediately resumed his newspaper career, editing *Il libero edificare* and then *La libera parola*, but illness and poverty dogged him. He died in miserable squalor at the age of fifty-four in 1893, curiously the very year of prophecy in *Regina o repubblica?* when a stupid and reckless Italy, according to the author's confident prediction, would be struck down.

Fate gave Sommaruga a longer life, but there would be no literary encore for him until many years after the unhappy events of 1885. All of the young publisher's hopes and dreams lay smothered under the 15 February government order that he desist from further publishing endeavors. Sommaruga was arrested on the night of 18 February, Ash Wednesday, the last night of Carnival. Shortly afterward the government granted him a provisional release; however, by 31 August, the day on which his trial commenced in the Convento dei Filippini, the publishing house had gone into receivership. All the publications were defunct. The severity of the Sbarbaro judgment made Sommaruga look toward his own trial with foreboding, but he did not lapse into a passive fatalism. To Carducci he expressed the desire "to work more than ever."[18] First, though, the trial had to be taken care of.

A team of three lawyers directed the defense, but Sommaruga put his own case in plain Italian when he explained to the judges: "I will only remind the Tribunal that my condemnation would mean four years of assiduous labor destroyed, that as the publisher of five publications and of a book per week I did not have time to control everything that I sent to press."[19] The prosecution listened to this and responded, in effect, "If you didn't, then who did?" In other words, where did final responsibility lie in the publishing business? It is odd that so much of the trial, lasting from 31 August to 18 September, dealt with this question of responsibility in publishing, whereas the final verdict did not even touch upon it.

The trial was conducted in an extremely tense atmosphere, and the judges frequently had to call the crowd to order. Every day the galleries were packed with reporters, with witnesses for the prosecution and the defense, and with the merely curious. People in Rome—indeed, people all over the country—had passionate feelings about Sommaruga because they sensed that he represented something much greater than himself. More than one man stood on trial in that courtroom. An entire cultural system was in the dock; and, by implication, an age, a society. Over one hundred witnesses testified for or against him, and dozens of depositions were read. The participants in the Sommaruga trial included the most influential and recognized literary, artistic, and political names in Umbertian Italy. For a writer, artist, or politician to remain outside the case was to have doubt cast upon his status in the intellectual, cultural, or political life of the country. These proceedings unquestionably amounted to what we would call a media event, with Sommaruga this time ironically generating the publicity from which other reputations would profit.

The format of the trial was simple and clear. The presiding judge read the charges: "You have been charged with misrepresentation and extortion. How do you plead?" Sommaruga answered, "Not guilty," and then the lawyers took over. For the next two weeks poets, painters, newspapermen, and politicians streamed in and out of the witness stand. No one should have been surprised to learn that, in his four years as a publisher, Sommaruga had made as many friends as enemies. The prosecution and the defense enjoyed equal success in finding the kind of testimony that each needed: Barrili and Carducci the most flattering of Sommaruga's faithful supporters; Scarfoglio and Davide Besana the star witnesses for the prosecution.

Carducci took the witness stand on 5 September; the defense lawyers had eagerly anticipated his appearance and now worked to derive maximum advantage from it for their client. Earlier in the year Carducci had suffered a stroke, but continuing ill health did not prevent him from making a last effort on Sommaruga's behalf. Shortly before the trial began, he had written to the imprisoned publisher: "Defend yourself as much as you can. I can do little for you, and perhaps nothing at all; but you know that I set great store in your ingenuity and also at bottom, in your spirit, which I know to be good."[20] The generous mood of this letter animated Carducci's formal testimony. "He has a good heart," Carducci began, "a wonderfully good heart. He has done much good for many people."[21] If Sommaruga's *reclame* occasionally had been in questionable taste, this was no reason to destroy him. Carducci made a powerful impression, at least on the gallery audience, easily offsetting the ill effects of the prosecution testimony given that day by Ferdinando Martini and later in a deposition by D'Annunzio, who was still carping about the *Libro delle vergini* cover design.[22]

In the three defense summations that began on 15 September, Sommaruga's lawyers took their cue from Carducci: the good that their client had done greatly outweighed the bad. *Cavaliere* Coboevich delivered the first summation. The session began early in the morning, but he spoke at such length that the judge ordered a lunch break before the peroration was half over. The lawyer hardly needed such a preamble to make his point, which was only this: the prosecution claimed that Sommaruga used the *Forche caudine* as a sword of Damocles over the heads of his enemies, and that Sbarbaro was his attack dog, to be unleashed at a signal upon victims of Sommaruga's choosing. Coboevich reminded the judges that in order to check-mate this prosecution tactic, the defense had brought Sbarbaro to the stand in Sommaruga's trial. Sbarbaro had entered the courtroom between two *carabinieri*, and he had declared under oath that the *Forche cau-dine* was "completely the blood of my blood, of my heart and soul." When the president of the tribunal read passages from a few *Forche* articles, Sbarbaro in-terrupted every few words with shouts of "It is mine! . . . My dear soul! . . . My heart! . . . Mine . . . of Pietro Sbarbaro!"[23] Indeed, the publisher and the editor of the *Forche caudine* never had been friends. Sbarbaro thought of Sommaruga as a "nice young man," but ignorant and uncultivated. When asked whether Som-maruga had played a decisive role in advising him on the *Forche caudine*, Sbarbaro laughed and replied: "That would have been like a duck giving advice to an eagle."[24] No, Coboevich concluded, the *Forche cau-dine* was the work of Sbarbaro, and since he had been tried and sentenced already that issue should be laid aside.

A second lawyer on the Sommaruga defense team, *cavaliere* Vitale, made the same point the next day, only he sprinkled his summation with long Latin pas-sages from Ovid's *Arts of Love*, to the wonder and ad-miration of the wildly applauding gallery crowd. Reverting to Italian for the serious legal points, he admitted that Sommaruga could not be described as "an ingenuous virgin"; but neither was his client "the vulgar delinquent against honor and propriety" ima-gined by the prosecution. The publisher was a busi-nessman who had taken a calculated risk in backing the *Forche caudine*. Such was his "crime." At this point Vitale asked the judges to consider that no less a man of honor than Silvio Spaventa, the grand old statesmen of the right, had proclaimed from the wit-

ness stand: "In truth the *Forche caudine* published
many things that were neither dishonest nor repre-
hensible."[25] Moreover, no evidence, apart from hear-
say, existed to prove that Sommaruga contributed to
the paper, or that he ordered Sbarbaro to go after
enemies of the publishing house. In fact, the prosecution had proven nothing at all. If the government
could not pin its *Forche caudine* case on Sbarbaro,
how could it expect to use that case against Sommaruga? Sbarbaro had been found guilty of having written threatening letters to government officials, but not
for anything he had done in connection with the
Forche caudine. The government was flogging a horse
that had died two months before. At the very worst,
Sommaruga was guilty of nothing more than "youthful imprudence."

On the penultimate day of the trial Carlo Panattoni, a parliamentary deputy reputed to be one of the
country's best trial lawyers, made the final defense
summation. Like his two colleagues, he devoted much
of his time to the prosecution's charges that the part-
nership of Sbarbaro and Sommaruga constituted "a
permanent danger for society," and that Sommaruga
was Sbarbaro's principal accomplice "in acts of black-
mail forming the scope of the scandalous and defama-
tory publications in the *Forche caudine*."[26] Chief
prosecutor Segala had declared that an avaricious
Sommaruga had engaged in "disgraceful and shame-
ful" speculation, and in the process had tried to per-
vert the moral sense of the country.[27] There it was: an
accusation that D'Annunzio, Depretis, Scarfoglio,
Crispi, Salvadori, Besana, and all the rest of Sommaruga's enemies, high and low, could chant in unison.
It was a strange chorus, and so loud that it easily
drowned out the voice of reason.

What about the other charge against Sommaruga,
that he had perpetrated acts of bribery and misrepre-

sentation while acting as the agent for different painters, principally Francesco Paolo Michetti? This activity had been a minor sideline for the industrious Sommaruga from his earliest days in Rome, and Panattoni
scoffed at the prosecution's bumbling attempts to turn
this red herring into a whale. Admittedly, the *concorsi*
system of art competition reeked of corrupt practices.[28]
Art judges were known to be venal. The awarding of
prizes was then, as it is now, largely a racket. To get
along in this world one had to push and shove, and no
one, not even the defense lawyers, would deny that
Sommaruga had pushed and shoved pretty hard.
Panattoni conceded all of these points, but then he
turned them around in defense of the accused. The art
world had been well known for its scandalous in-
trigues long before Sommaruga came upon the scene.
Not only had he done nothing wrong within the prevailing system of morality; he had not even done anything out of the ordinary. Panattoni asked the court to
consider the implications of the trial: if Sommaruga
were guilty, then the same judgment would have to
be rendered for the entire system under which art was
marketed in Umbertian Rome. Michetti himself, when
apprised of the charge against Sommaruga, had asked,
"Misrepresentation? What misrepresentation?" And
this was Panattoni's closing plea to the court. Let
alone the small matter of evidence, what, precisely,
had Sommaruga done wrong? After twenty days of
hearings, there was no clear question in the Sommaruga case. Therefore, it was impossible for the defense
to put forth any clear answers. The logic of justice
demanded the dismissal of all charges.

A spellbound audience erupted in a thunderous ova-
tion for the star advocate, but the next day Panattoni's
impassioned plea was denied. Judge Badò, the president of the tribunal, dumfounded everybody in the
courtroom by sentencing Sommaruga to six years in

jail and a fine of 506 lire. The date was 18 September 1885, and it marked the end of the Byzantine era in Italian cultural history.

Neither Sbarbaro's epistolary threats to government officials nor Sommaruga's shenanigans with Rome's art judges merited such draconian sentences.[29] The public reaction to both trials overwhelmingly favored the defendants. A tide of popular indignation swept Sbarbaro into public office, and, to judge from contemporary newspaper accounts, Sommaruga became a martyr. Even his enemies took no pleasure in the severity of the court's judgment. *L'Adige* of Verona conceded that Sommaruga might be guilty, but six years in jail and a heavy fine constituted cruelly unjust punishment. The *Gazzetta piemontese* quoted Panattoni as saying, "I knew that justice had abandoned the law courts, but I hoped that at least shame remained." Carducci denounced the sentence as "an infamy" possible only in a country like Italy, which everyone knew was feckless and immoral. *L'Adriatico di Venezia* hailed Sommaruga as "the hero of the day." *L'Italia* of Milan described the sentence "simply as an enormity." Had Sommaruga not been involved with the *Forche caudine*, Rome's *Messaggero* proclaimed, this disaster would not have befallen him; but the government had decided "to suppress the *Forche at any cost*, and the most rapid means of doing so was to arrest Sommaruga."[30]

Why "*at any cost*"? What motivated the government to bring the full force of its power down on the Sommaruga publishing house, by way of destroying the *Forche caudine*? To answer these questions, we must leave the smaller world of Sommaruga incorporated and turn to the larger world of Italian politics and society.

On 29 June 1885, when the Sbarbaro trial was near-

ing its climax, the sixth ministry of Agostino Depretis came to an end. His resignation was only a for-
mality, because on the same day he organized his
seventh ministry, which survived until 4 April 1887.
The personnel changes in the seventh ministry were
essentially cosmetic. Depretis himself retained the
crucial interior portfolio, and the controversial Magliani stayed on as his finance minister. Although a few
minor cabinet positions changed hands, as usual in the
Depretis years, *plus ça change, plus c'est la même
chose*.

Despite an unrivaled reputation for parliamentary
wiliness, Depretis has gone down in history in accordance with the prejudices of his contemporary enemies
on the left and right—as a bland, colorless time-server
whose only distinction lay in an uncanny capacity for
political survival. He managed to stay in power for
more than eight of the eleven years from 1876 to 1887.
Moreover, he was prime minister continuously from
1881 to 1887, and even during the two intervening
Cairoli ministries he remained the most powerful man
in Parliament. Depretis still awaits an impartial biographer, but this much can be said now: if he were not,
as his detractors claim, a truly gifted statesman, whatever that might entail, his political achievement was
unique; and when one thinks of what came after him,
in the ministries of Francesco Crispi and Luigi Pelloux, the Depretis record seems positively scintillating.[31]

Like Giolitti in the next generation, Depretis embodied what was best and worst in the Italian parliamentary system known as *trasformismo*. Generally
speaking, transformism evolved as the political defense of the dominant economic groups in Italian society, the long-regnant landowners and the emerging
industrialists. Even before unification, transformism
had been a conspicuous feature of Piedmontese parlia-

mentary life. In 1852 Cavour joined his right-center
following with Urbano Rattazzi's left-center group in
a *connubio*, or marriage; that maneuver set the future
pattern of Italian parliamentary politics as well. However, by the 1880s transformism meant something
much more than a parliamentary tactic to support this
or that ministerial combination. It had become a strategy against political extremism—particularly against
radicalism and socialism, which were much more important after the broadening of the suffrage laws of
1882, but against reactionary anticlerical threats as
well.[32] Depretis was the master builder of that strategy, and in the Sbarbaro-Sommaruga affair of 1884–
85 he saw an unorthodox though unmistakably real
political threat which, through shrewd handling,
might be turned into an opportunity to further his
design.

Considering his later political views, it is ironic that,
as a leader of the democratic left, Depretis heatedly
opposed the "immoral" *connubio* of 1852. Like nearly
all Italian leaders of his generation, Depretis (b. 1813)
experienced a youthful flirtation with Mazzinianism.
His political career began on 26 June 1848, when he
was elected to the Piedmontese parliament from Broni,
near his native Stradella, but even as a holder of public office he continued to foment Mazzinian rebellions,
as in 1853 at Milan. Very soon afterward, though,
signs of his natural moderation became apparent, as
he led the fight to temper democratic politics in Piedmont with an acceptance of the monarchy. Here was a
precocious statement of the fiery Crispi's political formula in the post-unification period. Characteristically,
his pioneering attitude received little notice—then or
since—for what the Sicilian did with such bombast,
Depretis did in a blandly ingratiating way. In Italian
politics, the lion upstages the fox every time.

After 1860, Depretis's Mazzinian background and

parliamentary connection made him an ideal mediating agent between Garibaldi and the king's government. He could not have done a worse job than his predecessor, the National Society's Giuseppe La Farina, who was expelled from Sicily by Garibaldi on 9 July 1860.[33] For a while Depretis ruled as pro-dictator in Sicily, but he resigned on 18 September over acrimonious disputes with the still antimonarchist Crispi, Garibaldi's secretary-general of the dictatorship. Depretis now resumed his parliamentary duties in Turin; there his support of Rattazzi resulted in a cabinet appointment, as minister of public works, in 1862. Four years later he became Ricasoli's naval minister, just in time to be blamed unfairly for the disaster at Lissa.[34] For the rest of his life this millstone weighed him down. Though not politically fatal, it caused acute discomfort, particularly at those moments when hecklers interrupted his speeches with the derisive salutation, "All hail the hero of Lissa." [35]

The public memory is short—and anyway, Depretis was a born survivor. From 1867 to 1876 he managed to strengthen his hold on the historic left. Meanwhile, the right had disintegrated under the weight of its own contradictions. As political labels go, "left" and "right" are misleading, not because no differences existed between the two, but because the differences between the various rightist factions were equally divisive, and perhaps even more important in Italian politics from 1860 to 1876. Certainly no later than 1864 the regional squabbles between the Piedmontese *permanente* and the Lombard-Tuscan *consorteria* within the right marked the passing of the old Cavourian majority. Moreover, the three major leaders of the right—Giovanni Lanza, Marco Minghetti, and Quintino Sella—held irreconcilably different views on foreign and domestic affairs. Minghetti and Sella, for example, never served in the same government.

In fact, after 1870, with the controversial issue of Rome removed from politics, the various right prime ministers combined with moderate members of the left even more frequently than before, and transformism became an increasingly prominent part of Italian political life.

The left eventually had to face similar internal problems. After 1860 it seemed to draw support from all over the political spectrum, and from all parts of Italy; however, what looked like support for the left was really opposition to the right. The difference was crucial.[36]

Until 1876 the eclectic left functioned as an opposition group, but its differences with the right were more rhetorical than real. Out of power, the left leaders (many of whom, like Crispi and Depretis, were ex-Mazzinians) spoke as champions of the injured classes and depressed areas of the country. As late as October 1875, when he gave his famous "Stradella Discourse," Depretis promised major reforms as soon as the left took power. These included extension of suffrage, decentralization of the administration, abolition of the grist tax (*macinato*), and state-run primary education for all.

The Stradella program seemed to promise a revolution, but nothing of the kind occurred. After Depretis had been in power for a few years, Sella, Minghetti, and Lanza were praising him—not without well-aimed satirical jabs—for adopting the program of the right. Even Silvio Spaventa, the paramount chief of the right's "spiritual aristocracy," in Croce's phrase, nodded with ironical approbation at the performance of Depretis, declaring in 1879: "In the three years that the Left has run the State, its administration has been called correctly a government of the right in decline."[37] And Spaventa's statement was largely true. For five years the left virtually stood pat in foreign and domestic affairs, finally bringing forth a moderate extension of suffrage and gradually eliminating the *macinato* tax. However, to those who had hoped for a real parliamentary revolution in 1876, such gains seemed trifling.

Depretis's moderation may have been prompted by the responsibility of office, but even though he managed to hold power through countless vicissitudes, his original coalition did not hang together. The spendthrift policies of Agostino Magliani prompted criticism from a mixed left-right group of financial conservatives known as the *Centro tecnico*. The distinguished leadership of this group included Sidney Sonnino and Giovanni Giolitti, but its total membership in Parliament never amounted to more than forty-five deputies.

More serious opposition to Depretis sprang up in 1882, when he promised to open his government to all "sincere progressives" of either the left or the right.[38] Here the prime minister drew attention to the most significant fact of Italian political life: the left and right were really one, because both represented the same social groups and opposed common enemies. This official acknowledgment signaled a more thorough transformation of the moderate right leaders into reliable members of the Depretis majority. Not everybody in the left took such a realistic view of the political situation. Crispi, ever chasing down the most fantastic conspiracies, indignantly denounced Depretis as the Judas Iscariot of the left's ideals and principles, of the Risorgimento itself; and he carried the intellectuals along with him.[39] Then in May 1883 Crispi, hitherto the *solitario* of Italian politics, joined with Benedetto Cairoli, Giovanni Nicotera, Giuseppe Zanardelli, and Alfredo Baccarini to form the *Pentarchia*, a splinter group that became known as the "pure left." For a time this faction controlled almost one hundred votes in the Chamber, and Depretis was constantly harried by the problems of either placating or blocking the Pentarchs.

Not until 1887 did Depretis successfully transform the opposition of the Pentarchy by wooing Crispi into the government. In Depretis's eighth and last ministry (4 April–29 July 1887) Crispi held the post of interior minister, putting him in line to succeed as prime minister when Depretis died that summer. This knowledge should not mislead us into thinking that the solution to Depretis's problems always lay close at hand, for it did not. In 1885, the time of the events that most concern us, Depretis enjoyed the support of the moderate historic right and the moderate historic left, but the anger and strength of the mutinous elements in his own party deeply worried him.[40] Bad as party disunity might be, however, it was only the tip of an iceberg that caused Depretis to fear not just for his ministry, but for the ship of state itself. Below the waterline lurked the far more serious threats of radicalism and socialism.

The origins of the extreme left parties lay in the country's Risorgimento past. By the time of Depretis's last few ministries, the *estrema* or ideological left, as opposed to the historic left, was made up of three groups: the Mazzinian Republicans, the Radicals, and the Socialists. A fourth group, Garibaldi's League of Democracy, was really a catch-all association of leftist parties; and with its leader's death in 1882, the League immediately began to flounder. The Republicans, even under the enterprising leadership of Giovanni Bovio, were also finished as an effective force in Italian politics. However, the other two extremist groups obviously had futures that Depretis could contemplate only with despair. The most forceful and impassioned orator of the day, Felice Cavallotti, led the Radicals, a republican splinter group founded in 1878 by Agostino Bertani, who accepted the monarchy for pragmatic reasons while working for advanced democratic social goals within the monarchical state. The ultimate Marxist destination of Italian socialism was by no means clear in the 1880s, and throughout the decade Mikhail Bakunin's surviving anarchist lieutenants, reformist socialists like Andrea Costa, and advocates of the Workers' party of Milan vied for power and influence on the socialist left, along with such odd Marxist bedfellows as Antonio Labriola and Filippo Turati. Although the ideological dissension of the 1870s and 1880s would continue during the twentieth century, weakening and dividing Italian socialism in periodic bloodletting over minimalist and maximalist programs, the din from these factional disputes has always sounded like a war cry in the ears of conservative opponents, not like what it really has been: a cry of futility. The most deceptive thing about Italian political life in the last century is that, in the moments of greatest crisis and turmoil, the showy socialist threat invariably evaporates, leaving only the specter of revolution to haunt the middle and upper classes, to terrorize them into giving their political agents the fullest authority to make the subversives shed, in Errico Malatesta's unforgettable image, "tears of blood."

Depretis did not have the benefit of one hundred years of socialist political failures from which to draw comfort; he gazed horror struck at this hydra-headed monster, and inevitably moved toward a confrontation with it. By 1883 the bespectacled prime minister, normally subdued in manner and reticent in speech, became quite excited and voluble on the subject of his *bête noire*, the political *estrema*. Although concerned, as Giolitti would be, with minimizing his losses on the left, Depretis had to agree with his old antagonist of the historic right, Marco Minghetti, who on 12 May 1883 declared that the radicals were "the real peril to the country's institutions."[41] Thereafter Depretis became even more bitterly critical of the extreme parties, and in the summer of 1885 he announced his intention to suppress every radical and socialist activity if any more subversions, i.e., strikes and demonstrations, occurred.

Despite his conservative attitude toward the labor movement and toward all the socialist factions then competing for power in Italy, Depretis was vilified by the extreme right for being soft on socialism. It is in the record of this criticism that the origins of the Italian ideological right may be found. If Sbarbaro's career has any political significance, it lies here, in his campaign to unmask the "false" liberals like Depretis (often spelled "Dei preti"—"of the priests"—in the *Forche*), who in their flaccid indecision would not be able to defend society against socialists, republicans, and the like. Other conservative liberals, men like Stefano Jacini, Sidney Sonnino, Leopoldo Franchetti, and Pasquale Villari, were saying the same thing in more literate language; but, unlike them, Sbarbaro reached a huge audience.

Depretis shared a trait with many Mazzinians of his generation: he grew to be a very conservative man. After 1882, with the new electoral law allowing greater working-class political participation, the prime minister welcomed support against the socialists wherever he could find it. In the beginning he seems to have tolerated Sbarbaro's appearance on the political scene.[42] Theoretically, the monarchism of the *Forche caudine* did not disturb him, even if Sbarbaro himself were a foolish old windbag. In time, the volume of the *Forche*'s anti-government diatribes began to drown out the theme of anti-socialism, but for a while Depretis continued to regard Sbarbaro as nothing more than a squalid nuisance.

Two related developments forced Depretis to change his mind about Sbarbaro and to take him seriously: first, the nearly incredible popularity of the *Forche caudine*; second, and simultaneously, *la grande peur* of 1884–85.[43] The 1880s witnessed the laggard takeoff of Italian society into the industrial age, and, in the words of Alexander Gerschenkron, "great delays in industrialization tend to allow time for social tensions to develop and to assume sinister proportions."[44] This is precisely what happened in Italy. In 1850 the Italian peninsula lagged far behind England and France in industrial development; it was considerably behind Germany, about even with Austria, and only a little ahead of Russia. Even after the Risorgimento, Italy remained a woefully backward country. The industrial progress that did occur during the 1860s and 1870s, always unhealthily dependent upon foreign capital, came at the expense of the South, which was forced to contribute a disproportionate share of its wealth for the country's economic unification.[45]

The high social cost of this industrialization reached a crescendo in 1884–85. The railroad conventions of those years shackled the South ever more securely to its position of economic subservience, and natural disasters further aggravated regional animosities. The 1884 cholera epidemic in Naples brought death and suffering to nearly 15,000 people. When the epidemic spread to Palermo the next year, thousands more died.[46] As usual during these years, the hated Piedmontese government was attacked as the cause of all the South's misfortunes, and troops had to be dispatched in order to put down rioters in the affected areas. However, agricultural discontent was not peculiar to the South. To pay for industrialization, the government imposed higher tariffs and taxes; these so enraged Italian farmers in both North and South that agrarian uprisings became commonplace throughout the country. Vast amounts of farm land were confiscated for non-payment of taxes, prompting violent demonstrations against the tax collector.[47] In addition, bread riots widened the social base of anti-government insurrection, particularly in the North. During the summer of 1885 rioting peasants in Cremona and Lodi got out of control, and terrified prefects telegraphed frantically to Rome for troop support. Southern peasants had been doing this sort of thing since the inception of the Italian state; now they were joined by northern peasants in a national rebellion against the government in Rome. The liberals had long dreamed of effectively uniting North and South, but this was a nightmare, with northerners and southerners finding the focal point of their unity in a mutual hatred of the liberal regime.

Although the social question took the form of a vehement nationwide agrarian crisis in the countryside, the government suffered its most severe anxieties over the revolutionary threat in the northern cities, as student agitators and workers' strikes broke out in every major industrial center.[48] This is not the place to explain why Germany in these years derived full advantage from being a relative late arrival in the field of industrial development, whereas Italy experienced only problems. However, the question itself serves to remind us that there was nothing inevitable about Italy's dismal performance in the transition from an agricultural to an industrial society. Perhaps comparisons of this sort are inherently invidious. Certainly the Italians had a longer way to go than the Germans. The peninsula's poor endowment in natural resources was a forbidding disadvantage. Then, too, the peculiarities of the national character have never been perceived as blessings by industrialists or economists.

To these very severe handicaps must be added the disgraceful failure of government leadership. Depretis was no Bismarck; but even if he had been, the Italian political system would have nullified his genius. No prime minister, however gifted or resolute, could have imposed a serious program of development on the Italian economy. The inherent contradictions of the historic left, made up at the top of a coalition of southern landowners and northern financiers, condemned the party to pursue contradictory policies. Hence Depretis simultaneously championed protection for steel and for wheat.[49] His sobriquet, "the magician" was well earned, as year after year he avoided political defeat by parliamentary sleights of hand that confounded his enemies and confused even his friends. The future prime minister, Rudinì, complained, "Depretis passes from the right to the left like an authentic constitutional monarch."[50] Through every vicissitude the main political problem never changed, and Depretis wrote, "The majority is numerous, perhaps too numerous, and to maintain it in its diverse gradations is extremely difficult."[51] In fact, the preservation of his majority became possible only in the absence of a government program, for any attempt at coherence immediately unmasked the warring elements within the party structure. The Depretis years, like the liberal period in general, were not distinguished by any real advance against Italy's tragic social and economic problems. Despite Depretis's good intentions, transformism gave Italy the appearance of government without the reality. Instead of government policies wisely thought out and consistently applied, there was little but drift. The unavoidable long-term results of such a flagrant abdication of responsibility were the polarization of Italian political life, the hemorrhage of emigration, and the nightmare of African imperialism.

The Sbarbaro case and the fall of the Sommaruga publishing house take on new meaning when viewed in the light of Italian politics. The jittery Depretis government was in the grip of what has been rightly called "the great fear" of 1884–85. It was as though Depretis had seen a battalion of goblins and now wanted to strike left and right, hoping to exorcise them from the body politic. The disorganized socialists on the left and the mad professor on the right could not have been more convenient outlets for the government's fury. Depretis went ahead against Sbarbaro with supreme confidence, because he could eliminate the *Forche caudine* without injuring any element of his coalition. For the same reason, the prime minister felt free to lay the bastinado on the socialists: they lacked sufficient power to strike back effectively. With Sbarbaro there was even less reason to temporize, for at that very moment Depretis wanted to break up the Pentarchy by luring Crispi into the government. Surely the proud Sicilian could not fail to be impressed, Depretis reasoned, if the government quashed such an annoying busybody as Sbarbaro. But this would be incidental to his main aim of stopping an antagonist whose power seemed to be building as the country careened toward the worst crisis in its history.

In retrospect, it is easy to see that Depretis overreacted. The turbulent summer of 1885 was followed by a calm autumn. Peasant outbreaks subsided, workers' strikes became fewer, and student demonstrations ceased. The great fear had ended, spent in the tremendous outburst of summer. Depretis was far too shrewd not to see that he had bungled the Sbarbaro and Sommaruga trials. His strategy in the Sbarbaro case especially nettled him, for the editor of the *Forche caudine* had now become a national hero and a member of Parliament. Depretis learned quickly from his mistake in the Sbarbaro matter, but he did not want to risk having a second parliamentary deputy emerge from the summer trials. Sommaruga would be free to leave prison only if he left Italy as well.

In the winter of 1886 Sommaruga boarded a night coach and began the long journey from Rome to Paris. He was completely unsure about his future, although at least it would include no more time spent in jail. Michetti had given him a case of paintings with a note that read simply, "Better luck." They might fetch him enough money for a new start elsewhere; and then, Sommaruga could make a triumphant return to Italy, once the "old bastard" was dead or out of office. The triumphant return never occurred, but those were the confused yet hopeful thoughts of a man still young enough to dream of better days ahead.

Only the day before, he had sent a telegram to Carducci: "Tomorrow evening, in the train that passes through Bologna, my thought will be of you." [52] The train carrying Sommaruga into exile was scheduled to stop there only long enough to pick up and to discharge passengers. He had no hope of exchanging farewells with Carducci. Still, when the lights of Bologna at last became visible in the dark, snowy night, Sommaruga felt desolate at the thought of passing through the city without at least a glimpse of the great man. Carducci's support had sustained him through the agonizing months of trial and imprisonment. The need to acknowledge that support nearly overwhelmed Sommaruga, almost forcing him to ignore the stern government directive that he leave the country at once. Carducci and the border were the twin poles of gravity that pulled on him now. Then, just as the train was getting up steam, Sommaruga spotted his old friend on the platform. Carducci stood there all bundled up, but not even a hat and an umbrella could completely conceal his distinctive leonine head. Sommaruga sprang from his seat and hurriedly opened the window of his compartment. The train was already pulling out of the station when Carducci saw him at last and started to wave vigorously. Speechless and crying, Sommaruga waved back. The last word, as always, belonged to Carducci, and he shouted: "Angiolino, remember that I have always liked you quite a bit!"

CHAPTER EIGHT

AFTER THE FALL: THE

POLITICS OF NOSTALGIA AND

D'ANNUNZIANISM, 1885–1897

*"It is necessary, my dear fellow, to persuade
the world that I am capable of everything."*
—D'Annunzio to his publisher,
  Emilio Treves (1897)

Edoardo Scarfoglio's 1911 "Ventisette anni dopo" preface for the second edition of *Il libro di Don Chisciotte* (1st edition, 1883) was meant to serve a dual purpose: first, as an act of contrition for his role in sabotaging Sommaruga's publishing house; second, as a forum for assessing the historical significance of the *periodo sommarughiano* in Italian cultural and intellectual history. This second consideration inspired him to ask a rhetorical question at the very end of the piece: "What remains of the *bizantina* parenthesis?" Scarfoglio's readers in 1911 would have known the answer, but he responded to his own question anyway: "Gabriele D'Annunzio remains."[1] If the *Cronaca bizantina*'s Umbertian chic now looked silly and affected, there was this one indisputable claim to excellence. For Scarfoglio's generation, the journal derived its chief significance as the "*Ca d'oro* of rising D'Annunzian glory."[2]

In 1885 D'Annunzio was twenty-two years old, already married, the father of a growing family, and driven by relentless financial pressure to write for immediate profit. Even at this early stage his career was characterized by qualities both anachronistic and modern. He had a nostalgic yearning for the old-style patronage system, and for the related social and political forms of that system. At the same time, D'Annunzio craved publicity as much as any writer of our own day, and he gauged his public perfectly.

People with D'Annunzio's own middle-class provincial background made up the bulk of his early audience. Italian literary culture had just begun to take on some of the modern characteristics that had long since achieved dominance in northern Europe and America—most importantly the gradual emergence of the professional man of letters whose livelihood depended on the sale of books in the open market. Italy was still far from the day when bookselling would become a mass-production industry catering to a mass public. Unlike England and the United States, where the nineteenth-century market for some kinds of literary works suddenly expanded from a limited part of the population to the vast majority of it, Italy lagged behind in an earlier socio-cultural stage. Illiteracy and a perilously slow industrial takeoff allowed the perpetuation of elitist aristocratic forms, with no serious competing democratic forms, longer in Italy than in most western European countries. When the Italian middle class finally made its presence felt, after the Risorgimento, that presence was inspired by class struggle only from below, against the dark, inarticulate masses. From above, the bourgeois struggle was marked by class envy.[3] In eighteenth-century England and France, the main obstacle to the cultural and political ambitions of the middle class had been the aristocracy. In contrast the Italian bourgeoisie began to wield decisive influence in a later and completely different historical epoch, when the only serious threat to middle-class economic liberty emanated from the left, not from the right. In reaction to this threat the Italian bourgeoisie looked to the aristocracy as a model for its own social pretensions, and as an ally against the mob. Here lay the social basis of cultural and political nostalgia in Umbertian Italy, and after 1885 no one better represented the aristocratic yearnings of the Italian middle class than D'Annunzio. Like Gilbert Osmond in Henry James's *Portrait of a Lady*, D'Annunzio must have cursed his stars that he had not been born a baronet, so great was his deference toward the aristocracy.

D'Annunzio was liberated at last from "the torture of the *Forche*," but how would he capitalize on Sommaruga's fall? For the young author this question took precedence over all others in the autumn of 1885, precisely when Sommaruga was beginning to serve his prison sentence. The offers were numerous, but the one that interested him the most came from Prince Maffeo Sciarra, described by one contemporary as "an adventurous patron, thoughtless and thriftless with regard to his personal fortune."[4] Prince Sciarra was the answer to a poet's prayer. Having bought Sommaruga's journal interests, the prince needed someone to direct the "new" *Cronaca bizantina–domenica letteraria.*[5] D'Annunzio took the job upon being assured that he would have complete editorial control. In practice, this meant that the *Cronaca bizantina–domenica letteraria* became little more than a celebration of its director's varied gifts. The celebration did not long continue, lasting only from November 1885 to March 1886. As an episode in the cultural life of Umbertian Italy, this *Cronaca bizantina dannunziana* would be hardly worth mentioning, except that it provides us with a concrete example of what the Scarfoglio-

Salvadori-D'Annunzio esthetes had in mind when they deserted Sommaruga in 1884.

In the introductory dedication, "Ai lettori," D'Annunzio wrote: "The renewed *Cronaca bizantina*, wishing principally to be a journal of good taste, will not present here a program either long or short."[6] What D'Annunzio intended by the phrase *buon gusto* was displayed in the journal's cover design, done in the Pre-Raphaelite style by Giuseppe Cellini. Under the title *Cronaca bizantina–domenica letteraria*, the three graces appeared, "garbed and bejewelled in the Byzantine manner."[7] Emblazoned on an oval shield, they stood on a magic carpet against a background of twinkling stars and swirling clouds. A bust portrait of tousle-haired Neptune in the left-hand corner, along with the zodiac sign of the month in the right, completed the effect of dreamy fantasy that suffused D'Annunzio's poetry in the mid 1880s.

With the conspicuous exception of Carducci, whose loyalty to Sommaruga stood fast against D'Annunzio's blandishments, the *Cronaca bizantina–domenica letteraria* enjoyed the support and collaboration of all major contemporary Italian writers. The names of Capuana, Verga, Serao, and Fogazzaro graced the cover, and from France Guy de Maupassant lent his name and prestige to the enterprise as a collaborator. D'Annunzio made a big show of dispensing with contracts and written agreements. The word of a prince would be sufficient guarantee for his "sodality" of writers; and, with obvious reference to that sharper, Sommaruga, "their payment would be "*most regular, without delays.*"[8] The new *Bizantina* would be, in D'Annunzio's own words, a publication by and for the "aristocratic," the "elegant," the "elect"; and all for just two lire.[9]

However, the public would not have it at any price.

From the ashes of the *Bizantina sommarughiana*, no phoenix arose. In his memoirs Sommaruga triumphantly documented the unmitigated failure of D'Annunzio's foray into the competitive world of Roman journal publication. D'Annunzio made the same mistake that Salvadori had pressured Sommaruga to make: that is, to produce "a review for the esthetes and the intellectuals." Sommaruga gloated that instead his successor achieved only "an annoying uniformity."[10] D'Annunzio the editor simply did not know what he was doing, and the failure of the *Cronaca bizantina–domenica letteraria* occurred in a way that Sommaruga had earlier predicted. Again the luckless publisher had been proven right, too late.

D'Annunzio tasted the bitterness of failure a second time in 1886, when the critics condemned a book of his poetry, *Isaotta Guttadauro*, as an inexcusably poor performance. The imperfections of his cut-glass-flower style were never more obvious than in this rhapsody of "bare breasts" and "dead nymphs." The unabashedly erotic *Isaotta*, distinguished throughout by a pseudo-Japanese delicacy that had been *à la mode* in Paris some years earlier, reminded Scarfoglio of the *Intermezzo di rime* disaster. He wrote a cruel spoof of "this silly little book" and signed it "Raphael Pannunzio:"

> Within the gardens that sing to you in chorus
> Within the fatal orchards where rubies
> Between leaves of silk embroidered with gold
> Mixed with pearls are born on penises
> For you matures, o my sweet Isaura
> Your fruit of love, the tomato.
>
> .   .   .   .
>
> I above an old china plate
> Where monsters mate with dragons
> Where in the midst of a cobalt blue glaze
> The poet Ko-Ko speaks with magicians

I conqueror of women and of enchantments
Before you that fruit I shall deposit.[11]

In its intention, at least, this piece is reminiscent of
Max Beerbohm's parody, "The Mote in the Eye of the
Flea," ridiculing the preciosity of Henry James. D'Annunzio's response to ridicule was characteristically
un-Jamesian, however; and he challenged Scarfoglio
to another duel over "Il giardino." "Ko-Ko" seems to
have been no match for Scarfoglio in swordplay, but
their encounters on the field of honor amounted to
hardly more than ritualistic indulgence in a form of
behavior associated with aristocratic privilege. The
always tempestuous friendship between the two men
resumed a short while later.

Unlike the critical disaster that D'Annunzio experienced with *Intermezzo di rime*, this time no consola-
tion could be drawn from high sales. Perhaps the
Italian reading public was distracted in 1886 by the
African crisis. Sommaruga might have been able to
do something with *Isaotta Guttadauro*, but Treves
could not. The commercial and critical failure of this
book only intensified D'Annunzio's earlier resolve to
strike out in a wholly new literary direction. In April
1886, immediately following the demise of the *Cronaca bizantina–domenica letteraria* and six months before the publication of *Isaotta*, he had written to his
benefactor, Prince Sciarra:

> I should, then, occupy myself in other ways, and
> return anew to write light "*cronache*" for the *Tri-
> buna* and to do hack work.
> This would be difficult for me because I have
> many other things to do, I have many works to
> finish. I have a great desire to begin working seri-
> ously on a long and important book. By my nature
> and my genius, daily collaboration on a journal

distracts me too much and scatters and unnerves
my strength too much.[12]

By the end of 1886 D'Annunzio had even less reason to stay in Rome, for he felt that his literary career
had come to a standstill. At the same time, his marriage had disintegrated in all but name, a casualty of
his inveterate womanizing. To hazard his fortunes on
a novelist's career away from the distractions of Rome
now became his heart's desire. Financial difficulties
and a torrid love affair with Barbara Leoni prevented
him from leaving the city until the summer of 1888,
when at last he retired with "Barbarella la bella romana" to Michetti's Adriatic villa, "Il convento," in
Francavilla. There, from July to December, he wrote
his first novel, *Il piacere*.

Like so much of D'Annunzio's writing, *Il piacere*
has not fared well at the hands of critics. A huge popular success which instantly established his reputation
as a major novelist, the book is usually marked down
as a poor man's *A Rebours*, with the hero, Andrea
Sperelli, somewhat snidely denigrated as an Italian
cousin of the Duc Des Esseintes.[13] To say this about *Il
piacere* is to tell the truth, but not the whole truth. The
novel was supremely decadent, perhaps the most pornographic "serious" book to be written in the nineteenth century.[14] D'Annunzio was already and irre-
vocably a willing prisoner of the decadent image that
Sommaruga had cast for him. One is reminded here
of Pirandello's autobiographical character, simply
called "xxx," in *Quando si è qualcuno* who loses his
real identity in the process of gaining a literary reputation. In complete contrast to the writer in Pirandello's play, however, D'Annunzio suffered no identity
crisis when fame arrived, and until World War I, the
image of decadent litterateur suited him perfectly.

Yet decadence does not provide the key to understanding D'Annunzio's work. The term itself is too
abstract and subjective. Like "romanticism," "decadence" is a semanticist's nightmare, and any attempt
to define it in schematic terms breaks down under a
welter of chronological and topical inconsistencies.
Decadence is one of those labels that we use for the
sake of convenience, but never for clarity. D'Annunzio
himself entertained ambivalent notions about "la decadence," sometimes hurling it as a malediction
against a society that he hated, and sometimes boast-
ing about himself as a "child of the nineteenth century, that is to say a decadent."[15] In 1889, for example,
he prefaced *Il piacere* with a dedicatory note to
Michetti: "I smile when I think that this book in
which I study with sadness so much corruption and so
much depravity and so much guile and falseness and
vain cruelties was written amidst the simple and
serene peace of your house."[16] Was D'Annunzio sincere when he wrote this? Was he ever sincere? Generations of critics have followed Croce's lead in denounc-
ing D'Annunzio's congenital *insincerità*, and it must
be allowed that the evidence for their case against him
is considerable. Nevertheless, this particular statement
to his friend Michetti should give us some pause before we accept as gospel the litany of clichés about
D'Annunzian decadence.

Anyway to define D'Annunzianism as the Italian
variant of the European decadent movement is, at
best, an incomplete and unnecessarily vague proposi-
tion. Decadence, dandyism, estheticism, and *l'art pour
l'art* were all outward manifestations of D'Annunzio's
protest against the soulless, mindless, banal torpor of
modern life. In other words, the ideological basis of
Il piacere, *L'innocente* (1892), and *Il trionfo della
morte* (1894)—the *Romanzi della rosa* trilogy—continued to be the politics of nostalgia. Andrea Sperelli,

Tullio Hermil, and Giorgio Aurispa all reflected the aristocratic value system in art and politics which D'Annunzio had derived from Carducci and the other *bizantini* before adding the highly personal stamp of his own style.

D'Annunzio's trilogy contrasts the superior refinements and sensibilities inherent in the aristocratic conception of life with the drab, faceless mediocrity of middle-class industrial society. *Il piacere* begins in a somber mood of nostalgic regret: "Under the gray democratic wave that daily submerges many beautiful and rare things, that special class of ancient Italian nobility, in which generation after generation upheld a certain family tradition of elect culture, of elegance, and of art is disappearing."[17] Pride of race and breed are primary sources of motivation for Tullio Hermil in *L'innocente*, no less than for Andrea Sperelli in *Il piacere*: "How many times did I, ideologist and analyst and sophist, take pleasure in being descended from Raimondo Hermil de Penedo, who had acted with such valor and ferocity for Charles V at Goletta." The latter-day Hermil is a decadent, but he soliloquizes, "The excessive development of my intelligence and of my sensibilities had not been able to change the essence of my substance, the hidden substratum in which were inscribed all the hereditary characteristics of my race."[18] Giorgio Aurispa, too, is an aristocrat— though as a Nietzschean he lays claim to this honor on the basis of inner merit, rather than as a result of noble birth. For him there never had been and never could be hope for men in the mass: "The human species was, then, at bottom entirely inert below the mobile zones of superiority. The ideal human type was not in the distant future, not at the unknown end of a progressive period, but could only reveal itself at the top of the human wave, in the more elevated beings."[19]

For all three of D'Annunzio's heroes in the *Romanzi della rosa*, an appreciation of art became the only way to distinguish the most exquisite spirits from the rude mass of men. The hero of *Il piacere* pinpointed the political function of culture in D'Annunzian fiction when he cried, "Art! Art! Here is the faithful lover." For Sperelli, art was "the fount of pure joy" because it would always be "forbidden to the multitudes, granted only to the elect; the precious food that makes man like unto a god."[20] On this point D'Annunzio spoke his true mind: the artist had his prerogatives, in fiction as well as in life. Hermil boasted that he was one of the superior souls who realized the dream of all intellectuals and artists, "to be constantly faithless to a constantly faithful woman."[21] Aurispa idealized his violinist Uncle Demetrio, a suicide whose elect spirit had been snuffed out by the thinness of *Abruzzesi* life.[22] Wagner's music—particularly the prelude of *Tristan und Isolde*, in which "insatiable desire exalts itself in a fever of destruction"—was the most sublime achievement of art, and throughout *Il trionfo della morte* the love of music served as the sign and precondition of true superiority.[23]

D'Annunzio described his political ideas in much greater detail when he wrote *Le vergini delle rocce* (1895), the novel of political nostalgia par excellence. The plot and symbolism of this novel have been a trial to generations of readers, but in the context of D'Annunzio's first trilogy the aspirations of Claudio Cantelmo are understandable enough. He is the first D'Annunzian hero who is no longer in the earliest flush of youth, and life has given this proud aristocrat a Nietzschean education: "The world is the representation of the sensibility and thought of a few superior men who have created and therefore amplified and ornamented it in the course of time, and who will go on amplifying

and ornamenting it in the future . . . a magnificent gift
by the few to the many, by the free to the slaves, by
those who think and feel to those who must work." It
follows in Cantelmo's mind that he must try "to bring
some ornament, to add some new value to this human
world that eternally grows in beauty and sadness."[24]

Alas, Cantelmo discovers that Umbertian Italy is
not a country where superior men can perform their
natural functions. Rome, he laments, has become a
den of iniquity, not only because of the "arrogant
plebes," but also because public life "is a miserable
spectacle of baseness and dishonor." Contemporary
Italy is the worst of all possible worlds, for on one
hand "the Great Beast" is vociferating in the public
assemblies, and on the other money-grubbing businessmen ("the new elect of fortune") are bringing
the country to its knees. The destruction of many beautiful Roman villas is only the most visible crime committed by this vicious and rapacious class of men. Cantelmo warns, "O Proci, o devourers of a patrimony not
your own, mind that Ulysses has already landed in
Ithaca."[25]

The warning comes a bit prematurely, for Cantelmo's as-yet-unborn son is to be the book's Ulysses figure. A mysterious Zarathustra-like spirit commands
him to beget a child ("Colui che deve venire") who
will become the leader of an aristocratic revival. The
remainder of the novel deals with the search for a
mother who will be worthy to give birth to this "King
of Rome."

The search takes Cantelmo to Trigento in Campania, where the ancient and aristocratic Montaga family lives. Here we meet old Prince Luzio, "a most beautiful example of superior humanity, manifesting in
every act of his diverse essence, the sentiment of absolute separation from the multitude, from common
duties, from common values."[26] However, he lives in

an irretrievable past, dreaming of a Bourbon restoration and a return to the good old days. The wheel of history cannot move backward, Cantelmo tells him: "Far from this world, enclosed in a dense cloud of sadness, you have been able to nourish until today the hope that dead things could be resurrected. Certainly the things that are dead will rise again, but transformed." [27]

Nietzsche had pointed the way for D'Annunzio: only the principle of aristocracy mattered, not any particular aristocratic regime. D'Annunzio, himself the quintessential personification of bourgeois *arrivisme*, wanted not to resurrect the dead aristocracy, but to copy it and adapt its class privileges to a new elite. Cantelmo's long-winded political speeches in *Le vergini delle rocce* elucidate this crucial distinction between unreflective traditionalism and modern radical conservatism. Unlike Prince Luzio, he does not call merely for a return to the past; on the contrary, Cantelmo fixes his gaze on the future. The change of historical direction had not come without effort, he confides to the prince. Once the spectacle of modern decadence had driven him nearly mad with rage, but now he realizes fully and happily that the dissolution must become complete before a renaissance can occur:

> When all is profaned, when all the altars of Thought and Beauty have been smashed, when all the urns containing the ideal essences have been broken, when daily life has been brought to such a limit of degradation that nothing worse seems possible, when in the great darkness the last flickering light has been extinguished, then the Mob will be arrested by a panic more severe than any that has ever terrified its miserable soul and . . . it will feel itself lost in the trackless desert, seeing no way, no light. Then it will realize the necessity of Heroes,

and it will invoke the iron rods that will have to discipline it anew. Then, dear Father, I think that these Heroes, these new Kings of the earth, must rise from our race, and that from today onward all of our energies must be coordinated in preparation of that event, whether it be near or far. This is my faith.[28]

Such a political credo, resting for the most part on literary prophesies and on the *ex cathedra* pronouncements of infallible spirits, is vague in every essential point, save D'Annunzio's characteristic reverence for "the value of blood."[29] Yet, ironically, Cantelmo's education in *Le vergini delle rocce* consists precisely in being disabused of this notion, at least insofar as the Montagas are concerned. He had come to them hoping to find a perfect woman, "an elect," to be the mother of Italy's savior; but they belong to a past beyond reclamation. When he asks Prince Luzio's daughter, Anatolia, to marry him, she who has sensed the grandeur of Cantelmo's mission declines. "But imagine, Claudio," she explains, "a conqueror who drags behind him a carriage full of invalids and who when preparing himself for battle must contemplate their wasted faces and listen to their lamentations."[30] Such a marriage, far from strengthening him, would be harmful, and she will not be a party to it. He must leave her in the verdant gloom of the Montaga garden and go forth into his brave new world alone.

At this point *Le vergini delle rocce* ends, with the prospect of Cantelmo continuing his search in the second novel of the *Romanzi del giglio* trilogy, *La grazia*. In 1895 D'Annunzio expected Cantelmo's quest to end at last in *L'annunciazione*, but neither of these latter two Novels of the Lily was ever written. *The Virgins of the Rocks* stands alone, as an elaborately detailed testament of the author's aristocratic political views and as his initial contribution to the foremost *fin de siècle* esthetic journal in Italy, *Il convito*.

The *Convito* is probably the best available source for a study of Italian esthetic politics during the 1890s. It certainly was an unusual publication, as the founder and editor, Adolfo De Bosis (1863–1924), intended that it should be. De Bosis wanted to publish the *Convito* in twelve monthly volumes, beginning in January 1895; but not until 1907 did the last volume go to press. The term *volume* (volume) is indicative of what he hoped to accomplish. De Bosis took care not to use the magazine term *fascicolo* (issue) in describing each *Convito* publication, for the twelve numbers were conceived and edited as twelve separate books. The whole series constituted an anthology of essays, stories, novels, and poems on the many variations of one theme, pure beauty.

The idea of a cultural journal had been on De Bosis's mind for several years, but nothing was done until October 1894, when, one night after a sumptuous dinner and plenty of wine at Michetti's villa, he and D'Annunzio vowed to begin working immediately on the *Convito*. One of the first things the two men did was make Carducci an honorary charter member. Next they issued appeals for patronage. These met with generous responses, including a donation from the royal family. The *Convito* was exactly the kind of reactionary cultural activity most favored by Queen Margherita and her intransigently antimodern "circle" of poets and artists, all clucking their disapproval of everything not expressly medieval in Italian society during the famous *giovedì della regina* gatherings at the Quirinale.[31] Although this auspicious beginning proved deceptive, November and December were months of intense excitement and limitless hope for the *convitati*, and they actually made their first deadline.[32]

The chief of the *convitati*, at least in terms of energy expended to keep the publication running, would always be De Bosis. Born just outside Ancona in 1863, the year of D'Annunzio's birth, De Bosis is a nearly prototypical representative of the esthetic tradition in Umbertian culture. He ran true to the form on every essential point. Like nearly all esthetes of his generation, De Bosis was of middle-class provincial origins, and he went off to Rome during the 1880s ostensibly to study at the university, but actually to establish himself as a writer. He enjoyed a modest success in this literary ambition and eventually received honorable mention from the critics as one of Italy's multitudinous *poeti minori*. The translator's art suited him perfectly, and his translations of Shelley drew abundant praise from contemporaries, but as a creative writer De Bosis lacked originality. He lived his entire life as the student of men more gifted than himself. From the art critic Angelo Conti, De Bosis absorbed the Pre-Raphaelite esthetic traditions of John Ruskin, Walter Pater, Dante Gabriel Rossetti, and John Everett Millais. These men never lost their intellectual authority over him. In the craft of poetry D'Annunzio became his teacher, and *Amori ac silentio sacrum* (1900), *Liriche* (1907) and *Le rime sparse* (1924) bear the mark of the master's *fin de siècle* style.

D'Annunzio could not long abide the company of most men—or most women, for that matter. He needed constant changes in the cast of his life's drama. However, De Bosis was an exception, always managing to stay in favor. When D'Annunzio wrote *Il trionfo della morte* in the early 1890s, De Bosis served as the model for a very sympathetic character, Adolfo Astorgi, described glowingly as "truly a fraternal spirit, the only one with whom he [Giorgio Aurispa] had been able to live for a time in communion without disagreement, ill feeling, or repugnance—which he usually experienced after prolonged familiarity with other friends."[33] D'Annunzio later remembered him in *Contemplazione della morte* as "The prince of silence, the most noble gentleman of the *Convito* . . . one of the few men of sense who opposed the new barbarism that menaced the Latin world. . . ."[34] The *Convito* experience was the high point of their friendship, and in the beginning they both shared the faith expressed by De Bosis in a letter to the painter, Cellini: the anthology would be a record of the age, embellished by "the clear thoughts and the lofty ideals of the elect few."[35]

De Bosis published his own work in the *Convito*, and numerous other writers, notably Giovanni Pascoli, contributed to the publication; but the cynosure of the *convitati* was unmistakably D'Annunzio. For his own part, D'Annunzio rested content in praising the acclaimed forerunner of the *convitati*, Giosuè Carducci, excerpts of whose *Canzone di Legnano* (1879) were republished in the *Convito*. D'Annunzio declared that Carducci was still "the whip of Italy," who gave the country all his love and fealty—"not the blind and miserable Italy that is in the hands of the swindlers and fools, but that divine and remote ideal country whose splendor is not hidden from the eyes of poets." Carducci the initiate, the advanced soul, became the object of D'Annunzio's most effusive prose in the *Convito*:

> We are happy and proud—we few who follow and sustain with all our force the cause of Intelligence against the "drunken slaves"—we are happy and proud that this opportunity is afforded us to express publicly our admiration and our profound reverence not only for a great master but also for

> him who, before a tumultuous and menacing crowd,
> knew how to affirm the sovereign dignity of the
> spirit and the necessity of intellectual leadership,
> serenely pronouncing the words: "Nature has
> placed me on high; you will never be able to lower
> me." [36]

D'Annunzio well understood the meaning of Carducci's remark, for it was nothing less than the proud boast of Claudio Cantelmo and the other "superior men" who dominated his early novels.

D'Annunzio could afford to be generous in praising Carducci, because he himself now received in the *Convito* the same adoring praise that had been given the older poet in Sommaruga's *Cronaca bizantina*. A published author for sixteen years, D'Annunzio at thirty-two had arrived as his generation's principal literary spokesman, and the *Convito* became the vehicle in which his work was held up for increasingly extravagant commendation. De Bosis took the lead in honoring his gifted friend and colleague. *Le vergini delle rocce* appeared serially as the lead piece in each of the first six *Convito* numbers, from January to June 1895. In the next three numbers published that year, his poetry and articles took page one precedence over the work of all other contributors. Moreover, De Bosis used the back pages of the *Convito*, in the *Cronache* section, to report on the reception of D'Annunzio's work abroad. The appearance of the *Convito* in 1895 coincided with D'Annunzio's conquest of the French literary establishment following Georges Hérelle's translations of the *Romanzi della rosa*, and De Bosis proudly hailed the triumphant advance of "le plus latin des genies latins." [37]

It is not surprising, then, that De Bosis should have asked D'Annunzio to write a "Proemio" for the *Convito* in order to explain what the *convitati* wanted to

do. D'Annunzio responded with a preachment in the
Carduccian tradition of political nostalgia. The ideals
of the previous generation had grown out of the Risorgimento, he began, but for the *convitati* the fruits of
the Risorgimento tasted bitter indeed: "We faced life
full of faith, believing ourselves to be in the presence
of a social Assumption. And instead we were specta-
tors looking on a tragic farce." [38] In 1895 the battle
was no longer between Italian patriots and Austrian
occupation troops; it was between Intelligence and
Barbarism:

> Gathering all their energies, the intellectuals
> must sustain in battle the cause of Intelligence
> against Barbarism if they have not lost the most
> profound instinct of life. If they want to live, they
> must fight and affirm themselves continuously
> against destruction, diminution, violation and con-
> tagion. Welcome is he, glowing like a furious flame
> with the zeal of art, who battles for a statue with
> greater energy than for a loved one. [39]

And to do so in the name of Venus Victrix, D'Annunzio exclaimed—this was the fondest wish of the esthetes who now gathered under the banner of *Bellezza*
"to defend against Barbarism the suffering intellectuals of the Latin Spirit."

D'Annunzio had a notoriously short attention span,
for causes as well as for people. That is why his heroic
war record later came as such a shock to the people
who knew him best. World War I was the only thing
in his life that he saw through to the end. His *Convito*
involvement had a more typical ending; he began to
lose interest after the first few numbers, especially
when the unpleasant problems of finance proved insoluble. The worship of De Bosis and the other *convitati* charmed him, but D'Annunzio never wasted time

trying to pay bills. That sort of thing he left to De Bosis, who manfully finished the course, paying for the *Convito*'s last three volumes out of his own pocket and learning from bitter experience that "literature does not pay in Italy."[40]

In the summer of 1895, while De Bosis struggled in his headquarters at the Villa Borghese to keep the *Convito* alive, D'Annunzio permitted himself to be lured away from Rome by an old friend. Edoardo Scarfoglio, now famous as the editor of *Il mattino* (an extremely conservative Neapolitan newspaper which he had founded with his wife, Matilde Serao) invited the poet to accompany him on a yacht cruise to the Greek islands.[41] It was not like D'Annunzio to refuse such an invitation, and it took very little pressure to persuade him to drop everything in favor of an extended holiday. Dropping everything meant disaster for De Bosis and eventual death for the *Convito*; but D'Annunzio was a poet, and what is bad taste for an ordinary person often passes for the manifestation of genius in an artist. De Bosis understood his friend too well to hold a grudge against him: he knew that D'Annunzio was an egotist who could rationalize any desertion, professional or personal, with the maxim that he had more than one life to live.

Sometime during the next two years D'Annunzio was overcome by the urge to test his aristocratic political ideas in an actual parliamentary campaign, and in the summer of 1897 he surprised even his closest friends by making a successful run for Ortona a Mare's seat. His decision to enter the campaign struck everyone as peculiar, even for so peculiar a man as D'Annunzio, and victory added an almost legendary dimension to the episode. His campaign speeches were utterly whimsical, as he addressed his future constituents in the hyperbolic mode of his own literary characters. Taxes, railroads, industrialization, foreign policy, and the social question were ignored in favor of higher considerations, expressed in statements such as "The Fate of Italy is inseparable from that of Beauty, of which she is the mother."[42] D'Annunzio's electoral rhetoric came straight from the pages of the *Convito*. In August 1897 he declared: "Gathering all their energies, the intellectuals must sustain militarily the cause of Intelligence against the Barbarians . . . they must end the disjunction that exists between thought and action: they must actively conquer their rightful place at the summit of society."[43] Not all of his campaign speeches were as fantastic as this, but in the wake of Adua fantasy was welcomed, at least in D'Annunzio's district, as a welcome respite from disturbing political realities.[44]

To the Milanese publisher Emilio Treves he explained the motive behind his foray into politics:

> I have just returned from an electoral swing; and I still have the acrid odor of humanity in my nose. This undertaking seems absurd, strange to my art, and contrary to my style of living; but to judge my attitude it is necessary to await the effect at which my will directly aims. Victory, in any case, is assured. It is necessary, my dear fellow, to persuade the world that I am capable of everything.[45]

D'Annunzio's prediction came true. This celebration of his ego was crowned with success; and, as expected, the Deputy of Beauty took his seat in Parliament on the last bench of the extreme right.

D'Annunzio attended to his parliamentary duties with characteristic nonchalance. He did not have the temperament to work at becoming an effective deputy; in any case, the "tremendously complicated" tangle of his private and literary affairs during this period would have kept him away from Montecitorio much of the time.[46] It turned out that 1897 was the year of the crucible for D'Annunzio, with continuing acrimony between him and his estranged wife, Maria; with a messy adultery trial in Naples, where the aggrieved husband of Maria Gravina named him as corespondent; with the beginning of the momentous Eleonora Duse affair; with the time-consuming promotion of his books in France; and with his old nemesis, debts. On the whole, D'Annunzio's experience as Ortona a Mare's representative seems to have confirmed his low opinion of Parliament.[47] One day, when asked by an usher to leave the Chamber library and to join the deputies in session for the purpose of making a quorum, he allegedly responded, "Tell the President that I am not a number," whereupon the Deputy of Beauty continued to read.[48] For most of his three-year term D'Annunzio might have been more accurately described as the *deputato mancato*, but in 1897 his appearance in Parliament enraptured those who hoped that the intellectuals might still save the Ideal of Italy.

CHAPTER NINE

THE POLITICS OF

NOSTALGIA IN CRISIS AND

THE GENESIS OF NATIONALISM:

ENRICO CORRADINI (1865–1931)

"...I incite the ruling classes to a national renewal
and to the doctrine of 'force for force,' the doctrine of
the continual struggle and the continual conquest of
the world."
—Gabriele D'Annunzio (1900)

"I was among those contemporary Italians who were
converted from literature in which I was dissolute and
blind. And my conversion was due to the disaster at
Adua."
—Enrico Corradini (1923)

D'Annunzio's esthetic politics of nostalgia
made a powerful appeal to Enrico Corradini,
the future founder of the right-wing Nationalist Association, who in the summer of
1897 was employed as the editor of a Florentine literary review, the *Marzocco*. Himself an aspiring playwright and novelist, Corradini departed from the customary esthetic editorial line of the journal on 6 June,
posing the following questions under the title, "Inquiry of the *Marzocco*":

   1. Do you think it suitable and proper for a literary

man to take part in the political life of our
country?

2. Do you think it useful or harmful for our country to have literary men in politics?

3. In the event of an affirmative response to the first
question, what should be the precise field of political action for the literary men, and under
what form should this action take place? [1]

Actually, scattered articles on the prospects of intellectuals participating in politics had appeared in Corradini's journal as early as the previous October, but
the *inchiesta* was exactly contemporaneous with D'Annunzio's parliamentary bid. Under Corradini's editorship, the *Marzocco* followed the D'Annunzio campaign very closely, and D'Annunzian political rhetoric
became the subject of numerous articles. Corradini
himself wrote, "If the artist is to see all the manifestations of life, he cannot close his eyes before the high
and complex things of civic responsibility." [2] Here he
echoed D'Annunzio's "I am capable of everything"
boast to Emilio Treves, the implication being that the
political involvement of intellectuals had value chiefly
as a *personal* experience. Corradini later developed a
much more social interpretation of cultural politics;
D'Annunzio did not, but political D'Annunzianism
was the point of departure for the Corradinian political synthesis known as nationalism.

Considering Corradini's bitter personal antagonism
toward D'Annunzio in the early 1890s, the relationship between nascent nationalism and D'Annunzian
political nostalgia is not immediately comprehensible.
Two years younger than D'Annunzio, Corradini was
born in the Tuscan town of San Miniatello in 1865.
His parents were small landowners belonging to the
same provincial bourgeois class from which D'Annun-

zio had come.[3] After some time in a Catholic seminary, where he trained for the priesthood, Corradini entered the University of Florence, took a degree in letters in 1889, and thereafter set about to become a professional writer.[4]

His debut was inauspicious. *Germinal*, a literary review that he helped found late in 1891, died out early in 1893, a passing regarded by no one then or since as a particularly sad loss. Corradini thought of it as a publication for esthetes, "for those who have faith in the future of Art—the highest manifestation and substantial need of the human spirit."[5] Although this was the language of traditional estheticism, Corradini did not begin his career as a typical representative of the poets and artists of his generation who took the high road to Parnassus in their escape from the *mal du siècle*. In the first place, Corradini had already passed his twenty-fourth birthday when he graduated from the university, and his rapidly receding red hair made him look much older. At that age, three or four years can make a great deal of difference in the relations between intellectuals, and Corradini seems to have emerged from his university experience as an authority figure for the esthetes among his classmates.[6] Second, the years he spent in the seminary, which had put him behind his chronological contemporaries to begin with, left an enduring mark on his mind and personality. Corradini never married, and all the reports of his friends suggest that he lived in monastic simplicity.[7] If he rejected the priest's life that the Church offered him, he held onto the image of that life and transposed it to fit his secular existence. Unlike Carducci and very much unlike D'Annunzio, Corradini was no pagan *poeta vate*. Instead, he reminds us of Giulio Salvadori turned inside out, with the Church a momentous starting point, rather than a peaceful destination.

Politics interested him little at first, and, ironically, when he did express a political opinion in *Germinal*, it was a far from conservative one. His sporadic rages against the *abbienti* ("haves") were coupled with glowing tributes to Italian literary celebrities, notably Edmondo De Amicis, upon their conversion to socialism.[8] Once Corradini even pleaded with the Italian government to cut its military budget—a request which, in contrast with his mature beliefs, stands out as a startling reversal of historical character.[9] In later years he came to regard these protests as youthful indiscretions, and the entire *Germinal* chapter of his life was allowed to disappear from view. Yet the political character of *Germinal*, however fragmentary, pointed toward the direction in which Corradini eventually would move.

Corradini's response to the social question provides the key to understanding the political potential of his *Germinal* editorials. A "Giornale d'Arte" it may have been, but editor Corradini never thought of art as the esthetic refuge of rentier capitalism. His convictions about the social responsibility of art led him into an inevitable confrontation with the traditional esthetes, despite the lip service that he had occasionally paid to their rhetoric in the beginning. Henrik Ibsen, the "potent innovator" and the "apostle of duty," towered above all other writers as his supreme intellectual hero. By comparison, D'Annunzio was merely a "derivative second-rater."[10] In Italy itself the "true social poetry" of Ada Negri put to shame the frivolous estheticism of her decadent critics. In her defense and in defense of social realism, Corradini dismissed the decadents, the *dannunziani*, and the *carducciani* as "those who make Art for Art and Verse for Verse . . . like children playing at their games."[11]

Corradini proclaimed the splendid ideal which art held out to man, but at the same time he condemned the betrayal of that ideal by D'Annunzio. Ibsen and Negri showed how art could strengthen man and improve society. Tragically for Italy, however, too many of her artists had succumbed to the siren call of D'Annunzio, in whose art "imitation takes the place of spontaneity, and falseness and artificiality that of sincerity and truth." [12] Corradini complained that what was best in the esthetic tradition had been compromised and spoiled by this "blasphemer in the true, pure, pristine temple of art."

Corradini's collegial sense of the art community, derived in part at least from his early Catholicism, suffered an unbearable affront in 1892, when D'Annunzio published a scornful review of Pietro Mascagni's *Cavalleria rusticana* in Scarfoglio's *Mattino*. Corradini read it incredulously. D'Annunzio the "parasite and Sybarite of Art" was bad enough, but D'Annunzio the music critic was simply grotesque. His mindless criticism, charged Corradini, proceeded in a direct line from his ridiculous vanity:

> Your apostles, your popes, your simple priests, your very simple worshippers, in the midst of whom you are adored, are crowing that you are the only poet, the only novelist, the only intelligent person in Italy; and you believe them, and you are drunk with vanity, and you dare everything against everyone with the certainty of being above everything and everyone. [13]

Astonishingly, within a few years after he wrote this derisive editorial Corradini came around, so to speak, and began to model his own work on D'Annunzio's. Corradini's extraordinary about-face, coming on the heels of his aggressive and unequivocal anti-D'Annunzianism during the 1891–93 *Germinal* period, can only be explained as further proof of D'Annunzio's irresistible appeal in Italy *after* the success of his novels in France became fully realized around 1895. Furthermore, it suggests that the mental development of the nationalist leader followed a more tortuous path than is usually described. Both of these matters must now be examined in some detail.

Although the publicity genius of Angelo Sommaruga produced numerous revolutionary changes in the marketing of literary culture in Italy during the 1880s, his claim to fame then and now has rested on his success in making D'Annunzio a national celebrity. By 1885 D'Annunzio had no rivals among Italy's younger writers, and in the country's entire literary establishment only Verga and Carducci took precedence over him. Still, outside Italy his fame was dimly perceived. Not until the mid 1890s, when his *Romanzi della rosa* were translated into French, did D'Annunzio's star shine on the whole of Europe. By 1897 William Butler Yeats had read D'Annunzio in translation, and he described the Italian as one of the few European writers who were "saying new things."[14] In the same year André Gide wrote, "M. D'Annunzio has drawn the attention of all Europe to Italy."[15] Remarks such as these were offered in praise of that rarest nineteenth-century phenomenon, an Italian writer of international stature.

The man most responsible for D'Annunzio's spectacular leap to continental prominence was Georges Hérelle, a philosophy teacher at a lycèe in Le Havre. While on a Neapolitan vacation in 1891, Hérelle chanced to read a serial installment of *L'innocente* in Scarfoglio's *Corriere di Napoli*.[16] He brought out a French translation of the novel, entitled *L'Intrus* which began to appear serially in *Le Temps* during September 1892, the same year as the Treves publication in Italy. A close friendship and an effective working relationship developed between the two men, and over the next four years all three of D'Annunzio's *Romanzi della rosa* were published in French: after *L'Intrus* came *L'Enfant de volupté* (*Il piacere*) in 1895, and *Le Triomphe de la mort* (*Il trionfo della morte*) in 1896.[17]

The novels created a sensation in France, and success there gave D'Annunzio entree elsewhere in Europe, including England. Arthur Symons, long the advance man for French symbolist literature and art in England, learned about D'Annunzio through the Hérelle translations. In 1898 Symons wrote a flattering introduction to Georgina Harding's translation of *Il piacere*, actually of *L'Enfant de volupté* (*The Child of Pleasure*), and D'Annunzio was brought to the attention of the English reading public.[18]

Still, the central question remains: Why did D'Annunzio's novels get such an enthusiastic reception in France? No Italian writer since Leopardi had been able to take the long stride from Italy to the intellectual capital of European civilization without falling down somewhere along the way, usually at the French border; but D'Annunzio took Paris as easily as he had taken Rome ten years before. How did he manage it?

Part of the answer lies in D'Annunzio's skill as a writer, but his Parisian success went beyond purely literary considerations. For the French, D'Annunzio's legend quickly became as important as anything that he ever wrote. His gaudy excesses appealed to the esthetes whose idol was the hugely influential Robert de Montesquiou, the real-life prototype for Joris-Karl Huysmans's Duc Des Esseintes in *A Rebours*. To them, D'Annunzio embodied the idea of Italian estheticism as much in his person and private life as in his poetry and prose. The relish with which D'Annunzio lived the role of *fin de siècle* decadent litterateur confirmed his French admirers in their view that he was the perfect symbol of the age. Moreover, the timing of his books was uncanny. The *Romanzi della rosa* appeared in Paris when the reaction against literary naturalism was reaching its highest pitch. Mysticism, sensuality, and exoticism—the principal traits of decadent romanticism—all flourished in *fin de siècle* Paris, and D'Annunzio blended them perfectly.[19]

L'Intrus enjoyed a much grander success in France than *L'innocente* had in Italy. The controversy attending the publication of *L'innocente* was comparable to the *Intermezzo di rime* imbroglio of ten years before. Treves judged *L'innocente* so grossly pornographic that he refused to publish it at first; when the book did appear in Scarfoglio's newspaper, the Italian reading public went into shock. However, *L'Intrus* met with a chorus of approving voices from nearly every important quarter in the French literary establishment.

D'Annunzio's handling of two elements in *L'Intrus* paved the way for his success with the French critics. First, the principal female characters—Teresa Raffo, Tullio Hermil's mistress; and Giuliana, his wife—were appealing specimens of the women most preferred by the decadent romantics: the murderous Cleopatra–Salome figure and the passive Ophelia–Madeline Usher figure, both pursued by the hero with typically D'Annunzian vigor.[20] Second, D'Annunzio had conceived *L'innocente* under a Tolstoian influence, and *L'Intrus* profited immensely from the Parisian vogue of the mystical Russian novel. The most significant element in Tolstoy's point of view was a pantheistic reverence for the land, which his contemporaries interpreted as a religious corollary of Rousseau's encomiums to Nature. D'Annunzio imbued his own novel with this very topical idea, without stooping to mere imitation.

Similarly, in 1889 *Il piacere* had outraged most Italian critics. It is true that some younger readers thought of it as "their book," but most Italian critics agreed that nothing quite like *Il piacere* had been published in Italy before.[21] However, in France *L'Enfant de volupté* provoked a very different reaction. There Andrea Sperelli's way had been paved ten years earlier by the Duc Des Esseintes. D'Annunzio admitted that Sperelli owed a considerable debt to Des Esseintes. In a letter to Hérelle, written on 14 November 1892, he conceded, "Here perhaps there is some relation with *A Rebours* by J. K. Huysmans."[22] There was really no "perhaps" about it, but D'Annunzio always took his themes wherever he found them. The important thing is that he never failed to transform completely, to *dannunziagiare*, whatever he borrowed in the alembic of his creative genius. Certainly in *L'Enfant de volupté* D'Annunzio wrote on themes made fashionable by "the decadence," but with a passion and energy that stood in complete contrast to the fiction of the decadents and the decadent romantics of Paris, where ennui *à la A Rebours* reigned as an unassailable convention. Thus, at a time when French intellectuals like Charles Maurras and Maurice Barrès were lamenting the decline of Latin civilization before the rising power of the Anglo-Saxon and German nations to the north, D'Annunzio's fiction was welcomed in Paris as a harbinger of a Latin renaissance.

Always alert to Europe's changing intellectual fashions, D'Annunzio displayed his knowledge of Nietzschean jargon in the preface to *Il trionfo della morte*: "We turn our ear to the voice of the magnanimous Zarathustra, o Cenobiarca, and we prepare in art with secure faith the advent of the UEBERMENSCH, of the Superman."[23] Again, D'Annunzio's timing was phenomenal. When *Le Triomphe de la mort* appeared in 1896, the Parisian vogue of Nietzsche had reached

its height, and this book became D'Annunzio's greatest French success. One triumph followed another in
his *annus mirabilis*: articles on his work appeared in
all the major French reviews, and there was no end of
lectures on the significance of the *Romanzi della rosa*
in European literature.[24] Obviously, D'Annunzio had
conquered Paris. With such a prize won, could the rest
of Europe long resist him?

D'Annunzio's recognition in the most prestigious
literary and intellectual circles of Paris was a decisive
success for him. Although Sommaruga had made him
prominent in Italy, his popularity in Italy increased
many times over when the French took him up. After
the success of the Hérelle translations, D'Annunzio
was not simply prominent in Italy; he was supreme.
During the next twenty years he served as the one successful model for all Italian writers who sought a continental audience. Here we have the real reason underlying the appeal of D'Annunzian decadence as a
literary standard for the coming generation. In this
way did D'Annunzio become a writer's writer and the
arbiter of literary taste for his countrymen—like
Shakespeare's Hotspur, "the glass wherein the noble
youth did dress themselves."

Throughout the 1890s Corradini lived for the day
when he would enjoy success as a creative writer, and
he became a conspicuous example of D'Annunzio's in-
escapable influence in Italy after 1895. Genuine literary success always eluded him, although in time, by
around 1910, he did win a sizeable following in conservative political circles. To put his professional advance in its proper historical perspective, the story of
Corradini's literary career is that of a third-string
writer who, by dint of unflagging effort and dedication, at last wins promotion to the second string. His
earliest efforts were frankly deplorable, but at the

height of his powers he attained the professional level of upper mediocrity. Through all of these vicissitudes D'Annunzio never stood far from the center of Corradini's consciousness.

Corradini's career as a dramatist began on a disastrous note, with a performance of *In riva all'Arno* at Florence's Regio Teatro Nuovo in January 1892. The play closed after one evening, and only a forgettable fragment of this maiden effort was ever published, in two of *Germinal*'s March issues. Even the friendly critics on his own staff were compelled to admit: "We must say immediately that it was a failure."[25] They hastened to add that *In riva all'Arno* boasted some undeniable merits, although what these were went nameless in the review. On the other hand, *Germinal*'s critics did enumerate the failings of the "indecent audience" which "comprehended nothing." Of course, "They didn't understand me" is the last refuge of the failed writer, but had he been able to peer into the future on that January night in 1892, Corradini would have recognized the whistling and the catcalls, however painful, as at least a form of recognition, which was more than he received for his next several dramatic works.

In the three years that followed, Corradini watched his plays fall into instant oblivion, a void from which none of them has ever emerged. Shaken and embittered by the hostile reception given his first play, Corradini decided to try out *Gli ultimi Elisei*, a three-act drama, on his friends in a private reading during the winter of 1893, at about the time of *Germinal*'s demise.[26] History is silent about the reaction to this private reading, but we do know that no one ever produced or published the play.

Le selve disappointed him scarcely less, although he did manage to get this play performed, at Florence's Arena Nazionale. Again Corradini had an embarrassing flop on his hands. The production closed quickly, publishers would not touch the play, and *Le selve* only added to its author's reputation for failure. Then, in late 1893, Corradini reached the nadir of his career as a playwright: all theaters and publishing houses turned down *Compleanno*, a comedy. At least his previous worst failure, *Gli ultimi Elisei*, had been featured at a private reading; but *Compleanno* never saw the light, and no fragment of it—hardly even a recollection of it—survives.

Finally, on 18 March 1895, opening night of the three-act drama, *Dopo la morte*, Corradini won his first measurable success in the theater. *Dopo la morte* was performed for the first time in Siena's Teatro dei Rozzi, and then the Compagnia Rosapina-Paradossi took it to Florence and to many other Italian cities. The next year Paggi published the play.

Since most of Corradini's earlier plays are lost, it is difficult to document how *Dopo la morte* differs from them. One obvious innovation in this modestly successful play, certainly in comparison with the surviving fragments of *In riva all'Arno*, was Corradini's reliance on D'Annunzian motifs and characters. By 1895 "the contagion of D'Annunzianism" was in the air, carried along by the prevailing winds of fashion from Paris. Writing at about this time, the young journalist and man of letters Ugo Ojetti complained:

This D'Annunzian contagion is today at its height. Everyone (myself included) . . . feels the nausea. Never has there been an imitation more dangerous and more diffuse in our art; not even the Baroque, not even Arcadianism. D'Annunzianism corrupts the mind and the heart, not only the style. Behind the pseudo-heroic poses of Claudio Cantelmo there are bloodless faces, sinister eyes—and what's worse—empty heads.[27]

Corradini complained, too, but he was no less infected by the disease of D'Annunzianism.

It would require a thick book to document all of Corradini's borrowings from D'Annunzio's work after 1895.[28] The protagonist of *Dopo la morte* is a young artist, Paolo Rosis. His love for Anna Gray is strikingly reminiscent of Giorgio Aurispa's passion for Ippolita Sanzio in *Il trionfo della morte*: "I feel myself invaded by her spirit (pointing toward his heart and forehead). She is here! . . . and here! . . . everywhere! . . . everywhere! . . . inside of me, outside of me, everywhere! I neither feel nor see anything but her!"[29] At this stage of his career Corradini attempted to suggest inexpressible depths of human pathos with dots and exclamation points. Eventually he rose above this impoverished artistic standard, but he never overcame his fundamental incapacity to set a mood or flesh out a character.

Paolo is little more than a stock D'Annunzian figure, drawn, to be sure, without the master's touch, but suffering from the curse of Sperelli, Hermil, and Aurispa (i.e., to be victimized by a "fatal destiny"). This became the key feature in the character development of all D'Annunzio's heroes, whose decadence was less a celebration of pagan delectation in bodily pleasure than the visible effect of a cruel, tragic, and overarching fate. D'Annunzio's heroes are, despite appearances, creatures upon whom events break. The men themselves initiate nothing, and in the end they are all disappointed, defeated, or killed. Paolo Rosis fits this pattern exactly, setting a trend that Corradini's other fictional characters would follow until after the turn of the century, when he began writing frankly political novels and plays.

Corradini's first novel, *Santamaura* (1896), has been accurately described as Ibsenesque in atmosphere and D'Annunzian in style, with Romolo Pieri, the hero, behaving like an *Abruzzese* Dr. Stockmann—not a wholly believable amalgam of conflicting tendencies, in the judgment of the book's critics. *La gioia* (1897) told the predictably tragic story of Vittorio Rodia, a D'Annunzian-style victim of forces completely beyond his control. Then, in *La verginità* (1898), Corradini went to the primal source of his imitation. Instead of extracting plots and situations from the *Romanzi della rosa*, he drew the two central male characters of his third novel on the model of D'Annunzio himself.[30]

All three of these remaindered novels were imitation D'Annunzio. The D'Annunzian style, a sophisticated compound of hyperbole and rococo preciosity, required great literary skill to be used effectively. D'Annunzio possessed that skill, and, because in his case the style faithfully reflected the man, *Il piacere*, *L'innocente*, *Il trionfo della morte*, and *Le vergini delle rocce* have a ring of authenticity. On the other hand, there is an unsettling artificiality about Corradini's *Santamaura*, *La gioia*, and *La verginità*. These novels are not, in the Italian phrase, *libri vissuti*. As Ettore Veo, his younger contemporary and colleague on *L'idea nazionale*, recalled in 1931, "One intuited that he was frugal, parsimonious and chaste." [31] This description reminds us that Corradini, the former Catholic seminarian, was hardly the man to follow in the footsteps of the Capponcina's amorous denizen. Corradini's "decadence," then, having no taproot in his mind, was largely an affectation and the adoption of a popular literary convention—hence the exasperating thinness of his early novels.

Following the dismal failure of *La verginità*, Corradini abandoned novel-writing for about thirteen years. Fortunately, his hiatus from the theater had begun on a positive note, with *Dopo la morte*. Now he proposed to return to that genre and to begin building on his earlier success.

In *La leonessa* (1899) Corradini presented the Italian theater audience with a new twist, insofar as the heroine was a Nietzschean character; however, the decadent romantic conventions made supreme in Italy by D'Annunzio were more obtrusively present than ever before. His friend and biographer, Pier Ludovico Occhini, who reviled *La leonessa* as a betrayal of the author's talent, bemoaned this influence:

> Here, in everything, in the same intonation, in the same rhetoric, in the same phrases, one hears the poet of the Abruzzi. And, indeed, he who wants some idea of all the bad influence that for a certain period was exercised by Gabriele D'Annunzio on the youth of Italy, who wants to see a precise document of that great D'Annunzian contagion that infected Italy around the turn of the century, has only to read this *Leonessa*.[32]

Another of Corradini's friends, Roberto Pio Gatteschi, recalled the premier performance of *La leonessa* at the Pergola Theater in Florence. He and a coterie of the young author's supporters arrived at the theater that night "with the idea of proudly contributing to the victory and to the glorification of their delightful friend." The audience liked Act I, but "by and by," Gatteschi rued, "there occurred here and there, at first with respectful discretion, then with less discretion a certain subtle coughing, a ripple of equivocal laughter, an ambiguous shuffling of feet." Corradini's *gruppetto* tried to help, but their cries of *Silenzio!* only exacerbated the worst instincts of the crowd, and a cacophony of catcalls and whistles drowned out the dialogue of the final act.[33]

The play, trite and mawkish even by the melodramatic standards of the age, might have escaped with its life had it not been for the reference, in the character of Paolo Emo, to Adua.[34] This "Apostle of Africa" is the very first distinctively Corradinian character up to 1899, made all the more intriguing because he never appears on stage. We see him only through the eyes of others, always as a hero who "is trying to establish among his barbarians the laws and customs of civilization."[35] Corradini's conception of imperialism as the white man's burden would change drastically later on, but Emo's exploits inspire Laura, the "lioness" in the play, to exclaim: "Oh, how this is beautiful and grand in an extraordinary way!" When informed that the heroic Paolo is expected to arrive home any day, Laura cannot contain her emotions: "What joy! What joy! What immense joy! Paolo Emo! The greatness of it! To be near him! Oh! how my soul is transformed! How clear everything is! I dreamt that I was miserable and trapped in the dust and mud of irreparable disasters and errors. Instead, now I seem to be climbing rung by rung on a ladder of gold to the heavens."[36]

The audience could not be expected to share Laura's girlish enthusiasm, for in the aftermath of Adua the word "Africa" produced the bitterest distress in the minds of most Italians. In foreign affairs the crushing defeat of General Baratieri's troops at the hands of King Menelik's tribesmen on 1–2 March 1896 had caused the Italians unbearable humiliation. On the home front, the consequences of this defeat were even more shattering. Adua touched off a period of internal strife without precedent in modern Italian history; indeed, the domestic motives behind Italian imperialism were never more in evidence than in the events leading up to the crisis of March 1896.

The Italians had taken up the fashionable but dangerous game of imperialism in the mid-1880s, and from the start Africa had given them one disagreeable surprise after another. First came the massacre at Dogali on 26 January 1887, when more than four hundred Italian soldiers were killed—"four hundred brutes brutally murdered," in Andrea Sperelli's contemptuous phrase.[37] The shock of this calamity all but killed Depretis. He called it an "irreparable disaster," and Ferdinando Martini noted in his diary that the prime minister "aged ten years in a single instant."[38] Although Crispi had not yet assumed power, his views mattered most in the long run, since the future belonged to him. He argued that Italy, a young nation with much to prove, could not imitate the British at Khartoum by simply withdrawing after a defeat. The "right" to retreat could be earned only after "centuries of military power demonstrated on a hundred battlefields."[39] At the same time, Crispi saw in Africa a safety valve for the pressures of Italian political and economic life. For the next two years, following his installment as prime minister in the summer of 1887, he exploited the political rivalries in east Africa between Negus Johannes and Menelik, and in 1889 scored an impressive diplomatic triumph with the Treaty of Uccialli, apparently setting up an Italian protectorate in Ethiopia. Of course, the wily Menelik intended no such thing. The king was merely playing for time until he could dispose of his African enemies. That substantially accomplished with the defeat and death of Negus Johannes, Menelik began to make a mockery of Italy's supposed authority in Ethiopia.

Meanwhile, Italy's honor had been put on the line. Everyone said so, no one more theatrically than Crispi and King Umberto himself. While deploring domestic strife, they solemnly pointed to Africa as the region where Italy's new Risorgimento would unfold, where the nation's character would receive its most severe test. The "mission of civilization" was not yet a phrase to provoke scornful derision; it still had the power to quicken the pulse of that naive generation. Nevertheless, one had to look behind the verbal draperies to see what was really going on. Though a tragic waste for the country as a whole, African imperialism meant enormous profits for special commercial and shipping interests.[40] Still, the economic factor was only a small part of the story. By the early 1890s Africa had become the elixir of Italy's leaders, a patent medicine guaranteed to cure all political ills. Huge doses of *africanismo* were prescribed after 1891, as the banking scandals and then the Sicilian *fasci* disturbances threatened the nation's established order. For a while the prescription seemed to work. Crispi's energetic attempts to reacquire Italy's protectorate over Ethiopia had the desired side effect of distracting the Italian people from their plight at home. The killing of a few dervishes also did wonders for the country's morale and at the same time gave added support to the other pillar of Crispi's policy, repression of left-wing political dissidents.

In reality, however, nothing was as rare in Africa as a genuine Italian victory. The government bragged a lot. A dropped decimal here and an added zero there created an illusion of "Roman" victories, but, beginning on 8 December 1895, at Amba Alagi, Italy's cause in Africa began to sink under an ever-mounting wave of defeats that were only too real. The final catastrophe broke on the Italians at Adua on the night of 1–2 March 1896, when 289 officers and 4,600 enlisted men were killed, victims of a military strategy designed primarily with the home front in mind.[41] Every war has a political dimension, but few commanding generals have ever suffered from as much political interference as General Baratieri did. Although Menelik enjoyed an overwhelming numerical superiority at Adua, his greatest advantage, unknown to him, lay in Italy's rapidly worsening political situation which in

Crispi's judgment, could be saved only by a decisive victory in Africa. The harried general read Crispi's increasingly threatening telegrams, and at last tried to save his career and the monarchy's prestige by a daring night march against the enemy; but he only succeeded in confusing his own soldiers, with bloodier results than the Italian public was willing to accept. News of Italy's defeat reached Rome that very day, and, despite Baratieri's attempt to save face by resorting to the peculiar euphemisms that have become characteristic of all government language in the twentieth century, there was no hiding those casualty figures. Within hours insurrections swept the peninsula, and the first head to roll was Crispi's.

Corradini was present in the Chamber galleries when Crispi resigned. He described the prime minister as "grandly pathetic," obviously suffering under the volley of invective that greeted his announcement.[42] Crispi had always been a hesitant speaker. Ferdinando Martini once remarked of him, "Was there ever a less effective speaker than Crispi? He would grind out three words and then pause."[43] On this occasion the deputies hardly waited for that first pause: "To the door, to the door . . . we don't want to hear any more; we've had enough!" they shouted.[44] Although it was too late to save those thousands of lives lost in Africa, the deputies had their courage now. In the timeless tradition of Montecitorio, they had remained silent enough while the government's imperialist ambitions appeared close to being realized. Defeat, not imperialism, galled them, and their noisy sanctimoniousness in 1896 gave no assurance that they had learned the only lesson Africa could teach them.

At the time, Corradini commented sarcastically on the hypocrisy of the Chamber, but many years later, in 1923, he described his personal reaction to the tragic days of 1896: "I was among those contemporary Ital-

ians who were converted from literature in which I
was dissolute and blind. And my conversion was due
to the disaster at Adua." [45] History has chosen to honor
this myth. In fact, even after 1896 Corradini continued to write novels and plays in the decadent style.
Moreover, Corradini was, from his *Germinal* days on,
always a moralist, given to fuzzy preachments, and
neither as dissolute nor as blind as he later liked to
imagine.

Still, Adua did bring to a boil his long-simmering
indignation about conditions in Italy. On 8 March
1896 Corradini published a memorial article on the
Adua dead, "Abba Carima," in *Il marzocco*, the literary journal that he had begun to edit in the previous
month. All of his anguish welled up in the opening
sentences:

> We would like these transitory pages to acquire
> the consistency of bronze tablets, and in them to be
> inscribed the lamentation of a sovereign poet capa-
> ble of transmitting down through the centuries the
> sadness of our defeat.
> Abba Carima! The flower of our youth struck
> down by a humiliating calamity; so many millions
> of hearts shaken by a common sadness made per-
> sonal to everyone by domestic factionalism; our
> highest thoughts, all our purest ideals brought low. [46]

This was the kind of rhetoric Mussolini had in mind
when he praised Corradini as a fascist of the "very
first (*primissima*) hour." [47] During the 1920s, when
the fascists were looking for precursors in an attempt
to confer upon fascism a quality of historical inevitability, Corradini's "Abba Carima" earned him high
praise from the regime. Properly explained, Adua
could be made to look like the blinding light on his
road to Damascus—although, for the sake of historical

continuity, Corradini's assigned role in fascist hagiography was that of St. John the Baptist to Mussolini's Christ. From either historical perspective, however, Corradini offered limitless possibilities to fascist propagandists.

Actually, "Abba Carima" was a very isolated piece.[48] Always sensitive to the charge of being merely one of the provincial *dannunziani*, Corradini explained his conversion to politics exclusively in terms of Adua instead of giving D'Annunzio sufficient credit. Abundant evidence suggests that Corradini suffered moral outrage because of Adua, but the genesis of his political response to that calamity occurred only the following year, when the implications of D'Annunzio's political example became clear to him.

It was the parliamentary campaign of 1897, in which D'Annunzio had abjured at last the "*grandi errori*" of his decadent past, that excited Corradini's political imagination.[49] Moreover, D'Annunzio had proven that an artist could succeed in politics. At the same time, Corradini appreciated the difference that politics had made in D'Annunzio's art, and his *Marzocco* reviews of *Il sogno di un tramonto d'autunno* (1898), *La gloria* (1898), and *Le laudi* (1899) were adulatory. These works, Corradini rhapsodized, augured a new Italy, and in the noble enterprise of regenerating the country's dreams of greatness *Il marzocco* could do no less than fight alongside the valorous poet.[50]

Corradini's ambitions to politicize the *Marzocco* came to nothing. Angiolo and Adolfo Orvieto, the co-proprietors of the *Marzocco*, and Angelo Conti (1860–1930), the journal's art critic, took exception to Corradini's political enthusiasm, and before long they were openly deriding it. For them, Pascoli's dictum had the force of law: "A poet is a poet, not an orator, not a preacher, not a philosopher, not a historian, not a teacher, not a tribune or a demagogue, not a man of state or court."⁵¹ The split did not appear particularly meaningful at first; but in fact it opened the way for the demise of traditional right wing intellectual politics in Italy, the politics of nostalgia. All of these *marzocchisti* had started out in the same general direction, as esthetes deploring the aimless drift of modern Italian life. It was the usual *fin de siècle* esthetic lament, with hardly a variation on the theme articulated by the enormously more influential *convitati*. From the beginning *Il convito* cast its shadow across the pages of *Il marzocco*, and the Florentine journal abounded with admiring references to D'Annunzio, De Bosis, and Pascoli. Although *Il marzocco* survived into the 1930s and became a publishing institution in Italy, it started out as a somewhat threadbare gospel in the religion of art. On this point the prologue, said to have been written by D'Annunzio himself, was very clear: "to oppose with all our force that production of literary and artistic works that have their origin outside pure beauty."⁵² As an editorial policy this formulation was comfortably vague enough to allow many divergent minds to begin working together, but within months the *Marzocco* became a battleground for the warring staff factions.

From 1897 on, the struggle for editorial control over the *Marzocco* became increasingly bad tempered. The trigger event of this crisis was D'Annunzio's parliamentary campaign, which instantly unmasked the contradictions and the inconsistencies within the esthetic political tradition. The potential for such a conflict had always been present, as the *Cronaca bizantina* factionalism showed; but as long as the esthetes merely discussed political theory, it remained possible to accommodate many different viewpoints. However, D'Annunzio's political action of 1897 set in motion forces that produced the crisis from which, simultaneously, the politics of nostagia died and the politics of nationalism took primal shape.

Corradini blazed the trail as a transitional figure between the two movements. At this decisive moment in his life Corradini was deeply influenced by the sociological and political writings of young Mario Morasso (b. 1871), whose most famous book, *L'imperialismo artistico*, would appear in 1903. He was a *Marzocco* staff member and Corradini's staunchest ally in the campaign to raise the journal's political consciousness. Morasso's *Marzocco* articles on politics and literature, particularly "La politica dei letterati" (1897), inspired Corradini to launch the famous "Inchiesta del *Marzocco*." In 1898 Morasso wrote *Uomini e idee del domani: l'egoarchia*, in which he denounced socialism ("the leveling menace both terrible and devastating") and the ruling class in Italy ("the decrepit edifice of sordid bourgeois society").[53] Only the intellectuals had a prayer of saving the country now, he observed. Corradini took away a good deal from *Uomini e idee del domani: l'egoarchia*, as he freely admitted, but all the same the editor of the *Marzocco* had been moving toward a politically *engagé* position since *Germinal* days. In 1892 he had proclaimed: "O, art and literature either place yourselves in the first line among the other potent factors of human progress . . . or you do not have the right to exist."[54] Morasso became useful to the extent that he gave Corradinian hyperbole the trappings of a system. At the same time, D'Annunzio performed a related service for Corradini by showing him in a concrete way how all of this theorizing about intellectuals in politics could work on the practical level.

In retrospect, it is plain that Corradini always felt out of place amidst the esthetes. It was the misfortune of the *Marzocco* esthetes to be close at hand when his

sullen disquiet suddenly yielded to aggressive contempt. Corradini had been spoiling for a fight with the
more rarefied spirits among the *marzocchisti*, and
when it erupted over the D'Annunzio business, he
blurted out his rage like one who had been biting his
tongue for a long while. The Orvietos and Conti
scarcely knew how to respond to such violence of language. All of Corradini's repressed hatred and scorn
seemed aimed at Conti in particular, the hapless "Dot-
tor mistico," Daniele Glauco, in D'Annunzio's autobiographical novel, *Il fuoco* (1900). Conti had been
involved in a minor way with the *Cronaca bizantina*
through his friendship with Giulio Salvadori.[55] In
books like *Rileggendo il Petrarca* (1892), *Giorgione*
(1894), and *La beata riva: trattato dell'oblio* (1900)
he defined the social role of the artist in religious
terms. The connection between such a definition and
Carduccian ideas on the subject was obvious, but Conti
represented the second generation of esthetes, which
in many ways stood at a distant remove from the first
generation. For the Conti-inspired esthetes on the
Marzocco, modern life had become too painful to be
endured and too corrupt to be reformed. Art beckoned
them as the *consolatrice*, offering a brief respite of un-
consciousness (*oblio*) from the tragedy of life. The
politics of nostalgia gave way to the theology of nostalgia. "I have already said that art is a prayer, and
here I add that it is a prayer of souls dissatisfied with
our terrestrial existence," Conti sermonized in *La
beata riva*.[56] Politics, society, and the visible world all
flickered like shadows on the wall of Plato's cave,
while the Truth lay outside, on a higher plane.

Conti seized upon D'Annunzianism as the perfect
literary expression of the modern religious spirit, and
his *Marzocco* column became yet another showcase for
the enhancement of D'Annunzio's fame. Corradini put
up with this "distortion" for a while—but what pain

it cost him to publish Conti's reviews, filled as they were with references to D'Annunzio the "mystic idealist" and the "Franciscan." Corradini retorted with rising heat in his own articles, asserting that only a man who was not listening very hard could fail to hear the ringing voice of the new D'Annunzio, the bard of war, conquest, and imperialism.

Finally, on 3 December 1899, Corradini could stomach no more. Conti's moral preachments, his insipid Tolstoianism, and his pitifully outdated Ruskinianism annoyed Corradini so much that he singled out his antagonist by name in an attack against conventional Christianity. A month later Corradini wrote the decisive "Lettera aperta a A. Conti." Regular *Marzocco* readers surely realized that the two men had their differences, but the polemic in Corradini's letter provoked a scandal. Conti found himself lumped with all the "sentimental, utopian, hypocritical dreamers" who were hopelessly out of touch with twentieth-century realities. Could anything be more ridiculous and pathetic, Corradini inquired of his readers, than Conti's "horror of the new machines and his love of 'the old ways' of doing things"?[57] He continued in the same vein:

> And here is the divide between those who think like you and those who think like me. You continue to propose a program that has always failed the test of facts; we would like to begin announcing a practical program, based on the conscience of man, one that is in harmony, insofar as possible, with the nature that makes men in their individual and social existences, their destinies and their morals . . . full of infinite and incomprehensible aims.

Shortly thereafter, as if to complete the immolation of his editorial job on the *Marzocco*, Corradini attacked Angiolo Orvieto as well, slashing away, in a dozen paragraphs or so, at the Tolstoian sensibilities of his boss. When the 18 February 1900 issue of the *Marzocco* carried an announcement of Corradini's departure from the journal's editorial office, it came as no surprise. The *Marzocco* ouster was the beginning of a vital new period in his career, however, and he had no regrets about leaving. Upon departing from Florence late in the winter of 1900, Corradini characterized the *Marzocco* as a "vehicle of the purest Christian and Tolstoian spirit."[58] For his own part, "the facts of life," not the "myths of the *Marzocco*" (i.e., the illusions of the Conti-inspired esthetes), would be the future. During the next several years, beginning with a brief interlude in Venice on the *Gazzetta di Venezia* staff, Corradini assembled these facts of life in a remarkable political synthesis known as nationalism.

One day before Corradini fired this parting shot at his former colleagues on the *Marzocco*, D'Annunzio, on 24 March 1900, made his famous "leap over the hedge." Addressing the deputies of the extreme left in Parliament, he declared, "I bring my congratulations to the extreme left for the fervor and tenacity with which it defends its idea. After the spectacle of today I know that on one side there are many dead who howl, and on the other a few quick and eloquent men. As a man of intellect, I go toward life."[59]

The spectacle to which D'Annunzio referred was the successful attempt of socialists and other antigovernment factions to block the repressive measures of Luigi Pelloux's ministry. Antonio di Rudinì had succeeded Crispi in March 1896; however, the "perpetual child prodigy" of Italian politics (in the damning phrase of Francesco De Sanctis), cracked under the pressure of Milan's May Days in 1898. Goaded on by bad harvests and soaring bread prices, the people of Milan, no doubt inspired by the example of the Sicilian *fasci* and influenced by the volatile political climate of Italy since Adua, took to the barricades. These riots were put down with extreme brutality by the House of Savoy's darling, General Bava-Beccaris. The next month Pelloux, himself a general, headed up a frankly reactionary ministry. It was *crispinismo* without Africa, but not for long. Pelloux's failure to impose a program tantamount to martial law doomed his ministry, and he fell late in the spring of 1900. The king's assassination a few months later so horrified the country that, at the time, some may have thought Sbarbaro's vision of catastrophe in *Regina o repubblica?* was coming to pass. In fact, however, the golden age of Giolitti lay only two innocuous care-taker ministries away.

Two days after his *salto della siepe*, D'Annunzio wrote a justificatory article, "Morti e vivi," for Luigi Lodi's *Il giorno*, and on 27 March returned to the Chamber, where he sat on the extreme left. The socialists wooed D'Annunzio assiduously, and Leonida Bissolati himself tried to deepen the poet's conversion experience. This attempt promised to succeed for a while, and in May the Socialists persuaded him to accept their nomination for a seat from Florence. The marriage of Beauty and the politics of nostalgia had created little in D'Annunzio's case, except occasional flamboyant speeches that set a new standard for long-winded exegesis in Italian political life. What would have been born of a union between Beauty and social-ism was never to be disclosed, for defeat terminated his parliamentary career in the May elections.

Although Corradini was almost certainly shocked by D'Annunzio's turnabout, he need not have been. From the beginning of his parliamentary bid, D'An-

nunzio had been completely candid about his unpre-
dictability. To the newspaper editor Luigi Lodi he explained on 15 July 1897:

> I am beyond the *right* and the *left* as I am beyond
> good and evil (!!!) .... I have seen that some news-
> papers present me as a ministerial candidate—of
> the right. But you know well, better than anyone,
> that the singularity of my attitudes will have a
> stupefying effect on the old benches of Monteci-
> torio. I will play my own part. I will be grateful to
> you, then, if, as you occupy yourself with this ad-
> venture, you will persist in making me appear
> abhorrent to the old labels. I am a man of life and
> not of formula.[60]

D'Annunzio was an incurable rebel, and in the end
the Socialists had no better luck with him than the
politically conscious *marzocchisti* had. Once more, in
1900, he chose *Il giorno* to explain his motives: "I
agree not with their [the socialist] idea . . . but with
their destructive force. And I incite the ruling classes
to a national renewal and to the doctrine of 'force for
force,' a doctrine of the continual struggle and the
continual conquest of the world."[61]

Here was the germ of Corradinian nationalism, and
it would be difficult to find, even in Corradini's political speeches and articles, a more pithily worded statement of what early nationalism represented in Italian
political and cultural life. At its moment of genesis,
nationalism was essentially a literary phenomenon,
making its first obstreperous appearance in cultural
journals with lofty intellectual pretensions. For form's
sake, anyway, this was all in keeping with the politics
of nostalgia. Nevertheless, Corradini's actions, hesitant
and confused though they surely were in 1900, represented a real advance in the evolution of Italian right-

wing intellectual politics. The theoretical points were made by D'Annunzio: the intellectuals of the right could no longer afford merely to be "beautiful souls" taking shelter in the ambiguous refuge of art; they had to learn from the left, to emulate its violence of language and action when necessary, to match its intellectual appeal with an equally compelling philosophy. D'Annunzio had a mental grasp of these issues, but for temperamental reasons he was unable or unwilling to act consistently in a politically practical way. Corradini absorbed the thought and around 1900 began to put it into action, stressing the need for violence as a tactic and imperialism as a world view. Above all, Corradini called for an organization of militants to implement these things in Italian political life; and the type of people he had in mind for such a task were the antithesis of the nostalgic esthetes among his former colleagues on the *Marzocco*. From these premises nationalism evolved as a bourgeois political reaction to the growing power of socialism and the deepening crisis of liberalism. The distinctive physiognomy of Italian fascism was already beginning to take shape.

CONCLUSION

"The claim . . . that every fluctuation of politics and ideology can be presented and expounded as an immediate expression of the economic structure must be contested in theory as primitive infantilism."
—Antonio Gramsci
The Prison Notebooks

To comprehend the ideological origins of Italian nationalism is to see that consciousness not only reflects the world of experience, but also helps shape that world. The early history of nationalism demonstrates how an important political movement can be generated from the tension within an ideological tradition, rather than from the immediate pressures of any recognizable socio-economic group. This does not mean that nationalism or any other ideology is ever free from socio-economic factors. There is a reciprocal action in history between social structure and intellectual activity, but it is not a relationship in which the underlying economic mode of production exerts an unmediated magnetic pull on the superstructural realm of ideas. Indeed, the entire substructural-superstructural model is quite misleading as a historical approach because economics and ideas can never be meaningfully separated. We do separate them for the purpose of analysis, but in the finished reconstruction of the past "substructure" and "superstructure" must be understood as diverse aspects of the same historical phenomenon.

Thus, ideas are more than mere epiphenomena. They are not a "second" signaling system simply reflecting a deeper economic reality below. In all their immense diversity ideas form society's consciousness and its range of mental possibilities, both reflecting and conditioning the institutions of society itself. On the *fin de siècle* Italian scene, for example, the traditions that we associate with liberalism, socialism, estheticism, and Catholicism were the main ideological choices for the country's politically active intellectuals. These four ongoing traditions were the constant factors in Italy's political and intellectual life at the time; their degree of acceptance at any particular moment were the variables. Class factors do not always help us understand why an intellectual would choose one tradition over another, for it is clear that, if all men are conditioned by class, they are not all conditioned in the same way. If they were there would be no need to write history.

The problem of ideological choice can be extremely elusive and untidy, but in the case of the nostalgic esthetes the facts are plain. The members of this group were overwhelmingly drawn from the provincial petit-bourgeois and middle-bourgeois classes. In the years following the Risorgimento these classes, traditionally the main suppliers of the country's intellectuals, were extremely hard hit by the fiscal policies of the new state. To an astonishing extent, amply documented in the work of Emilio Sereni and Salvatore Romano, the enormous economic and social costs of unification were borne by small provincial landowners who simply could no longer compete with large landowners in the national marketplace of post-Risorgimento Italy. As prices for farm produce fell, along with declining rent revenues, taxes swiftly mounted. Thousands of these farmers lost everything for nonpayment of taxes during the Umbertian period. Of course, in the end the agricultural proletariat suffered more than anyone else, but it was mute. Except for ineffectual rebellions, it could only express itself with its feet, and by the 1870s an epic Italian migration was under way. Thousands, followed by tens of thousands, and then hundreds of thousands of emigrants abandoned their native land; with them went the traditional structure of the country's agricultural life. However, the literary lament for its passing was voiced by the educated scions of the declining rentier class.

It is easy to miss this point, and even easier to misstate it. First, the myth of the Risorgimento betrayed was expressed in such high-flown, hyperbolic language that we might not hear the infrequently sounded note of class distress. Here Carducci's adaptation of Mazzini's "Third Rome" rhetoric was a decisive early development in the politics of nostalgia. Following Carducci's lead, the esthetes did not complain about prices and rents or taxes; rather, they raised their angry voices against "bourgeois vulgarity," the "vile majority," the "moral sickness" of the times, the threatening "mass civilization," the "merchandising of art," the "Great Beast," the "corruption of the banks and government." Theirs was a literature of exalted rejection. They took the high ground in defense of pristine Risorgimento ideals against the post-Risorgimento conglomeration of new money and brash ignorance, but only the most superficial student of this literature could believe that so much class wrath merely coincided with confiscatory taxes and a devastating downward spiral in prices and rents.

Second, although the appeal to nostalgia was certainly a middle-class phenomenon in Italian cultural and political life, it was not the only cultural and political possibility open to the middle class, or even to the provincial landowning element within it. The middle class was anything but monolithic in Umbertian Italy, socially or economically, culturally or politically. Moreover, its character, influence, and disposition toward the new order varied from region to region. The leading Italian socialist of this period, Filippo Turati, also emerged from a middle-class background, the son of a poetaster government official. Giulio Salvadori, a nostalgic esthete before he became one of the giants in the *fin de siècle* Catholic revival, was the son of a self-employed butcher. The Italian middle class produced apologists, like Pietro Sbarbaro, for *theoretical* liberalism, although the historian searches in vain for any contemporary Italian thinker who defended Umbertian liberalism as it actually was. The contemptuous disregard for the liberal establishment provides the key to understanding the political and intellectual life of the age. Benedetto Croce, the son of wealthy landowners, attempted such a defense after World War I, in *A History of Italy from 1871 to 1915*; but this was not the way he thought and wrote earlier, in the 1880s and 1890s, least of all during his Marxist phase when he, along with Georges Sorel and Antonio Labriola (himself descended from a patrician family), rounded out the trinity of Latin Marxism. Looking a little further down the social scale and moving north to Tuscany, we find Enrico Corradini and the Orvieto brothers, Angiolo and Adolfo, sharing identical class backgrounds; but as the *Marzocco* story makes clear, they ended up nearly as far apart politically as sons from the small to middle landowning class could.

Class, region, generation—all these factors are important in arriving at an understanding of any Italian thinker's mental life. Still, the class factor alone cannot bear much stress, primarily because, in the modern world all intellectuals are effectively middle class, but they do not all defend middle-class positions. Therefore it would be a major error to think of the esthetic invocations to the Risorgimento and Rome as insincere bourgeois machinations. Carducci and the middle-class writers who thought as he did were no

less sincere than the middle-class Turati or any of the
socialists invoking the proletariat. Sincerity, like beauty, is often in the eye of the beholder; but it is not very
helpful to argue that some middle-class intellectuals
profess political opinions which are merely rationali-
zations of their economic interests, whereas other intellectuals from the same class apprehend and act on
the Truth for the Truth's sake alone. Psychological
reductionism is not an answer, either. As Marx
pointed out (and as George Lichtheim has reminded
Marx's twentieth-century followers), history is always the record of particular events and particular
actors, whose appearance at a particular moment can
only be explained in concrete terms. I take this to
mean that each case in history is unique, and that to
understand a Corradini or a Turati one must study the
individual from the inside out, not the other way
around so that a career is made to fit alongside a well-
marked dialectical path. The true history of an individual might cause us to adjust the markers in the direction of new findings. Historians should always be
prepared to make those adjustments, lest they be led
into some new form of scholasticism much worse than
the old, though resting on the same pernicious anti-
intellectual frame of mind in which men no longer
would write history in a spirit of inquiry, but would
simply begin their investigations with conclusions already formed.

The choice of Corradini and Turati as examples
illustrating the thorny problem of class and ideological affiliation is not a random coupling. Their relationship in Italian politics suggests the violent union
throughout modern history between revolution and
counterrevolution. For the most part, the right was on
the defensive in Italy, responding to the left's initia-
tives and growth. Except for the menacing gestures of

the politically inactive clerical right, the development of extraconsensual politics in Umbertian Italy originated on the socialist-anarchist left. The esthetic politics of nostalgia, starting with Carducci and the *Cronaca bizantina*, arose as a secular antisocialist challenge to liberalism, marking the appearance, however hesitant and impractical, of a "new" right in Italian politics. Whereas the socialists attacked bourgeois society on economic grounds, the *bizantini* attacked it on esthetic grounds. Blaming the distress of modern life on the rule of businessmen, the esthetes looked back nostalgically to Italy's aristocratic past and longed for a revival of political traditionalism which alone, they thought, would bring Mazzini's vision of a Third Rome to pass. This was their high-brow way of condemning the liberal order, which had only succeeded in creating an *affarista* aristocracy of speculators and parasites. At the same time, the esthetes were terrified at the prospect of the new masses—or, rather, of the new visibility achieved by the masses after the Risorgimento. Thus the "vulgar businessmen" and the "vile mob" were the twin images of esthetic despair during the Umbertian period. Above all, the esthetes felt that the elite had to be surrounded with a *cordon sanitaire* in order to perform its intellectual and artistic functions unmolested by the masses. Culture would become, more emphatically than ever before, a device for social distancing, i.e., the arts would be useful as a means of preserving upper-class identity against the unwashed multitude, with the intellectuals appropriating for themselves the old aristocratic social models. *L'art pour l'art* functioned not only as an esthetic theory; it also involved an explicit political ideology. After 1885, no one better represented this union of art and politics in Italy than D'Annunzio. In his life and literature he embodied the disdain which one part of the middle class felt for another part and at the same time the envy which the middle class as a whole exhibited toward the aristocracy.

Corradini's break with the esthetes around 1900 drew attention to the many practical difficulties in nostalgic politics. It symbolized in a dramatically prophetic way the consolidation of heretofore antagonistic elements in the "old" and "new" ruling classes of the post-Risorgimento against what both sides by then recognized as an immeasurably more dangerous threat from the socialist left. The esthetic tradition had been under serious strain all the while, even during its heyday, as the *Cronaca bizantina* story illustrates. The history of the Sommaruga publishing house has been used here as a window through which to view what appear to be the distinctive elements in Italian culture and politics at the dawn of the Umbertian age. Sommaruga attempted to modernize the Italian publishing industry, and failed. His failure throws a glaring light on the backward conditions in the Italian cultural marketplace at this time. The younger *bizantini* represented the cream of Italy's writing talent in the 1880s, and their betrayal, as Scarfoglio himself later admitted, fatally undermined Sommaruga. What so distressed them was his commercialism— that is to say, his modernity. The irony here is striking: Sommaruga, denounced by the esthetes as an ignorant and ineducable parasite of culture, was the true revolutionary and the only member of the *bizantini* to see what the future held in store. D'Annunzio and his cohorts continued to pine for the vanishing patronage system. Everyone of them, a Wagner in embryo, looked for his Ludwig.

Although Sommaruga's business methods alienated the esthetes, the question of alienation is very complicated because Carducci, regarded by all *bizantini* as the maestro, refused to join the revolt. There were many reasons for his refusal. First, he genuinely liked Sommaruga, and we must not overlook the pull of emotion as a factor in history. Second, Carducci lived far from the scene of Sommaruga's so-called esthetic crimes which had dismayed the younger *bizantini*. Moreover, Carducci by this time had made his own way, and he had no cause to fear that his career might be jeopardized by the Sbarbaro imbroglio. Unlike the free-lance *bizantini* writers, Carducci had a safe institutional berth at the University of Bologna. He is an outstanding nineteenth-century precursor of a trend that has become dominant in the twentieth century: the channeling of intellectual life through a vast university network. Carducci could quite literally afford to relax at the time of the Sbarbaro scandal, whereas many of the *bizantini* felt they could not.

Finally, and most important, Carducci belonged to a different generation from the men who called themselves his disciples. While one generation can learn from another, the exact duplication of styles is historically impossible, because the experiences of any two generations are always different. By the mid-1880s Carducci more clearly perceived the distance that separated him from the younger *bizantini*, and he berated the "decadents" and "dandies" (i.e., the *dannunziani*), for their treatment of Sommaruga.

However, what mattered most during Sommaruga's glory years was the great shared idea that united the *bizantini* in a pledge of allegiance to Carducci. The idea had two faces: hatred of the "democratic" present, and nostalgia for the "aristocratic" past. This came to nothing less than social romanticism in the face of a society that was modernizing itself slowly and with excruciating pain. The seeming paradox of Sommaruga is that he founded the principal literary vehicle of nostalgic protest and then became the primary symbol of everything his writers despised most.

This contradiction disappears when it is fully understood that Sommaruga's intent in launching the
Cronaca bizantina was fundamentally practical. By
1884 the *bizantini* believed that, in breaking away
from a businessman as typically vile as Sommaruga,
they were upholding the true tradition of Carduccianism, while the master himself, far removed from
Rome, could not see the publisher's apostasy to the
original *Cronaca bizantina* ideals.

The Italian cultural crisis of the 1880s was accompanied by a parallel development in Italian political
life. Nostalgia for the disappearing patronage system
became coupled in the minds of the esthetes with nostalgia for the principle of aristocracy in politics.
Throughout the *fin de siècle* the esthetic politics of
nostalgia helped create a climate of hostility toward
liberal parliamentary institutions. The Socialists were
doing the same thing on the other side of the ideological spectrum, and by 1900 no institution in the country was as universally despised among intellectuals,
regardless of their ideological background, as Parliament.

In normal times radicals of the left and right tend
to be isolated, posing little threat to the stability of
society; however, the 1880s and 1890s did not constitute a normal period in Italian history. During the
1880s Italian industry reached the take-off stage of
development, and at the same time the country assumed its place as a power with imperialist pretensions. By the mid-1890s it was devastatingly clear to
every mentally alive person that neither of these developments was going at all well. The cause of socialism made a spectacular leap forward during these
years, profiting enormously from the losses and failures of liberalism; but it was not the only radical political cause to so prosper. As the Socialists advanced
and organized themselves into a militant anti-liberal

party, the right became increasingly desperate for more effective means to stop their enemies. As right-wing anxiety rose over the menace of socialism and the impotence of liberalism, the need for an explicit and aggressive doctrine of class survival became pressing. Nationalism was born of this need.

But the intellectuals led the way, not the land-owners or the industrialists who, in fact, resisted Corradini's antiliberalism for a long time. Inchoate nationalism emerged as another ideological option for Italy's politically conscious intellectuals; and the historical circumstances of its emergence must make us question the by now traditional assumption, derived from orthodox Marxism, that in explaining the evolution of ideologies we are concerned primarily with locating the social forces which initially engender new ideas in a small circle of thinkers, and with tracing the vicissitudes which eventually influence a larger group of people to accept them. The early history of nationalism shows instead that the cultural and institutional traditions to which ideology gives rise tend to assume their own generative power in history, making it necessary to look not only for the origins of ideology in the economic substructure, but also for its additional and unintended ideological consequences. In this sense the *fin de siècle* crisis in the politics of nostalgia formed the intellectual precondition for early nationalism, just as the fear of the right in the face of organized militant socialism formed the essential social precondition. But the intellectual crisis came first.

Thus the relationship between the politics of nostalgia and nationalism illuminates the historical process by which a parent ideology rooted in the socio-economic changes of its period can, by the force of its crisis in a later period, generate ideological offspring which must find a satisfactory socio-economic connection of their own in order to survive. The history of nationalism from 1900 to 1910 turns on the search for this connection. However, the actual genesis of nationalist ideology is largely understandable in terms of Corradini's intellectual biography, which was dominated at every vital point in the 1890s, negatively as well as positively, by D'Annunzian estheticism. Corradinian nationalism arose as a direct result of the disappointment that a handful of Florentine intellectuals suffered when the ideology of nostalgia failed the test of practical politics. D'Annunzio's fiasco in Parliament, especially his highly publicized though essentially capricious conversion to socialism in 1900, left these intellectuals bewildered, frustrated, and in a mood to repudiate the past. Italian nationalism began at this moment.

Two different processes may be seen at work here: the intellectual process of idea formation in which economic considerations have only indirect importance, and the acceptance process by society in which economic considerations are paramount. Though interrelated, the two processes are distinct in the history of Italian nationalism. An understanding of both is necessary in order to explain the genesis of the movement and how it achieved a decisive following in Italy.

CODA

"I fear you will laugh when I tell you what I conceive to be about the most essential quality for a free people whose liberty is to be progressive, permanent and on a large scale; it is much stupidity."
—Walter Bagehot
Letters on the French Coup d'Etat

After 1900 the political sympathies of Italian intellectuals were divided between various forms of liberalism, Catholicism, socialism, and nationalism; estheticism gradually dropped from view as a serious political position until it surfaced again, outwardly transformed, in a futurist guise about a decade later. This dialogue had infinite possibilities, but only one historical conclusion: the triumph of a fascist dictatorship over parliamentary democracy. By 1922 the combative intellectuals had been speaking in their transcendental manner for so long that the humdrum parliamentary realities of everyday political life were held in the deepest contempt by nearly all who have recorded their impressions. It is true that intellectuals everywhere tend to compare present realities with abstract ideals, rather than with other realities; however, in Italy this tendency became the basic law of political life. There the intellectual organization of political hatred and bigotry achieved a phenomenal success. The effects of this achievement were not felt seriously until after the war. With Giolitti as prime minister, Italy managed to muddle through what for all European countries was a comparative golden age, in the prewar period; but when the stability of a country's political life depends upon the skill and resourcefulness of one man, that country has every reason to fear the future. The storm signals flashed insistently throughout the Giolittian and postwar periods, and no thinking person could have been completely taken by surprise when liberalism collapsed before the challenge of fascism. The real tragedy for Italy in 1922, though, was that few people, on the left as well as on the right, were sorry to see that collapse occur. As so often happens in history, the extremes met and became one.

This conjunction endures today, a product of Italy's past, but with contours that fit the needs of the present. The politics of nostalgia occupy an important place in the Italian political tradition, because the esthetes of the Umbertian age established the anti-parliamentary precedents which eventually characterized the opinions of most Italian intellectuals, whether on the right or the left. Although the times have changed, the conditions essential to political abstraction on the part of Italy's intellectuals have not. Italy is still perceived by its own people as a country suffering from a national decline, and in such countries the nostalgia for utopian values exerts a powerful attraction. The psychological impulse behind the present nostalgia is the same in Italy as it was a century ago: the pressing need of the intellectual to avert his gaze from the unbridgeable chasm between ideals and reality. The *fin de siècle* esthetes and the *brigatisti rossi* of today have that much in common, and it is a lot, although the vagaries of an unknown future are now preferred to the fantasies of a glorified past. Nostalgia, we are reminded, may connote something that is far away, as well as long ago.

The burden of twentieth-century Italian life has been made heavier by the failure of the country's intellectuals to realize that genuine progress of any kind is painful, piecemeal, and slow; that utopia is, in the end, chimerical. Their apocalyptic visions of a change both terrible and swift produce impatience in the young, the impressionable, the ignorant, and the foolish that continuously threatens to submerge the country under a wave of anarchy. Carducci, D'Annunzio, and Corradini threatened to do the same thing during the Umbertian age—but at least it can be said of the nostalgic esthetes that in the *fin de siècle* they did not have World War I, fascism, nazism, Stalinism, worldwide depression, Auschwitz and Dachau, World War II, Hiroshima, and the ruin of Europe to contemplate. Comparatively speaking, the esthetes were innocents. The voice of Giuseppe Prezzolini, who began his yet unfinished career as a *fin de siècle* esthete, speaks to us across the decades. Writing about Umbertian and Giolittian Italy in his autobiography, *L'italiano inutile*, he expressed disbelief at his youthful impetuosity: "To think that we didn't appreciate it, that we tried to destroy it, and that it seemed impossible for us to live if there were not at least a revolution or a war." That statement might serve as the epitaph for an entire generation—not that succeeding generations have been able to learn anything from it. Intellectuals have had a continued and crucial responsibility for making the twentieth century the worst century yet, but that historical fact does not dull the ardor of the dogma-filled men and women who profess their willingness to reduce the world to "a weary and unbright cinder" in the fanatical pursuit of their abstractions.

NOTES

Introduction

1. Filippo Crispolti, "Ricordi su due re: Vittorio Emanuele II e Umberto I."
2. "The Statuto: The Constitution of Piedmont-Sardinia," in Denis Mack Smith, ed., *The Making of Italy, 1796–1870*, p. 136.
3. This was Quintino Sella's phrase. He also told the story of how Vittorio Emanuele was depressed after the conquest of Rome. When asked why, the king answered: "In the years that I have left there will be nothing left to grab" (cited by Ferdinando Martini in *Confessioni e ricordi, 1859–92*, p. 152).
4. In late 1855 Vittorio Emanuele visited France and England, a trip which gave rise to some legendary anecdotes. For an amusing account of the king's gaffes on this tour, see Denis Mack Smith, *Victor Emanuel, Cavour and the Risorgimento*, ch. 2.
5. "Cronaca Contemporanea: Cose Italiane," *Civiltà cattolica*, 19 Jan. 1878. This Catholic publication is an excellent source for journalistic commentary on monarchical politics. Usually the press put the monarchy on the social page and gave it deferential treatment; not *Civiltà cattolica*, which trained a sharply skeptical eye on the Italian government and its institutions. Its coverage of Umberto's coronation is unique among that of major publications for an absence of the "grand style" then common in reporting anything to do with the monarchy.
6. Ibid., 2 Feb. 1878.

7. Vittorio Bersezio, "Re Vittorio Emanuele," *Gaz-zetta letteraria*, 12–18 Jan. 1878.
8. Cited in Crispolti, "Ricordi."
9. E.g., see Barbara Tuchman's handling of the *fin de siècle* wave of anarchist terror in *The Proud Tower*, ch. 2.
10. In *Dynamics of Counterrevolution in Europe, 1870–1956*, ch. 2, Arno J. Mayer calls attention to the dearth of historiography on themes dealing with reaction, conservatism, and counterrevolution in politics.
11. This is Fritz Stern's apt phrase in *The Politics of Cultural Despair*.
12. See William J. McGrath, *Dionysian Art and Pop-ulist Politics in Austria.*
13. Luigi Federzoni, *L'Italia di ieri per la storia di domani*, ch. 1. Federzoni was a major figure in the Italian Nationalist movement. In the same chapter he writes, "Enrico Corradini, between 1903, the year his review *Il regno* was founded, and 1922, was the founder and genial leader of Italian nationalism" (p. 9).
14. Irving Howe, *Politics and the Novel*, p. 19.
15. Benito Mussolini, "Enrico Corradini."

Chapter One

1. Giovanni Papini, *L'uomo Carducci*.
2. Cited in "Inchiesta su l'arte e la letteratura," *Il Marzocco*, 28 Nov. 1897–13 Feb. 1898. Enrico Corradini, editor of this journal, published the responses of numerous French intellectuals and artists regarding their opinions of Italian litera-ture. Whereas they all had great respect for D'An-nunzio, hardly any of them bothered to read Carducci.

3. These are Carducci's words about his father. Cited by Augusto Dalgas, "Ripose o no il Carducci amore alla Versilia?"

4. Mario Biagini, *Il poeta della terza Italia*, pt. 1, contains much highly detailed information about Carducci's childhood.

5. Carducci to Giuseppe Torquato Gargani, 29 Oct. 1853, *Lettere di Giosuè Carducci*.

6. Carducci to Gargani, 11 Sept. 1853, ibid.

7. Ettore Caccia, *Poesia e ideologia per Carducci*, p. 53.

8. Carducci's anti-Christianity, like so much anti-Christian thought of this period, was colored by anti-Semitic prejudice. "Christianity," he wrote, "is a Semitic religion, that is to say it is Jewish; and the Semites, the Jews, do not understand and even hate plastic beauty. Now even we are lacking this sense because we, Greco-Latins, a noble Aryan race, have been injected with a Semitic religion; we, children of the sun, adorers of the sun and sky. This unnatural inoculation has ruined us, has made us false, sad, cowardly, and indolent. Believe me . . . the cause of Greek and Italian decline was Christianity" (Carducci to Lidia, 17 May 1874, *Lettere*).

9. Giuseppe Chiarini, *Memorie della vita di Giosuè Carducci*, p. 120.

10. Caccia, *Poesia e ideologia*, p. 74.

11. Upon learning of his appointment to the University of Bologna, Carducci expressed regret about leaving Florence. To his close friend Dr. Luigi Billi he wrote on 27 Aug. 1860, "I am not a local patriot, and furthermore I pride myself on being broadly Italian; but Tuscany will always be Tuscany" (*Lettere*).

12. Papini, *L'uomo Carducci*, p. 236.

13. Carducci to Gargani, 15 June 1860, *Lettere*.

14. Cited in Biagini, *Il poeta*, p. 100.
15. Carducci, "Gli Austriaci in Piemonte," *Edizione nazionale delle opere*, vol. 2.
16. Carducci, "Dopo Aspromonte," ibid.
17. Carducci also referred to Venice as the city given "by one General Leboeuf to I don't know what Italian general" (*Confessioni e battaglie*, 3:64–65).
18. This line comes from "Congedo" in *Levia gravia*.
19. Carducci, *Confessioni e battaglie*, vol. 3, ch. 2.
20. In line with Carducci's claims, it is well to remember that not until 1895, in Crispi's second ministry, was 20 September declared a national holiday for the Italian people. Then, as part of the Lateran Treaty, Mussolini dropped the day from the national calendar in deference to the Church. See Giovanni Spadolini, *Autunno del risorgimento*, pt. 2.
21. Carducci, "Per la morte di Giuseppe Mazzini," *Confessioni e battaglie*, 2:220.
22. Carducci, "Levia Gravia," ibid., p. 8.
23. This lady had a weakness for literary men: Ruggiero Bonghi, Enrico Panzacchi, and Giovanni Verga all enjoyed her favors. Although Carducci found in her "the Hellenic and pagan ideal of my life," signora Cristofori-Piva nearly drove him mad with her infidelities.
24. The quoted phrase is from a letter of Carducci to Giuseppe Chiarini, 15 Oct. 1863, *Lettere*.
25. Filopanti's critique was reprinted in Carducci, *Confessioni e battaglie*, 1:59.
26. Ibid., p. 65.
27. Caccia, *Poesia e ideologia*, p. 175.
28. Carducci, *Confessioni e battaglie*, 1:149.
29. Carlo Casalegno's book, *La regina Margherita*, contains a detailed and uniformly unflattering portrait of King Umberto.

30. Ibid. See ch. 4.
31. Carducci, "Discorso politico carducciano," 22 Aug. 1880, in Alberto Lumbroso, ed., *Miscellanea carducciana.*
32. Carducci, *Confessioni e battaglie*, 1:109.
33. Carducci to Camillo Antona Traversi, 13 Sept. 1897, *Lettere.*
34. Mario Vinciguerra, *Carducci, uomo politico*, p. 37.
35. Carducci, *Confessioni e battaglie*, 2:13.
36. Ibid., 1:309.
37. Ibid., 3:239.
38. Ibid., 1:159.
39. Carducci articulated the exasperation of many intellectuals with the cautious foreign policy of Italy's transformist governments when he claimed that "it would be better to die in glory against the cannons of Austria or France" than to endure any further humiliations in Africa and in *Italia irredenta* (ibid., 3:63).
40. Cited in Vinciguerra, *Carducci*, p. 55. The religious imagery here is significant, because Carducci employed it repeatedly in describing his political views.
41. Mazzini's position on the monarchy during the Risorgimento was not consistent. However, during the critical year 1860, as Luigi Salvatorelli explains, "Mazzini yielded and accepted the dominant participation of the monarchy, and in fact promoted it, even though he foresaw a result contrary to his republican ideals because his desire for unity prevailed over everything else" (*The Risorgimento: Thought and Action*, p. 164).
42. Cited in Massimo Grillandi, *Francesco Crispi*, pt. 2, ch. 12.
43. Arturo Carlo Jemolo argues in *Crispi*, ch. 3, that differences in temperament made a split between

Crispi and Mazzini inevitable.

44. Grillandi, *Crispi*, pt. 3, ch. 4.

45. This bitter polemic did not prevent Crispi from revering Mazzini's memory in later years. In 1876, at a private dinner party in Rome, he told Ferdinando Martini and Benedetto Capponi, two parliamentary deputies, that Mazzini was the greatest European of the nineteenth century: "Within one hundred years he who writes our history will call our time the century of Mazzini" (Martini, *Confessioni e ricordi*, ch. 8).

46. Alessandro Luzio's *La massoneria e il risorgimento italiano* is an extremely polemical work. Badly flawed by its unremitting anti-Masonic bias, it still offers a vast amount of information that, separated from the author's hysterical interpretation, is useful, particularly concerning the power struggles within Italian masonry.

47. Writing in an 1893 issue of *The Political Science Quarterly*, the Italian sociologist Vilfredo Pareto conceded that political parties existed in Italy, "but the names serve only to designate bodies of men united by certain strictly personal interests or by a certain community of temperament." This article, "The Parliamentary Regime in Italy," was reprinted in his book *The Ruling Class in Italy before 1900*.

48. Horst Frenz, ed., *Nobel Lectures*, p. 47.

49. Benedetto Croce, *Giosuè Carducci*.

50. Luigi Lodi, *Giornalisti*, p. 11.

51. Carducci to Cecioni, 19 Feb. 1881, *Lettere*.

Chapter Two

1. In 1893 his former competitor, Luigi Arnaldo Vassallo, exulted when Sommaruga's fortunes

collapsed in Latin America: "The bank, the emporium, and the *Patria lontana* in Buenos Aires have suspended payments, and Sommaruga has fled." In a final cruel swipe he added: "Pear trees always make pears" ("Angelo Sommaruga").

2. C. G. Sarti, "Il secondo editore del Carducci."

3. Diego Angeli, "Lettere inedite di Giosuè Carducci ad Angelo Sommaruga."

4. Eventually Sommaruga himself wrote about his publishing house, first in an article, "Il Carducci e la *Bizantina*" (1934), and then in a book, *Cronaca bizantina (1881–1885): noti e ricordi* (1941).

5. In 1909 the artist Serafino Macchiati had told Sarti that Carducci's approval and support meant everything to Sommaruga: "He had never felt himself lost; in the same hour in which half of Italy was enjoying his defeat, Giosuè Carducci shook his hand, and he has lived for more than twenty years on that memory and he feels secure in that judgment" (Sarti, "Il secondo editore").

6. Alberto Lumbroso visited Sommaruga's apartment in May 1911 and described it as "a genuine gallery of modern art" (in "Una pagina del diario carducciano").

7. C. G. Sarti, "La resurrezione di Angelo Sommaruga."

8. Sommaruga, *Cronaca bizantina,* p. 21.

9. Luigi Lodi, "Ciarle della domenica: *La farfalla,*" *Domenica letteraria,* 3 Aug. 1884.

10. Giuseppe Squarciapino, *Roma bizantina,* p. 77. For a detailed account of *La farfalla,* see Adriana Chemello, *"La farfalla" di Angelo Sommaruga.*

11. The *scapigliatura* literary movement flourished in Turin and Genoa, but the main center was always Milan. Eventually the style spread southward to include Naples. See Francesco Bruno, *La scapig-*

liatura napoletana e meridionale.

12. Arrighi's real name was Carlo Righetti (1830–1906). His influence on the younger generation of *scapigliati* writers was important, but Giuseppe Rovani (1818–74), called the "father of the Scapigliatura," had an even greater impact on their style through books like *Cento anni* (1857). See Edoardo Gennarini, *La scapigliatura milanese.*

13. Giacomo Puccini (1858–1924), the composer of *La Bohème* (1896), was a student of Amilcare Ponchielli (1834–86), a habitué of *scapigliatura* circles. Pietro Mascagni (1863–1945) also studied under Ponchielli.

14. Sommaruga, *Cronaca bizantina*, p. 24.

15. Ibid., p. 25.

16. Ibid., p. 26.

17. Ibid., p. 27.

18. The Italian army, led by General Cadorna, was 50,000 strong, whereas the papal army of General Kanzler numbered about 13,000. See Alberto Ghisalberti, "Settembre 1870" in *Roma capitale.*

19. Ugo Pesci, *I primi anni di Roma capitale, 1870–78*, p. 202.

20. See Fiorella Bartoccini, *La Roma dei romani.*

21. Pesci, *I primi anni*, p. 669.

22. See Edward R. Tannenbaum, "Education," and Leonard W. Moss, "The Passing of Traditional Peasant Society in the South," both in *Modern Italy*, ed. Edward R. Tannenbaum and Emiliana Noether.

23. Many statistical studies document the relatively high literacy rate in Rome. One of the oldest and most thorough is Aristide Gabelli's "Istruzione primaria e secondaria nella città e provincia di Roma," in *Monografia della Città di Roma e della Campagna Romana.*

24. See Valerio Castronovo's *La stampa italiana*

dall'unità al fascismo for a detailed account of
Roman journalism in this period.

25. Francesco Flora, "*Il fanfulla della domenica* I-II."
26. Olga Majolo Molinari, *La stampa periodica ro-
    mana dell'ottocento.* See the entry for *Fanfulla
    della domenica.*
27. Carducci to Martini, 29 May 1881, *Lettere.*
28. Vassallo, "Sommaruga."
29. See Edoardo Scarfoglio, "Introduzione: ventisette
    anni dopo," in *Il libro di Don Chisciotte.*
30. For a penetrating analysis of the changing liter-
    ary marketplace in nineteenth-century Europe,
    see César Graña's *Modernity and Its Discontents,*
    esp. ch. 4.
31. Cited by Pesci in *I primi anni,* p. 481. The career
    of Gian Pietro Vieusseux (d. 1863) is yet another
    earlier example of commercialization in Italian
    literature. Of Swiss origin, Vieusseux settled in
    Florence and established a publishing house
    "more for commercial reasons than for a genuine
    program of cultural diffusion." See Spadolini,
    Autunno del risorgimento, pt. 1.
32. *Cronaca bizantina,* 15 June 1881. Carducci re-
    sponded to the first issue of the *Cronaca bizantina*
    with warm praise, assuring Sommaruga that it
    was "exceptionally beautiful" (Carducci to Som-
    maruga, 15 June 1881, *Lettere*).
33. Cited by Sommaruga in "Il Carducci e la *Bizan-
    tina.*"
34. Carducci to Sommaruga, 23 Nov. 1882, *Lettere.*
35. *Cronaca bizantina,* 30 Sept. 1881.
36. At the same time, the *Fanfulla della domenica*
    went into a steep sales decline over Ferdinando
    Martini's resignation.
37. Francesco Flora, "*La Cronaca Bizantina.*" Flora's
    article is very important because while preparing
    it he actually interviewed Sommaruga.

38. Carducci to Sommaruga, 24 Feb. 1882, *Lettere*. Even earlier Carducci had complained that he was not "a writing machine" (Carducci to Sommaruga, 15 June 1881, *Lettere*).
39. C. G. Sarti, "Fra Giosuè Carducci e Sommaruga."
40. C. G. Sarti, "Sommaruga e le sue idee."
41. The phrase belongs to Edoardo Scarfoglio, one of Sommaruga's writers. See "Introduzione: ventisette anni dopo" in *Il libro di Don Chisciotte*.

Chapter Three

1. Sommaruga, *Cronaca bizantina*, p. 41.
2. Carducci, *Confessioni e battaglie*, 3:274.
3. Ibid., pp. 283–84. Costanzo Chauvet (1844–1918) was the owner and editor of *Il popolo romano*, a pro-Depretis daily newspaper.
4. Emanuella Scaranno, *Dalla cronaca bizantina al convito*, p. 27 and ff.
5. Benedetto Croce, *Storia d'Italia dal 1871 al 1915*, ch. 3.
6. Sommaruga, *Cronaca bizantina*, p. 29.
7. Squarciapino, *Roma bizantina*, p. 102.
8. Ibid., p. 256.
9. Ibid., p. 104.
10. Cesario Testa, "Ciò che si dice," *Cronaca bizantina*, 31 July 1881.
11. I. L'Angelo [Testa], "Ciò che si stampa," *Cronaca bizantina*, 6 June 1883.
12. Papiliunculus [Testa], "A Gabriele D'Annunzio," *Cronaca bizantina*, 1 Mar. 1882.
13. Benedetto Croce, *La letteratura della nuova Italia*, vol. 4, ch. 42.
14. Giuseppe Chiarini, "A proposito di un nuovo poeta."

15. Enrico Nencioni, a member of Carducci's and Chiarini's circle since their *liceo* days together in Florence, immediately entered into correspondence with D'Annunzio on the strength of the *Primo vere* review. D'Annunzio wrote back, "Your letter will make my mother weep with joy" (D'Annunzio to Nencioni, 9 Dec. 1880, in Roberto Forcella, "Lettere di Gabriele D'Annunzio a Enrico Nencioni").

16. D'Annunzio to Carducci, Mar. 1879. Cited in Guglielmo Gatti, *La vita di Gabriele D'Annunzio*, pp. 23–24.

17. Giuseppe Chiarini, "In memoriam."

18. Scarfoglio, *Il libro di Don Chisciotte*, p. 162.

19. D'Annunzio to Giselda Zucconi, cited in Gatti, *Vita*, pp. 45–46.

20. Pietro Pancrazi, *Scrittori italiani dal Carducci al D'Annunzio*. See the essay on Scarfoglio.

21. Scarfoglio, "Novelle nuove," *Cronaca bizantina*, 16 Aug. 1882.

22. Scarfoglio, "Contro i Raffaelisti," *Cronaca bizantina*, 1 Apr. 1883. He wrote this wrathful article to protest Italy's failure to honor the fourth centenary of Raphael's birth: "Neither Urbino, which witnessed his birth, nor Rome, which witnessed his death, know when Raphael was born, but there is not a single German high school student who is ignorant of this event. In the name of God, what do you want when the Germans cover us with vituperations!"

23. Scarfoglio, "Un nuovo poeta," *Cronaca bizantina*, 1 Aug. 1883.

24. Scarfoglio, "Demi Monde," *Cronaca bizantina*, 16 Nov. 1882.

25. See Nello Vian, *La giovinezza di Giulio Salvadori*, for background on Salvadori's conversion.

242 Notes to Pages 68–72

26. Salvadori to Fogazzaro, 18 Jan. 1883, in *Lettere di Giulio Salvadori*, eds. Pietro Paolo Trompeo and Nello Vian.

27. Salvadori adored Fogazzaro's first novel, *Malombra* (1882), for its "strong mystical character" (Salvadori to Fogazzaro, Oct. 1882, ibid.). At the same time, Salvadori was dabbling in "spiritualist experiments," as indicated by the editors' note after this letter.

28. After breaking with Salvadori, D'Annunzio, and Scarfoglio, publisher Sommaruga declared, "Leaving apart literary merit, if they had left sooner, how many cookies and bouquets we would have saved" (cited in Vian, *La giovinezza di Giulio Salvadori*, ch. 3).

29. Salvadori, "Roma," *Cronaca bizantina*, 1 June 1882.

30. Ibid.

31. Salvadori, "*La Conquista di Roma* di Matilde Serao," *Fanfulla della domenica*, 5 July 1885.

32. Nello Vian documents Salvadori's strong aversion for Sommaruga, "that American merchant," in *La giovinezza di Giulio Salvadori*, ch. 3.

33. Salvadori, "Nuovo ideale," *Cronaca bizantina*, 1 Sept. 1882.

34. Salvadori, "Le confessioni d'una donna," *Domenica letteraria*, 4 Feb. 1883. The woman in question was "Contessa Lara," a pseudonym for Evelina Cattermole Mancini, one of Sommaruga's most commercially successful writers.

35. Salvadori, "Nuovo ideale."

36. Ibid.

37. Salvadori, "La vil prosa: lettera a 'Chiquita' del *Capitan Fracassa*," *Cronaca bizantina*, 16 Aug. 1882. Here he was criticizing a review of Catulle Mendès's *Monstres parisiens* by Matilde Serao.

38. Sommaruga, *Cronaca bizantina*, p. 46.

39. Squarciapino cites this phrase in *Roma bizantina*, pt. 3.

Chapter Four

1. This was Albi Orazio's *Peccati di gioventù*. See Squarciapino's indispensable "Catalago ragionato delle edizioni sommarughiane" in the appendix of his *Roma bizantina*.
2. Guglielmo Gatti writes, "Usually the debts of newspapers are absorbed by industrial and commercial financiers whose interests these newspapers serve. Sommaruga had no financiers" ("Sommarughiana," p. 219).
3. Squarciapino's *Roma bizantina* is a lawyer's brief for Sommaruga, but the book fully documents the historical reality of the publisher's challenge to the Italian publishing industry. See the book's "Epilogo" for a summary of this crucial argument.
4. The modern English equivalent of *reclame* is "hype."
5. Although Contessa Lara had been writing verses since she was fourteen, the public remained apathetic until 1875, when her husband killed her lover in a duel. From then on she was "the fatal woman, the woman of tragedy" (see Luigi Lodi's review, "*La Contessa Lara* di Maria Borgese"). Sommaruga made her famous, and she continued to write until her death in 1896 at the age of forty-six. True to her public image, she died as she had lived—in the midst of scandal and notoriety, the murder victim of a psychotic painter who was her last lover.
6. Cited in Squarciapino, *Roma bizantina*, pt. 3.
7. Martini formally withdrew from the *Domenica*

letteraria staff on 15 July 1883, but he had been inactive for several months before that. See "Carissimo Signor Sommaruga," an open letter by Martini in *Domenica letteraria*, 15 July 1883.

8. Sommaruga, *Cronaca bizantina*, p. 57.

9. Carducci to Sommaruga, 10 Nov. 1883, *Lettere*.

10. Carducci to Sommaruga, 12 Dec. 1882, ibid.

11. Carducci to Sommaruga, 10 Nov. 1883, ibid.

12. Carducci to Sommaruga, 1 Dec. 1883, ibid.

13. Scarfoglio, "Ça ira," *Domenica letteraria*, 5 May 1883.

14. Carducci to Sommaruga, 18 Feb. 1883, *Lettere*.

15. On 21 July 1883 Carducci wrote a long letter to Lodi in which he praised the young man's *Letteraria* articles. However, a telling phrase indicates the poet's true feelings about his disciple's present position: "I desire and I hope and I believe that *in the end* you will enjoy the success that you merit" (*Lettere*; my italics).

16. See Alessandra Briganti, *Intellettuali e cultura tra ottocento e novecento*, esp. ch. 10.

17. Ferdinando Martini, "Analfabeti" (7 Jan. 1883) and "Perchè ci sono gli analfabeti?" (14 Jan. 1883), both in *Domenica letteraria*. These two articles were random shots with few echoes in later issues, and the *Domenica letteraria* remained primarily a literary journal.

18. Lodi, "La nuova battaglia del Carducci," *Domenica letteraria*, 9 Dec. 1883.

19. Lodi, "Quello che siè fatto," *Domenica letteraria*, 30 Dec. 1883.

20. See Carducci's 1884 correspondence with Sommaruga and with Chiarini in *Lettere*.

21. Croce touches on these points in his essay on "Antonio Barrili" in *La letteratura della nuova Italia*.

22. In 1895 Barrili wrote a trenchant memoir of the Mentana campaign, *Con Garibaldi alle porte di*

Roma. See F. Ernesto Morando, *Anton Giulio Barrili e i suoi tempi.*

23. Barrili, "Ai lettori della *Domenica letteraria*," *Domenica letteraria*, 4 Jan. 1885.
24. Squarciapino, *Roma bizantina*, p. 433.
25. In his old age Sommaruga wrote nostalgically of *Nabab*: "I regarded it so highly because it seemed to me the most aristocratic among the newspapers of that period and the best staffed. . . . It fell, in fact, when it was impossible for me to look after it any longer. [When it ceased publication] I was greatly saddened because, as I have said, *Nabab* was my pride; I could say that I was the inspiration for it because I easily succeeded in convincing Panzacchi who was good and timid, to undertake the enterprise." In later years the two men always reminded each other in their correspondence of "il *Nabab* di gloriosa memoria" (see *Cronaca bizantina*, pp. 164–68).
26. Panzacchi, "Presentazione," *Nabab*, 21 Dec. 1884. The actual name of the newspaper was taken from Alphonse Daudet's novel, *Nabab* (1877), which described the sordid political and moral life of the Second Empire.
27. See the essay entitled "Jorik" in *Giornalisti*, especially p. 20 where Lodi describes Italian journalism as "politics, nothing but politics."
28. The conservative position was expressed by Giulio Agricola in "Il partito agrario: lettera di un agricoltore," *Nabab*, 22 Jan. 1885. He urged the creation of an agrarian party to oppose the spread of socialism.
29. Crispi recalled this phrase many years later in an article entitled "Dopo diciotto anni" for *Nuova antologia*, 1 Oct. 1900.
30. Biagini, *Il poeta*, pt. 6.
31. For the civilian background of Italy's imperialist

involvement in Africa, see Roberto Battaglia, *La prima guerra d'Africa*, pt. 1.

32. Antonio Gramsci, *Il risorgimento*. See "Il problema della direzione politica nella formazione e nello sviluppo della Nazione e dello stato moderno in Italia." In this essay Gramsci, with his usual brilliance, illuminates the whole problem of Italian imperialism with a phrase: "one is speaking here of the necessity to resolve internal politics" (p. 77).

33. Federico Chabod analyzes the idea of Rome and its impact on Italian culture and foreign policy in *Storia della politica estera italiana dal 1870 al 1896*, vol. 1, ch. 2.

34. Actually, Carducci opposed the African expedition of 1884. He rightly saw Africa as a distraction from irredentism, and in 1887 he wrote: "The Abyssinians were right to drive us out, as we drove out and will drive out the Austrians" (see Biagini, *Il poeta*, ch. 33). By 1893, however, Carducci was fully converted to Crispi's way of thinking about Africa, describing himself as "proudly Africanist" (see *Lotta politica in Italia dall'unità al 1925*, ed. Nino Valeri, pp. 203–4).

35. Arturo Colautti, "L'Africa irredenta," *Nabab*, 9 Jan. 1885. Colautti eventually became a prominent member of the imperialistic Nationalist party.

36. Doremi, "La nota politica," *Nabab*, 21 Feb. 1885.

37. Cited in Battaglia, *La prima guerra d'Africa*, ch. 5.

38. Henriquez developed this theme in a number of his "La nota politica" columns for *Nabab*, 27 Dec. 1884–7 Jan. 1885.

39. Oriani is listed by Squarciapino as one of *Nabab*'s writers. See the "Catalago ragionato delle edizioni sommarughiane" in *Roma bizantina*, p. 444.

40. Orao, "Vediamo un po," *Nabab*, 8 Feb. 1885.
41. Castronovo, *La stampa italiana*, ch. 2.

Chapter Five

1. In addition to *Vita segreta di Gabriele D'Annunzio*, Antongini wrote *D'Annunzio aneddotico*, *Gli allegri filibustieri di D'Annunzio*, and *Quarant'-anni con D'Annunzio*. *Vita segreta* was published in French and English translations.
2. Cited in Frances Winwar, *Wingless Victory*, ch. 4.
3. This episode is recounted on pp. 722–23 of Antongini, *Vita segreta*.
4. Chiarini, "A proposito di un nuovo poeta."
5. D'Annunzio, *Canto novo*, "Canto dell'ospite," 11: 73.
6. Cited in Squarciapino, *Roma bizantina*, p. 338.
7. Scarfoglio, *Il libro di Don Chisciotte*, p. 167.
8. Cited in Giuseppe Chiarini, "Alla ricerca della verecondia," *Domenica letteraria*, 19 Aug. 1883. Carducci agreed with his old friend, but added in a letter written on 1 September 1883: "in my opinion . . . you are making too much of this business" (*Lettere*).
9. Just before arriving in Rome, D'Annunzio asked Enrico Nencioni to find him a room "where I can also eat because I cordially hate restaurants with their noises, their unpleasant clientele, and suffocating tobacco smoke" (D'Annunzio to Nencioni, 1 Nov. 1881, in Forcella, "Lettere"). D'Annunzio's letters to Nencioni in 1880–81 reinforce Scarfoglio's image of him in *Il libro di Don Chisciotte* as an earnest, rather priggish young man.
10. Forcella, "Lettere."
11. D'Annunzio lashed out most vehemently at Chiarini. To Nencioni he wrote, "I confess to you . . .

that the *horrid, supremely vulgar* prose of the
good and fatherly Professor Chiarini inspired my
pity" (D'Annunzio to Nencioni, 17 Apr. 1884,
ibid.).

12. Many of these early poems were collected in *Canto novo* (1882).

13. Scarfoglio's concern with D'Annunzian decadence
found echoes in Arthur Symons's later claim that
the term "decadence" was "in place only when
applied to style, to that ingenious deformation of
the language, in Mallarmé, for instance, which
can be compared with what we are accustomed to
call the Greek and Latin of the Decadence" (*The
Symbolist Movement in Literature*, p. 4).

14. Scarfoglio, *Il libro di Don Chisciotte*, p. 166.

15. Scarfoglio, "Da parte degli amici (a Gabriele
D'Annunzio)," *Domenica letteraria*, 20 May
1883.

16. Scarfoglio wrote a number of poems satirizing the
preciosity of D'Annunzio's new Oriental style.
See Pietro Paolo Trompeo, *Carducci e D'Annunzio: saggi e postille*, ch. 2.

17. D'Annunzio to Nencioni, 24 June 1884, in Forcella, "Lettere." D'Annunzio was still outraged
more than a month later when he wrote, "I have
been attacked by a fit of invincible hatred and
languor for the hideous atrocity that now is slowly
diminishing after a great torrential storm"
(D'Annunzio to Nencioni, 27 July 1884, ibid.).

18. D'Annunzio to Sommaruga, 24 June 1884. Cited
by Sommaruga in *Cronaca bizantina*, pp. 130–31.

19. D'Annunzio to Sommaruga, 24 Mar. 1884, cited
ibid., p. 127.

20. Ibid., p. 130.

21. Sommaruga carried this announcement in the
Cronaca bizantina.

22. Nello Vian points out that Salvadori had con-

tributed nothing to the *Cronaca bizantina* since 1 August, and that he had stopped writing for the *Domenica letteraria* as of March 1884. Salvadori's signature on the secessionists' declaration merely made public a long-standing animosity between him and Sommaruga. See *La giovinézza di Giulio Salvadori*, pp. 228–29.

23. Sommaruga's open letter was appended to the secessionists' "Declaration," *Cronaca bizantina*, 1 Oct. 1884.

24. See "Catalogo delle lettere di Gabriele D'Annunzio al Vittoriale," vol. 1 in *Quaderni dannunziani*, fasc. 42–43, p. 151.

25. Scarfoglio to Carducci, 8 Oct. 1884. Cited by Vian in "Sommaruga, ruga, ruga . . . ruga." *Strenna dei romanisti*, vol. XII, 1951.

26. Carducci to Sommaruga, 4 Oct. 1884, *Lettere*.

27. Carducci to Chiarini, 5 June 1884, *Lettere*.

28. Cited by Sommaruga in *Cronaca bizantina*, p. 138.

29. Cited by Carmelo Trasselli, *Le Forche caudine (Pietro Sbarbaro e Angelo Sommaruga): 1884–1885*, p. 145.

30. Alessandro Guiccioli, "Diario del 1884: II," *Nuova antologia*, 1 Oct. 1937.

31. Scarfoglio, *Il libro di Don Chisciotte*, p. 7.

32. Ibid.

33. Sommaruga, *Cronaca bizantina*, p. 18.

Chapter Six

1. Croce, "Pietro Sbarbaro," *La letteratura*, 3:371.

2. See Sommaruga, *Cronaca bizantina*, ch. 8.

3. Trasselli, *Le Forche caudine*, see ch. 1, "Dove si Parla di Libri."

4. Vilfredo Pareto attacked the dependence of university professors on the government as one of the

most illiberal features of Italian society during the Umbertian period. See "The Parliamentary Regime in Italy," in *The Ruling Class in Italy*.

5. Giuseppe Mazza's *Sulla vita e sulle opere di Pietro Sbarbaro* is the best source of information for Sbarbaro's early life, but it is very biased. A useful corrective to Mazza's unctuously flattering interpretation is Augusto Pierantoni's *Sub lege libertas*.

6. Croce subjects this work to a merciless critique in "Pietro Sbarbaro," *La letteratura*.

7. *Enciclopedia italiana*, 30:982.

8. Mazza, *Sulla vita*, p. 47.

9. Pierantoni, *Sub lege libertas*; see "Signor Magistrati di Appello."

10. Mazza, *Sulla vita*, p. 77.

11. Sbarbaro, *Sulle opinioni di Vincenzo Gioberti intorno all'economia politica e alla questione sociale*, p. 438.

12. Ibid., p. 440.

13. Ibid., p. 47.

14. Mazza, *Sulla vita*, ch. 10.

15. This book or pamphlet is lost, but it was extant when Mazza wrote *Sulla vita*; see ch. 12.

16. Cited by Trasselli, *Le Forche caudine*, p. 65.

17. In his completely discredited anti-Sommaruga diatribe, *Sommaruga occulto e Sommaruga palese*, Davide Besana quotes from a telegram sent by the publisher to Sbarbaro: "Come, we will make money" (p. 436). Knowing what we now do about the unreliable Besana, the telegram was probably apocryphal, although it does reflect the spirit in which Sommaruga dealt with Sbarbaro.

18. Sommaruga, *Cronaca bizantina*, p. 64.

19. Ibid., p. 171.

20. Pietro Sbarbaro, *Re travicello o re costituzionale?*, p. 20.

21. Ibid., p. 129.
22. Despite his warm praise for King Umberto and Queen Margherita, Sbarbaro's hesitancy to affirm the ultimate utility of the crown was not lost on the House of Savoy. The royal family never supported him.
23. Pietro Sbarbaro, *Regina o repubblica*, see ch. 3, "Ai critici del *Re travicello*—Margherita ante porcos. Colpi di stato o di frustino."
24. Ibid., p. 147.
25. Ibid., p. 180.
26. Ibid., p. 206.
27. Ibid., p. 210.
28. Ibid., p. 56. Lanza had died in 1883. After Sella's death in 1884, Sbarbaro transferred his political loyalties to Giuseppe Zanardelli.
29. The Forche Caudine, or Caudine Forks, is the name of a narrow pass in Campania where the Samnites under Gavius Pontius defeated the Romans in 321 b.c., during the Second Samnite War. Sbarbaro chose this name for its image as a place where his Roman enemies, too, would perish.
30. Sommaruga, *Cronaca bizantina*, p. 169.
31. Vian, "Un manifesto contro le *Forche caudine.*"
32. Trasselli, *Le Forche caudine*, see ch. 5.
33. Sommaruga, *Cronaca bizantina*, p. 173. Besana, no friend of Sommaruga, makes a similar estimate in *Sommaruga occulto*, ch. 39. Also see Castronovo, *La stampa italiana*, ch. 2.
34. Sbarbaro, "Per intenderci," *Forche caudine*, 15 June 1884.
35. Sbarbaro, "Tremano tutti," *Forche caudine*, 15 June 1884.
36. Sbarbaro, "Chi sono io?," *Forche caudine*, 13 July 1884.
37. Sbarbaro, "Verità e avvisi," *Forche caudine*, 25 Jan. 1885.

38. Arturo Carlo Jemolo is very balanced and almost tender in his judgments; even he admits that, as a result of "the incessant need for money," Crispi took advantage of his political position to make a financial profit. See *Crispi*, ch. 5.
39. Grillandi, *Crispi*, ch. 7.
40. Sbarbaro, "Vita privata ed interesse pubblico," *Forche caudine*, 7 Sept. 1884.
41. Sbarbaro, "L'adulterio impunito," *Forche caudine*, 6 Nov. 1884.
42. This was the observation of Guiccioli, "Diario del 1884: II."
43. Sbarbaro, "Il 20 settembre," *Forche caudine*, 14 Sept. 1884.

Chapter Seven

1. Sommaruga, *Cronaca bizantina*, p. 175.
2. Sommaruga, *Giudicatemi!*, p. 9.
3. Ibid.
4. Ibid.
5. There was no general election in 1885, and Sbarbaro's entry into Parliament could only occur under the following special circumstances. The Collegio of Pavia had five parliamentary deputies, and on 22 November 1885 one of them, Pasquale Valsecchi, became a senator. A special election was held to replace him on 27 December. The results were: Sbarbaro, 8,153; Luigi della Croce, 3,621; Giuseppe Reminolfi, 2,219. See *Storia dei collegi elettorali*, vol. 2.
6. *L'illustrazione italiana* followed the Sbarbaro affair in sensationalistic detail. See "La Settimana" in the issue for 3 January 1886.
7. Pietro Sbarbaro, "Per intenderci bene," *Forche caudine: nuova serie*, 18 June 1885.

8. Ugo Pesci, "Corriere: Odi Sbarbare," *L'illustrazione italiana*, 17 Jan. 1886.

9. Edoardo Perino, "Una Dichiarazione," *La penna: effemeride settimanale*, 4 Apr. 1886.

10. Pietro Sbarbaro, "Le elezioni generali," *La penna d'oro di Pietro Sbarbaro*, 8 Apr. 1886.

11. Pietro Sbarbaro, "La riforma del Senato," ibid., 25 July 1886.

12. Pietro Sbarbaro, "Salute e Denaro," ibid., 8 Aug. 1886.

13. Pietro Sbarbaro, "Dichiarazione," ibid., 29 July 1886.

14. Edoardo Perino, "Passione e morte di Pietro Sbarbaro," *La penna*: *effemeride settimanale*, 18 Apr. 1886.

15. Edoardo Perino, "La fuga di Sbarbaro in Svizzera," ibid., 18 Apr. 1886.

16. Pietro Sbarbaro, "Programma," *La penna d'oro di Pietro Sbarbaro*, 15 July 1886.

17. Casalegno, *La regina Margherita*, p. 131.

18. Carducci claimed, in a letter to Chiarini, that Sommaruga had used this phrase (24 June 1885, *Lettere*).

19. Sommaruga, *Giudicatemi!*, "Udienza del 18 settembre 1885."

20. Carducci to Sommaruga, 25 Aug. 1885, *Lettere*.

21. Sommaruga, *Giudicatemi!*, "Udienza del 5 settembre 1885." For Carducci's testimony at the trial, see also Roberto Forcella, *D'Annunzio: 1884–85*, p. 247. Carducci was attacked in the press for his defense of Sommaruga. On 22 September 1885 he wrote a stinging public letter against these critics, remarking about his action in the trial, "I was not inspired by prudence or piety, but by my conscience" (Sarti, "Il secondo editore").

22. For D'Annunzio's deposition, see *Giudicatemi!*,

"Udiènza del 12 settembre 1885."

23. Cited by Trasselli, *Le Forche caudine*, see ch. 7.

24. For the Cobevich summation, see *Giudicatemi!*, "Udiènza del 15 settembre 1885."

25. For the Vitale summation, see ibid., "Udiènza del 16 settembre 1885."

26. For the Panattoni summation, see ibid., "Udiènza del 17 settembre 1885."

27. Ibid.

28. The planning of the Vittorio Emanuele II monument in Rome during these years resulted in a profusion of scandals. This project is really the best example of how the *concorsi* system of art competition worked in Italy. The government asked architects to submit models for the monument. Hundreds were submitted to the commission of judges, and all Italy was rife with speculation that the one chosen might have been honored for other than purely esthetic reasons. Looking at the garish white Brescia marble structure today, few can be absolutely certain that the suspicions of the critics were groundless. Art competitions of this kind, though usually on a lesser scale, were routine in Umbertian Italy, and the system encouraged lobbying. A man of Sommaruga's special talents would be much in demand for work such as this, although he never considered it significant or especially worthy of mention. Consequently, we really do not know the extent of his involvement in the *concorsi* system. But in the public eye Sommaruga's lobbying activities added another lurid dimension to his image as a flesh peddler.

29. No social critic exposed the dependence of Italian judges on the government more effectively than Vilfredo Pareto. About the vulnerable judges he wrote, "The government rewards its friends by

promotion and punishes its enemies by transferring them from courts situated in the principal towns to smaller and less desirable places" ("The Parliamentary Regime in Italy," in *The Ruling Class in Italy before 1900*). Moreover, the *Civiltà cattolica* could be expected to draw maximum advantage from the scandals and corrupt practices revealed by the Sommaruga trial, which "unmasked the most Italian revolution [la rivoluzione italianissima] and exposed it in its deceits, in its perfidies, in its baseness, and in its shame," 19 September 1885.

30. For the newspaper accounts of Sommaruga's trial, see *Giudicatemi!*, "La sentenza e la stampa," and Squarciapino's *Roma bizantina*, pp. 234–45. Guiccioli commented in his diary that if Sommaruga had not been perceived as "jointly responsible" (*corresponsàbile*) for the injuries of Sbarbaro, "all would have passed unnoticed; but one does not with impunity attack the plebeian oligarchy that governs us." See "Diario del 1885: II," *Nuova antologia*, 1 Nov. 1937.

31. A spirited and convincing defense of Depretis is to be found in Giovanni Giolitti's *Memorie della mia vita*. He lauded Depretis for his common sense and statecraft. As for the old bugbear, that Depretis was "cunning" (*furbo*), Giolitti asked, "Is it really obligatory for a statesman to be an ingénue?" (1:37–38).

32. As a result of the 1882 electoral reform law, the number of eligible voters rose from 600,000 to 2,000,000. See Carlo Morandi, *I partiti politici nella storia d'Italia*, ch. 2, for the immediate consequences of this change in the suffrage requirements. Depretis's attitude toward the electoral reform law was nearly schizophrenic, as Ferdinando Martini clearly saw: "He wanted it, he

proposed it, he obtained it, but having obtained it (as he himself later admitted) he became frightened by its effects" (*Confessioni e ricordi*, ch. 11).

33. See Raymond Grew, *A Sterner Plan for Italian Unity*.

34. Depretis had been naval minister for only a month when the Lissa disaster occurred in the Austrian War of 1866.

35. There is a recorded instance of Sbarbaro himself heckling Depretis on 7 October 1876. This was the start of the bilious hatred between the two men. See "Pietro Sbarbaro e il suo processo," *L'illustrazione italiana*, 19 July 1885.

36. As Martini later remarked in his *Confessioni e ricordi*, "The left, compact and harmonious in Parliament so long as it fought as a party of opposition, fell apart as soon as it took power" (p. 119).

37. Silvio Spaventa, "Discorso pronunziato all' Associazione Costituzionale Romana nell' adunanza del 21 marzo 1879," in *La politica della destra*, ed. Benedetto Croce.

38. Depretis used this phrase in an electoral discourse before his constituents in Stradella on 8 October 1882. See *La lotta politica*, ed. Valeri.

39. Somewhat later, on 19 May 1886, Crispi spoke about transformism to his constituents in Palermo: "Since 1878 there have not been political parties in Italy, but political men. . . . I deplore this state of things, and I stand apart from it, with a few faithful friends" ("Il riordinamento dello stato," in *Scritti e discorsi politici di Francesco Crispi, 1849–1890*). On that very day Carducci spoke on the same subject in Pisa's Teatro Nuovo, repeating his famous epigram, "*Trasformismo* is an ugly word for an even uglier thing." Depretis had imposed this system on the country and thereby had corrupted Italian political life. What a fall

from "the days of sunshine, of liberty and of glory in 1860! Oh the battles of the giants between Garibaldi and Cavour in 1861! What have we become? An infinitely grand epic has been succeeded by an infinitely small farce (in *Carducci, Edizione nazionale*, 25:34–35).

40. Even in the late 1870s Depretis feared the opposition within his own party more than he did the right. Giampiero Carocci, *Agostino Depretis e la politica interna italiana dal 1876 al 1887*, ch. 2.

41. Giampiero Carocci, ed., *Il parlamento nella storia d'Italia*, pt. 4, p. 203.

42. Carocci says as much in *Agostino Depretis*, pp. 607–8.

43. Carocci uses this phrase and explains why ibid., ch. 10.

44. Alexander Gerschenkron, *Economic Backwardness in Historical Perspective*, p. 28.

45. Rosario Romeo, *Risorgimento e capitalismo*, pt. 2.

46. During 1884, 14,233 people came down with cholera in Naples; 6,971 of them died. During 1885 there were 5,535 cases of the disease in Palermo, with 2,959 deaths. These statistics were published by *Nuova antologia* (16 Dec. 1885) in an article entitled "La politica sanitaria d'Italia nelle epidemie coleriche 1884–1885."

47. The South was especially hard hit by land expropriations. See Gino Luzzatto's expropriations chart in *L'economia italiana dal 1861 al 1894*, p. 172. E.g., from 17 January 1885 to 30 June 1897 there were 52,060 expropriations in Sardinia, meaning that the region suffered an expropriation for every 14 inhabitants. By contrast, there were only 128 expropriations in Piedmont, or one for every 26,906 inhabitants.

48. The annual strike rate rose in Italy from an average of 13 during the period 1860–69 to 96 in 1886,

with the number of participants steadily climbing. Ibid., p. 139.

49. This is a good example of what Pareto had in
mind when he wrote, "It is characteristic of the
Italian political regime that it tends always to
sacrifice reality to appearances" (*The Ruling
Class in Italy before 1900*, p. 69).

50. Carocci, ed., *Il parlamento*, pt. 4, p. 222.

51. Carocci, *Agostino Depretis*, ch. 3.

52. Sommaruga, *Cronaca bizantina*, p. 114.

Chapter Eight

1. Scarfoglio, *Il libro di Don Chisciotte*, p. XIV.

2. This is Squarciapino's phrase in *Roma bizantina*,
p. 110.

3. Pareto commented on the class envy of the Italian
bourgeoisie. He was struck, for example, by the
increased budget allowances for the army which
made possible "additional aristocratic employ-
ments" for the sons of the bourgeoisie, raising
them in effect "to the level of the aristocracy and
at the same time [giving] them a secure income"
(*The Ruling Class*, p. 67).

4. Trompeo, *Carducci e D'Annunzio*, p. 180.

5. Technically, the *Cronaca bizantina dannunziana*
was the third incarnation of the journal. The last
issue of the *Cronaca bizantina sommarughiana*
appeared on 16 March 1885. *La tribuna* took over
the defunct journal and brought it back to life on
3 May 1885 under the name *Cronaca bizantina–
domenica letteraria*; twenty-eight numbers were
published, until 7 November. On 15 November
the so-called third *Cronaca bizantina*, or *Bizantina dannunziana*, was born; its last issue appeared on 28 March 1886.

6. D'Annunzio, "Ai lettori," *Cronaca bizantina– domenica letteraria*, no. 1, 15 Nov. 1885.
7. Ibid.
8. D'Annunzio to Nencioni, 26 Oct. 1885, in Forcella, "Lettere."
9. D'Annunzio to Nencioni, 24 Oct. 1885, ibid.
10. Sommaruga, *Cronaca bizantina*, p. 56.
11. Scarfoglio, "Il giardino," cited in Trompeo, *Carducci e D'Annunzio*, p. 183.
12. D'Annunzio to Sciarra, Apr. 1886. Cited by Guglielmo Gatti in *Le donne nella vita e nell'arte di Gabriele D'Annunzio*, p. 69. Throughout the 1880s D'Annunzio worked as a society reporter for the *Tribuna*.
13. See Eurialo De Michelis, "D'Annunzio e i plagi," pp. 859–65. See also the same author's "D'Annunzio e Huysmans."
14. E.g., see ch. 14, in which Sperelli is shown the erotic book collection of his paramour's husband, Lord Heathfield. He owns all the "voluptuous vignettes," including the masterworks of Sade, the *Erotopaegnion* of Petronius, and John Wilkes's *Essay on Woman*. But Heathfield's pride and joy is his complete collection of Francis Redgrave's art, especially the English artist's phallic studies: " 'Poor Redgrave,' Lord Heathfield remarked, reentering the room with a folio of the artist's designs. 'Without doubt, he was a genius. No erotic fantasy exceeds his. Look! Look! What style! No artist, I think, in the study of human physiognomy comes close to the profundity and acuteness that Redgrave achieved in the study of the phallus. Look!' " (*Il piacere*, pp. 402–3). This was the most shocking scene in a brazen book. For the erotic impact of *Il piacere* on the younger generation in Umbertian Italy, see Trompeo's description of "the voluptuousness I experienced when as

a boy I read that forbidden literature" (*Carducci e D'Annunzio*, p. 173).

15. In 1893 D'Annunzio wrote a series of three newspaper articles in which he defended Wagner against Nietzsche's charge, that "Wagner *est une nevrose.*" The series, entitled "Il caso di Wagner," after Nietzsche's book of the same name, was run originally in Scarfoglio's *Mattino*. The articles were later republished in Alighiero Castelli, ed., *Pagine disperse di Gabriele D'Annunzio*, pp. 572–88.

16. Gabriele D'Annunzio, *Il piacere*, p. vi.

17. Ibid., p. 38.

18. Gabriele D'Annunzio, *L'innocente*, p. 219.

19. Gabriele D'Annunzio, *Il trionfo della morte*, pp. 327–28.

20. D'Annunzio, *Il piacere*, p. 175.

21. D'Annunzio, *L'innocente*, p. 65.

22. Much ethnic material, particularly regarding the religious fetishism of the Abruzzi, is brilliantly incorporated into the plot of *Il trionfo della morte*. See Books 4 and 5, especially the stunning scene in the Sanctuary of Casalbordino, where "there was a deafening clamor, more atrocious than the screams of someone who is burning alive with no escape, more terrible than the cry of shipwrecked persons in a nocturnal sea who are condemned to certain death" (pp. 320–21). As early as 1884 D'Annunzio had been gathering material on the bizarre religious customs in his native region. On 6 May of that year he wrote to Nencioni, "I participated in certain strange festivals in the sanctuaries around here. If you saw the singular spectacles of barbarism! Incredible!" (in Forcella, "Lettere").

23. D'Annunzio, *Il trionfo della morte*, pt. 2.

24. Gabriele D'Annunzio, *Le vergini delle rocce*. Of these "few superior men," Socrates is Cantelmo's supreme intellectual hero, above all because he opposed the "plebeian tyranny" in Athens (p. 33).

25. Ibid., p. 105.

26. Ibid., p. 378.

27. Ibid., pp. 358–59.

28. Ibid., pp. 366–67.

29. Ibid., p. 374. The full quotation is as follows: "The value of blood is not only the boast of our patrician pride, it is also recognized by the most severe doctrine. The highest example of conscience can only appear at the topmost part of a race that has been elevated in time by a continuous accumulation of forces and works: at the topmost part of a race in which are born and conserved for a long run of centuries the most beautiful dreams, the most vigorous sentiments, the most noble thoughts, and the most imperious desires."

30. Ibid., p. 443.

31. Casalegno, *La regina Margherita*, ch. 4.

32. An excellent source of information about *Il convito* and D'Annunzio's role in it is Valeriano Cianfrani's "*Il convito*"; See also Scaranno's *Dalla cronaca bizantina al convito*.

33. D'Annunzio, *Il trionfo della morte*, p. 393.

34. Gabriele D'Annunzio, *Contemplazione della morte*, p. 11.

35. De Bosis to Cellini, 31 Oct. 1894. Cited in Cianfrani, "*Il convito*," p. 155.

36. D'Annunzio, introduction to "Della canzone di Legnano" by Giosuè Carducci, in *Il convito* 8 (Apr.–June 1896). D'Annunzio was referring to Carducci's well-publicized confrontation with a

group of leftist students at the University of Bologna on 11 March 1891, when his classroom was invaded to the cries of "Abasso Carducci!"

37. René Doumic used this phrase in his Sorbonne lecture on D'Annunzio (reported by De Bosis in "Le Cronache," *Il convito* 2 [Feb. 1895]). De Bosis delighted in using "Le Cronache" section of *Il convito* as a scrapbook of foreign praise for his famous friend. D'Annunzio studies in France by Charles Maurras, Jacques Mesnil, and Eugène-Melchior de Vogüé, and in Germany by Robert Saitschick, were all highly acclaimed in *Il convito*.

38. D'Annunzio, "Proemio," *Il convito* 1 (Jan. 1895).

39. Ibid.

40. The phrase is Pascoli's, in a letter to Antony De Witt, 15 June 1897. See Antony De Witt, "Giovanni Pascoli: lettere al pittore Antony De Witt."

41. A substantial body of literature has grown up around this legendary trip—"*un' orgia dionisiaca*," as Scarfoglio called it. Gatti's account is excellent; see *Vita*, pp. 140–41. D'Annunzio occasionally contributed to *Il convito* after returning from Greece, but De Bosis was left to tie up all the loose ends of the project that both men had launched.

42. Cited by Enrico Corradini in "Ancora della politica dei letterati," *Il marzocco*, 29 Aug. 1897. This quotation appeared again in *Il fuoco* (1900), p. 101.

43. This statement was part of an electoral discourse published by *La tribuna*, 23 Aug. 1897. Cited in Francesco Pariset, "L'esperienza parlamentare di Gabriele D'Annunzio."

44. D'Annunzio's campaign speeches charmed deposed prime minister Francesco Crispi, who wrote

to a friend: "And I tell you that the discourse of Raffaele [*sic*] d'Annunzio was very pleasing to me. In the midst of such cowardice, in the degradation of modern youth, I feel Italian greatness palpitating in my heart" (Gatti, *Vita*, p. 164).

45. Ibid., p. 163.

46. This is Gatti's phrase in *Vita*.

47. During the Fiume adventure D'Annunzio devised a constitution for the city, "La carta del Carnaro," in which the two deliberating bodies—the "Consiglio degli ottimi" and the "Consiglio dei provvisori"—were advised to dispatch their business "with distinctly concise brevity" and to use "in debate the laconic mode." No one was less likely to observe these guidelines than their formulator, but it is no doubt true that the poet had his *fin de siècle* parliamentary experience in mind when he wrote "La carta del Carnaro." See Pariset, "L'esperienza."

48. Gatti, *Vita*, p. 180.

Chapter Nine

1. Enrico Corradini, "L'inchiesta del *Marzocco*," *Il marzocco*, 6 June 1897.

2. Corradini, "Ancora della politica dei letterati," *Il marzocco*, 29 Aug. 1897.

3. The known facts pertaining to Corradini's private life are few. In the absence of thorough biographies, I have turned to the obituary pages of Italian newspapers and magazines in the issues following his death in 1931.

4. Robert Pio Gatteschi's "Umanità di Enrico Corradini" and Angiolo Orvieto's "Enrico Corradini: i primi passi" contain interesting observations

about these early years in Corradini's life.

5. Enrico Corradini, "Spigolature e notizie," *Germinal*, 14 Feb. 1892.

6. Orvieto, "Enrico Corradini."

7. Ettore Veo, "Qualche ricordo su Enrico Corradini all'*Idea nazionale*."

8. Enrico Corradini, "Per la conversione di Edmondo De Amicis," *Germinal*, 3 Apr. 1892.

9. Enrico Corradini, "Napoleone Colaianni—*La difesa nazionale e le economie nelle spese militari*," *Germinal*, 9 Oct. 1892.

10. Beginning on 17 July 1892 Corradini ran his own three-part biographical and critical article on Ibsen in *Germinal*. Parts 2 and 3 were published on 24 July and 7 August.

11. Enrico Corradini, "Per una giovanissima poetessa," *Germinal*, 3 Apr. 1892.

12. Enrico Corradini, "Elegie romane," *Germinal*, 10 July 1892.

13. Enrico Corradini, "Un ebbro di vanità," *Germinal*, 11 Sept. 1892.

14. Cited by Edmund Wilson in *Axel's Castle*, pp. 22–23.

15. Cited by Philippe Jullian in *D'Annunzio*, p. 116.

16. In the same year Scarfoglio and his wife, Matilde Serao, founded *Il mattino*.

17. *Episcopo et Compagnie* (*Giovanni Episcopo*) also appeared in 1895, and although this novel enjoyed a more enthusiastic reception in France than in Italy, it never has been regarded as one of D'Annunzio's major works.

18. Symons also translated the poetry in *Il piacere*. *The Child of Pleasure* was not a success in England, probably due to the puritanical reaction following the Wilde affair.

19. Philippe Jullian's *Dreamers of the Decadence*

contains some good descriptive passages on the esthetic fashions in *fin de siècle* Paris.

20. For more on these decadent prototypes, see Mario Praz's *La carne, la morte e il diavolo nella letteratura romantica*, esp. ch. 4. A vigorous critique of Praz's decadence as the "dying agony" of romanticism thesis may be found in A. E. Carter's *Idea of Decadence in French Literature.*

21. See Trompeo, *Carducci e D'Annunzio*, p. 173.

22. Eurialo De Michelis, "D'Annunzio e i plagi."

23. D'Annunzio, *Il trionfo della morte*, p. xi.

24. See Giovanni Gullace, *Gabriele D'Annunzio in France*, ch. 1.

25. Gli altri della redazione, "*In riva all'Arno*," *Germinal*, 30 Jan. 1892.

26. Apparently *Germinal* died of inanition. The last issue came out on 15 January 1893 with this announcement: "Not being able to eliminate some insoluble differences of opinion concerning the direction of the journal between Messrs. Luigi Rasa, Carlo Cordara, and Enrico Corradini, co-proprietors and collaborators on *Germinal*, *Germinal* ceases publication with this number."

27. Ugo Ojetti, "Il contagio dannunziano," *Il marzocco*, 20 Feb. 1898.

28. There is some speculation, chiefly by Pier Ludovico Occhini, that in this delicate business of plagiarism D'Annunzio was equally light fingered, e.g., "And it is certain that even D'Annunzio was struck by this drama [*Dopo la morte*] because in *Gioconda* he substantially repeated the theme of Corradini" (*Enrico Corradini e la nuova coscienza nazionale*, p. 89).

29. Enrico Corradini, *Dopo la morte*, act 3, scene 4, pp. 83–84.

30. In *La verginità*, Ercole, the older cousin of At-

tilio, is described as a bald decadent novelist and playwright whose latest work is centered around a character named Tullio, an obvious reference to *L'innocente*. Attilio, on the other hand, might easily have been perceived by Corradini's readers as a younger D'Annunzio: "The young man now wanted his mama who was far away under the blue of his Abruzzi sky, by the blue of his Adriatic sea" (p. 12).

31. See Veo's "Qualche ricordo."

32. Occhini, *Enrico Corradini e la nuova coscienza nazionale*. *La leonessa* was published originally by Riccardo Forster in *Flegrea*, a Neapolitan journal of letters, sciences, and arts. *Flegrea* first appeared on 5 February 1899 and survived until 20 December 1901, distinguishing itself as the most long-lived of the *Marzocco*'s imitators. Prominent among the journal's contributors were Forster himself, Angelo Conti, Ugo Ojetti, Diego Angeli, Mario Morasso, and Corradini, who offered *Flegrea* his *Leonessa*, a short story entitled "Beniamino Nicosia," and a pair of articles, one of which, "La missione dell'Italia" (20 Dec. 1901), was among his earliest nationalist writings.

33. Gatteschi, "Umanità di Enrico Corradini." However, Occhini remembered that the first performance of *La leonessa* was given at the Regio Teatro Nuovo in Florence.

34. The historical significance of the name Emo would not be lost on Corradini's audience. In 1784 the Venetian admiral Angelo Emo had engaged in heroic action off the north African coast, raising for the last time in glorious offensive combat the red-and-gold standard of the winged lion.

35. Corradini, *La leonessa*, act 2, scene 2, pp. 333–34. Even the peasants join in the hosannas to this all-conquering hero: "What a glory for our *paese*

is this great Paolo Emo!'' they shout, saluting the triumphant return of their native son.

36. Ibid.

37. D'Annunzio, *Il piacere*, p. 361.

38. Commenting on Depretis's death in July 1887, Martini wrote that, although the doctors diagnosed the fatal malady as a stomach disorder, ''the truth is that the piazza in Rome called 'The Five Hundred Dead of Dogali' could be called the Five Hundred and One Dead of Dogali. Among the victims of that slaughter was Agostino Depretis'' (*Confessioni e ricordi*, p. 212).

39. Cited in Battaglia, *La prima guerra d'Africa*, p. 278.

40. See Richard Webster, *Industrial Imperialism in Italy*.

41. See Battaglia, *La prima guerra d'Africa*, pt. 3, ch. 6.

42. Grillandi, *Crispi*, ch. 7.

43. Martini, *Confessioni e ricordi*, ch. 7.

44. Grillandi, *Crispi*, ch. 7.

45. Enrico Corradini, *Discorsi politici*, p. 8.

46. Corradini, ''Abba Carima,'' *Il marzocco*, 8 Mar. 1896. Abba Carima was the first phase of the battle at Adua.

47. Mussolini, ''Corradini.''

48. From 2 February 1896 to 8 February 1900, the period of his *Marzocco* editorship, Corradini wrote no fewer than sixty signed articles, and his total contribution to the journal was close to two hundred articles. (See Giuseppe Ulivi's *Indice del Marzocco*.) I looked at all of his articles written after ''Abba Carima'' and did not find a single additional reference to Adua in particular, or to Africa in general.

49. Enrico Corradini, ''*La gloria*,'' *Il marzocco*, 4 June 1899.

50. Enrico Corradini, "*Le laudi*," *Il marzocco*, 3 Dec. 1899.

51. Giovanni Pascoli, "Pensieri sull'arte poetica," *Il marzocco*, 17 Jan. 1897. Pascoli developed these views in greater detail when he answered Corradini's *inchiesta* with the claim that "politics is a beautiful nothing."

52. Orvieto, "Corradini."

53. Mario Morasso, *Uomini e idee del domani: l'ego-archia*, introduction.

54. Corradini, "L'arte nel momento attuale," *Germinal*, 1892.

55. Vian, *La giovinezza*, ch. 3.

56. Angelo Conti, *La beata riva*, p. 92.

57. Enrico Corradini, "Lettera aperta a A. Conti," *Il marzocco*, 4 Feb. 1900. Conti had claimed, for instance, that of all the regions in Italy he liked the South best because it had the fewest miles of railroad track.

58. Enrico Corradini, "Ama il prossimo tuo," *Il marzocco*, 25 Mar. 1900.

59. Cited in Gatti, *Vita*, p. 181.

60. Ibid., p. 163.

61. Gabriele D'Annunzio, "Della mia legislatura," *Il giorno*, 29 Mar. 1900.

BIBLIOGRAPHY

Alatri, Paolo. *Carducci giacobino; l'evoluzione dell'-ethos politico*. Palermo: Libreria Prima, 1953.

Amoruso, Vincenzo. *Il sindacalismo di Enrico Corradini*. Palermo: Società Editrice Orazio Fiorenza, 1929.

Angeli, Diego. "L'ambiente del *Convito*." *Il marzocco*, 7 September 1924.

————. "Lettere inedite di Giosuè Carducci ad Angelo Sommaruga." *Il giornale d'Italia*, 27 March 1910.

Antongini, Tom. *D'Annunzio aneddotico*. Milano: Mondadori, 1939.

————. *Gli allegri filibustieri di D'Annunzio*. Milano: Martello, 1951.

————. *Quarant'anni con D'Annunzio*. Milano: Mondadori, 1957.

————. *Vita segreta di Gabriele D'Annunzio*. Milano: Mondadori, 1938.

Arcari, Paolo Maria. *Le elaborazioni della dottrina politica nazionale fra l'unità e l'intervento, 1870–1914*. 3 vols. Firenze: Casa Editrice Marzocco, 1939.

Are, Giuseppe. *Economia e politica nell'Italia liberale (1890–1915)*. Bologna: Il Mulino, 1974.

Aron, Raymond. *The Opium of the Intellectuals*. New York: Norton, 1955.

Barbieri, Lodovico, et al., eds. *Il risorgimento nell' opera di Giosuè Carducci*. Roma: Vittoriano, 1935.

Bartoccini, Fiorella. *La Roma dei romani*. Roma: Istituto per la storia del risorgimento italiano, 1971.

Barzini, Luigi. *The Italians*. New York: Atheneum, 1964.

Barzun, Jacques. *Darwin, Marx, Wagner*. New York: Doubleday, 1941.

————. *The House of Intellect*. New York: Harper, 1959.

Battaglia, Roberto. *La prima guerra d'Africa*. Torino: Einaudi, 1958.

Baumer, Franklin L. *Modern European Thought: Continuity and Change in Ideas, 1600–1950*. New York: Macmillan, 1977.

Benda, Julien. *The Treason of the Intellectuals*. New York: Norton, 1969.

Besana, Davide. *Sommaruga occulto e Sommaruga palese*. Roma: Giovanni Bracco, 1885.

Biagini, Mario. *Il poeta della terza Italia*. Milano: Mursia, 1961.

Binni, Walter. *Carducci e altri saggi*. Torino: Einaudi, 1960.

————. *La poetica del decadentismo*. Firenze: Sansoni, 1968.

Bobbio, Aurelia, *Le riviste fiorentine del principio del secolo, 1903–1916*. Firenze: Sansoni, 1936.

Bonomi, Ivanoe. *La politica italiana da Porta Pia a Vittorio Veneto, 1870–1918*. Torino: Einaudi, 1966.

Borgese, Giuseppe Antonio. *Gabriele D'Annunzio*. Napoli: Ricciardi, 1909.

————. *La vita e il libro: prima serie*. Bologna: Zanichelli, 1923.

Braudel, Fernand. *The Mediterranean and the Mediterranean World in the Age of Philip II*. 2 vols. New York: Harper and Row, 1972–73.

Briganti, Alessandra. *Il parlamento nel romanzo italiano del secondo ottocento*. Firenze: Le Monnier, 1972.

————. *Intellettuali e cultura tra ottocento e nove-*

cento: nascita e storia della terza pagina. Padova: Liviana, 1972.

Bruers, Antonio. *Gabriele D'Annunzio: il pensiero e l'azione*. Bologna: Zanichelli, 1943.

Bruno, Francesco. *La scapigliatura napoletana e meridionale*. Napoli: La Nuova Cultura Editrice, 1971.

Busetto, Natale. *Giosuè Carducci: l'uomo, il poeta, il critico, e il prosatore*. Padova: Liviana, 1958.

Caccia, Ettore. *Poesia e ideologia per Carducci*. Brescia: Paideia, 1970.

Cammett, John M. *Antonio Gramsci and the Origins of Italian Communism*. Stanford: Stanford University Press, 1967.

Cannas, Dino. "*La Cronaca Bizantina* e le sue battaglie." *Il giornale d'Italia*, 24 April 1910.

Caprin, Giulio. "*Il marzocco.*" *L'otto-novecento*. Firenze: Sansoni, 1957.

Caracciolo, Alberto, ed. *La formazione dell'Italia industriale*. Bari: Laterza, 1969.

Carducci, Giosuè. *Confessioni e battaglie*, 3 vols. Roma: Sommaruga, 1883–1884.

———. *Edizione nazionale delle opere di Giosuè Carducci*. Bologna: Zanichelli, 1939.

———. *Lettere di Giosuè Carducci: edizione nazionale*. Bologna: Zanichelli, 1938.

Carocci, Giampiero. *Agostino Depretis e la politica interna italiana dal 1876 al 1887*. Torino: Einaudi, 1956.

———, ed. *Il parlamento nella storia d'Italia*. Bari: Laterza, 1964.

———. "La polemica antidecadentistica di Giosuè Carducci." *Belfagor*, May 1949.

Carter, A. E. *The Idea of Decadence in French Literature, 1830–1900*. Toronto: Toronto University Press, 1958.

Casalegno, Carlo. *La regina Margherita*. Torino: Einaudi, 1956.

Casnati, Francesco. "Il sodale bizantino." *Quaderni dannunziani XX-XXI*, 1961.

Castelli, Alighiero, ed. *Pagine disperse di Gabriele D'Annunzio*. Roma: Bernardo Lux, 1913.

Castronovo, Valerio. *La stampa italiana dall' unità al fascismo*. Bari: Laterza, 1970.

Chabod, Federico. *Storia della politica estera italiana dal 1870 al 1896*. 2 vols. Bari: Laterza, 1971.

Charlesworth, Barbara. *Dark Passages: The Decadent Consciousness in Victorian Literature*. Madison: University of Wisconsin Press, 1965.

Chemello, Adriana. *"La farfalla" di Angelo Sommaruga*. Roma: Bulzoni, 1977.

Chiarini, Giuseppe. "A proposito di un nuovo poeta." *Fanfulla della domenica*, 2 May 1880.

———. "In memoriam." *Fanfulla della domenica*, 24 October 1880.

———. *Memorie della vita di Giosuè Carducci*. Firenze: Barbèra, 1907.

Chiarini, Luigi. "Le prime poesie del Carducci: lettere del poeta a Giuseppe Chiarini (1857)." *Pègaso* 3, pt. 1 (1931).

Chiti, Luca, ed. *Cultura e politica nelle riviste fiorentine del primo novecento, 1903–1915*. Torino: Loescher, 1972.

Cianfrani, Valeriano. *"Il convito." Ricordi romani di Gabriele D'Annunzio*. Roma: Palomba, 1938.

Civiltà cattolica. Roma.

Consiglio, Alberto. "Edoardo Scarfoglio: lettere a Olga Lodi Ossani." *Pègaso* 3, pt. 2 (1931).

———. "Edoardo Scarfoglio scrittore." *Pègaso* 2, pt. 1 (1930).

———. "Matilde Serao e Edoardo Scarfoglio." *Pègaso* 3, pt. 2 (1931).

————. *Napoli: amore e morte: Edoardo Scarfoglio e Matilde Serao*. Napoli: Bianco, 1959.

————, ed. *Le più belle pagine di Edoardo Scarfoglio*. Milano: Treves, 1932.

————. "Ricordo di Angelo Conti." *Pègaso* 2, pt. 2 (1930).

Conti, Angelo. *La beata riva: trattato dell'oblio*. Milano: Treves, 1900.

————. *Giorgione*. Firenze: Alinari, 1894.

————. *Rileggendo il Petrarca*. Firenze, 1892.

Il convito. Roma: Adolfo de Bosis, director, Libro I (January 1895) through Libro XII (December 1907).

Coppola, Francesco. "Dal liberalismo al nazionalismo: in morte di Enrico Corradini." *Politica* 36 (1932).

Cornell, Kenneth. *The Symbolist Movement*. New Haven: Yale University Press, 1951.

Corradini, Enrico. *L'apologo delle due sorelle*. Firenze: Barbèra, 1929.

————. *Carlotta Corday*. Firenze: Barbèra, 1929.

————. "Dalle carte inedite." *Nuova antologia*, 16 January 1932.

————. *Discorsi politici: 1902–1923*. Firenze: Vallecchi, 1923.

————. "Domenico trentacoste." *Nuova antologia*, 16 November 1905.

————. *Dopo la morte*. Firenze: Paggi, 1896.

————. *Fascismo vita d'Italia*. Firenze: Vallecchi, 1925.

————. "Gabriele D'Annunzio." *L'illustrazione italiana*, 10 January 1904.

————. "*Giacomo Vettori*." *Nuova antologia*, 16 January 1901.

————. *La gioia*. Firenze: Paggi, 1897.

————. *Giulio Cesare*. Roma: Rassegna Internazionale, 1902.

————. *Giulio Cesare*, rev. ed. Milano: Mondadori, 1926.

————. "Il Giulio Cesare di Shakespeare all'Argentina." *Nuova antologia*, January 1906.

————. *La guerra lontana*. Milano: Treves, 1911.

————. "Intorno alla *Fiaccola sotto il moggio*." *Nuova antologia*, 16 April 1905.

————. *La leonessa. Flegrea* 3, nos. 3–6 (1899).

————. *Maria Salvestri*. Milano: Treves, 1907.

————. *L'ombra della vita: costume, letteratura, teatro e arte*. Napoli: Ricciardi, 1908.

————. *La patria lontana*. Milano: Treves, 1910.

————. *Santamaura*. Firenze: Paggi, 1896.

————. *Le sette lampade d'oro*. Torino: Renzo Streglio, 1904.

————. *La verginità*. Milano: Vitagliano, 1922.

Coser, Lewis A. *Men of Ideas: A Sociologist's View*. New York: Collier-Macmillan, 1965.

Crispi, Francesco, "Dopo diciotto anni," *Nuova antologia*, 1 October 1900.

————. *Scritti e discorsi politici di Francesco Crispi, 1849–1890*. Roma: Unione cooperativa editrice, 1890.

Crispolti, Filippo. "La regina Margherita." *Pègaso* 5, pt. 1 (1933).

————. "Ricordi su due re: Vittorio Emanuele II e Umberto I." *Pègaso* 4, pt. 2 (1932).

Croce, Benedetto. *Aesthetic: As Science of Expression and General Linguistic*. Trans. Douglas Ainslie. New York: Farrar, Straus and Giroux, 1922.

————. *Essays on Marx and Russia*. New York: Ungar, 1966.

————. *Giosuè Carducci: studio critico*. Bari: Laterza, 1920.

————. *La letteratura della nuova Italia*. 4th ed. 5 vols. Bari: Laterza, 1943.

————. *Storia d'Italia dal 1871 al 1915*. Bari: Laterza, 1943.

————, ed. *La politica della destra*. Bari: Laterza, 1910.

Cronaca bizantina. Roma: Sommaruga journal, 15 June 1881–16 March 1885.

Cronaca bizantina–domenica letteraria. Roma: Gabriele D'Annunzio, director, 15 November 1885–21 March 1886.

Cunsolo, Ronald. "Enrico Corradini and Italian Nationalism." Ph.D. dissertation, New York University, 1962.

Dalgas, Augusto. "Ripose o no il Carducci amore alla Versilia?" In Lumbroso, Alberto, ed. *Miscellanea carducciana*. Bologna: Zanichelli, 1911.

D'Annunzio, Gabriele. "Dell'arte, della critica e del fervore." Introduction to Angelo Conti's *La beata riva: trattato dell'oblio*. Milano: Treves, 1900.

————. *Canto novo, Intermezzo* (1881–83). Milano: Treves, 1920.

————. *Contemplazione della morte*. Milano: Treves, 1912.

————. *Il fuoco*. Milano: Mondadori, 1967.

————. *Giovanni Episcopo*. Sesto S. Giovanni: Casa Editrice Modella, 1913.

————. *L'innocente*. Roma: Oleandro, 1934.

————. *Intermezzo di rime*. Roma: Sommaruga, 1884.

————. *Isaotta Guttadàuro*. Sesto S. Giovanni: Casa Editrice Modella, 1913.

————. "Italia in te sola: lettere a Enrico Corradini." *Nuova antologia*, August 1943.

————. *Lettere a Barbara Leoni*. Firenze: Sansoni, 1954.

————. *La nave*. Milano: Treves, 1908.

————. *Il piacere*. Milano: Treves, 1918.

————. *Il poema paradisiaco, Odi navali* (1891–93). Milano: Treves, 1899.

————. *Il trionfo della morte.* Milano: Treves, 1903.

————. *Le vergini delle rocce.* Milano: Treves, 1916.

De Bosis, Adolfo. *Amori ac silentio, le rime sparse.* Milano: Studio editoriale Lombardo, 1914.

DeGrand, Alexander J. *The Italian Nationalist Association and the Rise of Fascism in Italy.* Lincoln and London: University of Nebraska Press, 1978.

Delzell, Charles F., ed. *The Unification of Italy, 1859–61.* New York: Holt, Rinehart, and Winston, 1965.

De Michelis, Eurialo. "D'Annunzio e Huysmans." *Rassegna di cultura e vita scolastica.* Roma, July–August 1961.

————. "D'Annunzio e i plagi." *Quaderni dannunziani XX-XXI*, 1965.

————. *Novecento e dintorni: dal Carducci al neorealismo.* Milano: Mursia, 1976.

————. *Tutto D'Annunzio.* Milano: Feltrinelli, 1960.

De Rosa, Gabriele, et al. *Roma capitale.* Roma: Istituto di Studi Romani, 1972.

De Witt, Antony. "Giovanni Pascoli: lettere al pittore Antony De Witt." *Pègaso* 4, pt. 1 (1932).

Dizionario biografico degli italiani. Roma: Istituto della enciclopedia italiana, 1964.

Dizionario enciclopedico della letteratura italiana. Bari: Laterza, 1966.

Dizionario storico politico italiano. Firenze: Sansoni, 1971.

Domenica del fracassa. Roma: Giuseppe Chiarini, director, 28 December 1884–14 February 1886.

Domenica letteraria. Roma: Sommaruga journal, 14 December 1884–1 February 1885.

Edel, Leon. *Literary Biography.* New York: Anchor, 1959.

Eickhorst, William. *Decadence in German Fiction.*
Denver: Alan Swallow, 1953.
―――. *Significant Types of Decadent Character in
Modern German Fiction.* Urbana: University of
Illinois Press, 1946.
Enciclopedia Italiana. Roma: Istituto della Enciclope-
dia Italiana, 1949.
Encyclopedia of Philosophy. New York: Macmillan,
1967.
Erikson, Erik. *Childhood and Society.* New York:
Norton, 1963.

Falqui, Enrico. *Bibliografia dannunziana.* Firenze: Le
Monnier, 1941.
―――. *Nostra terza pagina.* Roma: Canesi, n.d.
Fanfulla della domenica. Roma.
Federzoni, Luigi. *L'Italia di ieri per la storia di do-
mani.* Verona: Mondadori, 1967.
Finer, S. E. *Vilfredo Pareto: Sociological Writings.*
London: Pall Mall Press, 1966.
Flegrea: rivista di lettere, scienze ed arti. Napoli: Ric-
cardo Forster, director, 5 February 1899–20 De-
cember 1901.
Fleming, William. *Art and Ideas.* New York: Holt,
Rinehart, and Winston, 1974.
Flora, Francesco. *D'Annunzio.* Napoli: Ricciardi,
1926.
―――. "*La cronaca bizantina.*" *Pègaso* 2, pt. 2
(1930).
―――. "Il decadentismo." *Questioni e correnti di
storia letteraria.* Ed. Attilio Momigliano. Mi-
lano: Marzorati, 1949.
―――. "*Il fanfulla della domenica* I-II." *Pègaso* 2,
pts. 1-2 (1930).
―――. *La poesia e la prosa di Giosuè Carducci.* Pisa:
Nastri-Lischi, 1959.
Forcella, Roberto. *D'Annunzio 1863–1883.* Roma:

Fondazione Leonardo per la cultura italiana, 1926.

————. *D'Annunzio 1884–1885*. Roma: Fondazione Leonardo per la cultura italiana, 1928.

————. *D'Annunzio 1886*. Firenze: Sansoni, 1936.

————. *D'Annunzio 1887*. Firenze: Sansoni, 1937.

————. "Lettere di Gabriele D'Annunzio a Enrico Nencioni (1880–1896)." *Nuova antologia*, May 1939.

Forche caudine. Roma: Sommaruga journal, Pietro Sbarbaro, director, 15 June 1884–15 February 1885.

Forche caudine: nuova serie. Roma: Pietro Sbarbaro, director, 18 June 1885–6 August 1885.

Frateili, Arnaldo. "Vita e Poesia di Giulio Salvadori." *Pègaso* 1, pt. 1 (1929).

Frenz, Horst, ed. *Nobel Lectures: Literature (1901–1967)*. Amsterdam: Elsevier, 1969.

Fried, Robert C. *Planning the Eternal City: Roman Politics and Planning since World War II*. New Haven: Yale University Press, 1973.

Friedman, Maurice. *To Deny Our Nothingness: Contemporary Images of Man*. New York: Delacorte, 1967.

Frigessi, Delio, ed. *La cultura italiana del '900 attraverso le riviste: Leonardo, Hermes, Il regno*. Vol. I. Torino: Einaudi, 1960.

Frye, Northrup. *The Critical Path: An Essay on the Social Context of Literary Criticism*. Bloomington: Indiana University Press, 1971.

————. *The Anatomy of Criticism*. Princeton: Princeton University Press, 1957.

Fucilla, Joseph G., and Joseph M. Carrière. *D'Annunzio Abroad: A Bibliographical Essay*. 2 vols. New York: Institution of French Studies, 1935–37.

Fusco, Enrico M., ed. *Scrittori e idee: dizionario critico*

della letteratura italiana. Roma: Società editrice
internazionale, 1956.

Gabelli, Aristide, "Istruzione primaria e secondaria
nella città e provincia di Roma." In *Monografia
della città di Roma e della campagna romana.*
Roma: Tipografia Elzeviriana, 1881.

Gaeta, Franco, ed. *La stampa nazionalista.* Rocca San
Casciano: Cappelli, 1965.

Gargano, G. S. "Adolfo De Bosis." *Il marzocco,* 7 September 1924.

Garin, Eugenio. *La cultura italiana tra '800 e '900.*
Bari: Laterza, 1963.

Gatteschi, Roberto Pio. "Umanità di Enrico Corradini." *Nuova antologia,* December 1941.

Gatti, Guglielmo. *Correzioni e aggiunte alla vita di
Gabriele D'Annunzio.* Pescara: Giuseppe Ferret-
ti, 1969.

————. *Le donne nella vita e nell'arte di Gabriele
D'Annunzio.* Modena: Guanda, 1951.

————. *Gabriele D'Annunzio: studi e saggi.* Rocca
San Casciano: Cappelli, 1959.

————. "Sommarughiana." *Strenna dei romanisti* 24
(21 April 1963).

————. *La vita di Gabriele D'Annunzio.* Firenze:
Sansoni, 1956.

Gaunt, William. *The Aesthetic Adventure.* New York:
Harcourt, Brace, 1945.

Gazzetta di Venezia. (A daily newspaper directed
by Ferruccio Macola; Corradini was associated
with it as a reporter for a few months in 1900.)

Gazzetta letteraria. Torino.

Gennarini, Edoardo. *La scapigliatura milanese.* Napoli: Scalabini, 1961.

Germinal. Firenze: Enrico Corradini, director, 20 December 1891–15 January 1893.

Gerschenkron, Alexander. *Economic Backwardness in Historical Perspective*. Cambridge: Harvard University Press, 1966.

Getto, Giovanni. *Carducci e Pascoli*. Bologna: Zanichelli, 1957.

Ghisalberti, Alberto, "Settembre 1870." In *Roma capitale*. Roma: Istituto di Studi Romani, 1972.

Giolitti, Giovanni. *Memorie della mia vita*. 2 vols. Milano: Garzanti, 1967.

Il giorno. Roma.

Golzio, Francesco, and Augusto Guerra, eds. *La cultura italiana del '900 attraverso le riviste: L'unità e La voce politica (1915)*. Vol. V. Torino: Einaudi, 1962.

Graf, Arturo. "Preraffaelliti, simbolisti ed esteti I-II." *Nuova antologia*, January 1897.

Gramsci, Antonio. *The Modern Prince and Other Writings*. Trans. and introduced by Louis Marks. New York: International Publishers, 1957.

————. *Il risorgimento*. Torino: Einaudi, 1952.

————. *Selections from the Prison Notebooks*. Ed. and trans. Quentin Hoare and Geoffrey Nowell Smith. New York: International Publishers, 1971.

Graña, César. *Modernity and Its Discontents*. New York: Harper and Row, 1964.

Greenfield, Kent Roberts. *Economics and Liberalism in the Risorgimento: A Study of Nationalism in Lombardy, 1814–1848*. Baltimore: Johns Hopkins University Press, 1965.

Grew, Raymond. *A Sterner Plan for Italian Unity: the Italian National Society in the Risorgimento*. Princeton: Princeton University Press, 1963.

Grillandi, Massimo. *Francesco Crispi*. Torino: UTET, 1969.

Grilli, Alfredo. "Carducci, Oriani, e Albicini: tre fedeli di Crispi." *Nuova antologia*, September 1959.

Guabello, Mario. *Catalogo ragionato della raccolta dannunziana di Mario Guabello*. Billa: Guabello, 1948.

——. *Documenti d'amore: lettere di Gabriele D'Annunzio a una Beatrice*. Billa: Guabello, 1936.

Guiccioli, Alessandro. "Diario del 1883–86." *Nuova antologia*, 16 August–1 December 1937.

Gullace, Giovanni. *Gabriele D'Annunzio in France: A Study in Cultural Relations*. Syracuse: Syracuse University Press, 1966.

Hales, E. E. Y. *Pio Nono: A Study in European Politics and Religion in the Nineteenth Century*. London: Eyre and Spottiswoode, 1956.

Hauser, Arnold. *The Social History of Art*. 4 vols. New York: Vintage, 1951.

Hayes, Carlton J. H. *A Generation of Materialism*. New York: Harper, 1941.

——. *The Historical Evolution of Modern Nationalism*. New York: Macmillan, 1931.

——. *Nationalism: A Religion*. New York: Macmillan, 1960.

Hearder, H. *Europe in the Nineteenth Century, 1830–1880*. New York: Holt, Rinehart and Winston, 1966.

Hibbert, Christopher. *Garibaldi and His Enemies*. New York: New American Library, 1965.

Hostetter, Richard. *The Italian Socialist Movement: Origins (1880–82)*. Princeton: Van Nostrand, 1958.

Howe, Irving. *Politics and the Novel*. New York: Horizon, 1967.

Hughes, H. Stuart. *Consciousness and Society*. New York: Vintage, 1958.

——. *The United States and Italy*. New York: Norton, 1965.

Huysmans, Joris-Karl. *Against the Grain*. New York: Lieber and Lewis, 1922.

L'Illustrazione italiana. Milano.
Insolera, Italo. *Roma moderna: un secolo di storia urbanistica*. Torino: Einaudi, 1962, 1971.

Jemolo, Arturo Carlo. *Crispi*. Firenze: Le Monnier, 1970.
Joad, C. E. M. *Decadence: A Philosophical Inquiry*. London: Faber and Faber, 1948.
Joll, James. *Europe since 1870: An International History*. New York: Harper and Row, 1973.
――――. *Three Intellectuals in Politics*. New York: Pantheon, 1960.
Jullian, Philippe. *D'Annunzio*. New York: Viking, 1971.
――――. *Dreamers of the Decadence: Symbolist Painters of the 1890's*. New York: Praeger, 1971.
――――. *Prince of Aesthetes: Count Robert de Montesquiou (1855–1921)*. New York: Viking, 1968.

Kostof, Spiro. *The Third Rome, 1870–1950*. Berkeley: University Art Museum, 1973.
――――. "The Third Rome: The Polemics of Architectural History." *Journal of the Society of Architectural Historians* 32, no. 3 (October 1973).

Lampert, E. "Decadents, Liberals, Revolutionaries: Russia, 1900–1918." Inaugural lecture at the University of Keele, 18 November 1969.
Leoni, Francesco. *Origini del nazionalismo italiano*. Napoli: Morano, 1970.
Lichtheim, George. *The Concept of Ideology and Other Essays*. New York: Random House, 1967.
Lo Curzio, Guglielmo. *Ottocento minore: incontri e pretesti*. Palermo: Palumbo, 1950.

Lodi, Luigi. *Alla ricerca della verecondia*. Roma: Sommaruga, 1884.

———. *Giornalisti*. Bari: Laterza, 1930.

———. "*La Contessa Lara* di Maria Borgese." *Pègaso* 2, pt. 2 (1930).

Lumbroso, Alberto, ed. *Miscellanea carducciana*. Bologna: Zanichelli, 1911.

———. "Una pagina del diario carducciano." In his *Miscellanea carducciana*.

Luzio, Alessandro. *La massoneria e il risorgimento italiano*. 2 vols. Bologna: Forni, 1925.

Luzzatto, Gino. *L'economia italiana dal 1861 al 1894*. Torino: Einaudi, 1968.

Lyttelton, Adrian, ed. *Italian Fascisms from Pareto to Gentile*. London: Cape, 1973.

McGrath, Willian J. *Dionysian Art and Populist Politics in Austria*. New Haven: Yale University Press, 1974.

Mack Smith, Denis, ed. *The Making of Italy, 1796–1870*. New York: Harper and Row, 1968.

———. *Victor Emanuel, Cavour and the Risorgimento*. London: Oxford University Press, 1971.

Maffii, Maffio. "Corradini e *Il regno*." *Il marzocco*, 20 December 1931.

———. "Corradini e *Il regno*." *Politica*, August 1937. (This is a much longer article than the earlier *Marzocco* version.)

Majolo Molinari, Olga. *La stampa periodica romana dell'ottocento*. 2 vols. Roma: Istituto di Studi Romani, 1963.

Mannheim, Karl. *Essays on the Sociology of Culture*. London: Routledge & Paul, 1956.

———. *Ideology and Utopia: An Introduction to the Sociology of Knowledge*. New York: Harcourt, Brace and World, 1936.

————. *Systematic Sociology: An Introduction to the Study of Society*. New York: Philosophical Library, 1958.

Marcazzan, Mario. "Dal romanticismo al decadentismo." *Letteratura italiana: le correnti*. Milano: Marzorati, 1956.

Martini, Ferdinando, *Confessioni e ricordi, 1859–92*. Milano: Treves, 1928.

Il marzocco. Firenze: Enrico Corradini, director, February 1896–February 1900; thereafter Adolfo and Angiolo Orvieto, directors until its demise in 1932.

Marzot, Giulio. *Il decadentismo italiano*. Bologna: Cappelli, 1970.

Mayer, Arno J. *Dynamics of Counterrevolution in Europe, 1870–1956: An Analytic Framework*. New York: Harper and Row, 1971.

Mazza, Giuseppe. *Sulla vita e sulle opere di Pietro Sbarbaro*. Scansano: Tipografia editrice degli Olmi, 1891.

Meisel, James H. *The Myth of the Ruling Class: Gaetano Mosca and the Elite*. Ann Arbor: University of Michigan Press, 1958.

————, ed. *Pareto and Mosca*. Englewood Cliffs: Prentice-Hall, 1965.

Missiroli, Mario. "Anarchici e tribunali." *Il messaggero*, 10 June 1973.

————. *Gente di conoscenza*. Milano-Napoli: Riccardo Ricciardi, 1972.

Molinelli, Raffaele. *Per una storia del nazionalismo italiano*. Urbino: Argelia, 1966.

Monografia della città di Roma e della campagna romana. Roma: Tipografia Elzeviriana, 1881.

Montani, C. "Il primo editore di D'Annunzio." *Il messaggero*, 9 August 1924.

Morandi, Carlo. *I partiti politici nella storia d'Italia*. Firenze: Le Monnier, 1968.

Morando, F. Ernesto, *Anton Giulio Barrili e i suoi tempi* (Napoli, Perrelli, 1926).

Morasso, Mario. *L'imperialismo artistico.* Torino: Bocca, 1903.

———. *L'imperialismo nel secolo XX: la conquista del mondo.* Milano: Treves, 1905.

———. *La nuova arma (la macchina).* Torino: Bocca, 1905.

———. *L'origine delle razze europee.* Firenze: Landi, 1895.

———. *Uomini e idee del domani: l'egoarchia.* Torino: Bocca, 1898.

Mosca, Gaetano. *The Ruling Class.* Ed. and revised by Arthur Livingston. New York: McGraw-Hill, 1939.

Mosse, George L. *The Crisis of German Ideology: Intellectual Origins of the Third Reich.* New York: Grosset and Dunlap, 1964.

———. *The Culture of Western Europe.* Chicago: Rand-McNally, 1974.

Munro, John M. *The Decadent Poetry of the Eighteen-Nineties.* Beirut: American University of Beirut, 1970.

Musatti, Alberto. "La passione nazionale di Enrico Corradini." *Nuova antologia,* 16 April 1932.

Mussolini, Benito. "Enrico Corradini." *Nuova antologia,* 16 December 1931.

Nabab. Roma: Sommaruga journal, Enrico Panzacchi, director, 21 December 1884–27 February 1885.

Nardi, Piero. *Scapigliatura: da Giuseppe Rovani a Carlo Dossi.* Verona: Mondadori, 1968.

Neufield, Maurice F. *Italy: School for Awakening Countries (The Italian Labor Movement in Its Political, Social and Economic Setting from 1800 to 1960).* Ithaca: Cornell University Press, 1961.

Nolte, Ernst. *Three Faces of Fascism*. New York: Holt, Rinehart, and Winston, 1966.

Nordau, Max. *Degeneration*. New York: Fertig, 1968.

Occhini, Pier Ludovico. *Enrico Corradini*. Firenze: Rinascimento del Libro, 1933.

———. "Enrico Corradini: Africanista." *Nuova antologia*, 16 January 1936.

———. *Enrico Corradini e la nuova coscienza nazionale*. Firenze: Vallecchi, 1925.

———. *Enrico Corradini, scrittore e nazionalista*. Roma: Gaetano Garzoni, Provenzani, 1914.

Ojetti, Ugo. *Alla scoperta dei letterati*. Edited by Pietro Pancrazi. Firenze: Le Monnier, 1946.

———. *Cose viste*. 7 vols. Milano: Treves, 1923–39.

Olschki, Leonardo. *The Genius of Italy*. New York: Oxford University Press, 1949.

Omodeo, Adolfo. *L'età del risorgimento italiano*. Napoli: Edizione scientifiche italiane, 1965.

Oriani, Alfredo. *Fino a Dogali*. Bologna: Laterza, 1918.

———. *Le lettere*. Ed. Piero Zama. Bologna: Cappelli, 1958.

———. *La lotta politica in Italia*. Bologna: Cappelli, 1944–46.

———. *Memorie inutili*. Bologna: Licinio Cappelli, 1927.

Orvieto, Angiolo. "Enrico Corradini: i primi passi." *Il marzocco*, 20 December 1931.

Pancrazi, Pietro. *Scrittori italiani dal Carducci al D'Annunzio*. Bari: Laterza, 1937.

Papini, Giovanni. *Il crepuscolo dei filosofi*. Milano: Lombarda, 1906.

———. *Ritratti italiani*. Firenze: Vallecchi, 1944.

———. *L'uomo Carducci*. Bologna: Zanichelli, 1918.

————. *Un uomo finito.* Firenze: Vallecchi, 1932.

————, and Giuseppe Prezzolini. *La coltura italiana.* Firenze: Lumachi, 1906.

————. *Vecchio e nuovo nazionalismo.* Roma: Volpe, 1967.

Pareto, Vilfredo. *The Ruling Class in Italy before 1900.* New York: S. F. Vanni, 1950.

Pariset, Francesco. "L'esperienza parlamentare di Gabriele D'Annunzio." *Storia contemporanea,* March 1977.

Pavoni, Giacomo. *L'opera nazionale di Enrico Corradini.* Firenze: Vallecchi, 1928.

La penna d'oro di Pietro Sbarbaro. Roma-Lugano: Pietro Sbarbaro, director, 4 April 1886–23 September 1886.

La penna di Pietro Sbarbaro: deputato al parlamento nazionale. Roma: Pietro Sbarbaro, director, 10 January 1886–28 March 1886. (Edoardo Perino continued to publish the journal as *La penna: effemeride settimanale* with old Sbarbaro articles until 29 May 1886.)

Perowne, Stewart. *Rome: From Its Foundation to the Present.* New York: Coward, McCann & Geoghegan, 1971.

Pescetti, Luigi. "Giosuè Carducci: lettere a Olga Lodi Ossani." *Pègaso* 3, pt. 2 (1931).

Pesci, Ugo. *Come siamo entrati in Roma.* Preface by Giosuè Carducci. Milano: Treves, 1895.

————. *I primi anni di Roma capitale, 1870–78.* Firenze: Bemporad e Figlio, 1907.

Petrini, Mario. "Giovanni Pascoli, *Il convito,* e *Il marzocco.*" *Belfagor,* 31 July 1961.

Pierantoni, Augusto. *Sub lege libertas: contro Pietro Sbarbaro.* Roma: Fratelli Pallotta, 1884.

Pincus-Witten, Robert. *Occult Symbolism in France.* New York: Garland, 1976.

"La politica sanitaria d'Italia nelle epidemie coleriche 1884–85 (un ex-funzionario di sanità)." *Nuova antologia*, 16 December 1885.

Pompeati, Arturo. "Decadentismo straniero e italiano." Review of *La carne, la morte e il diavolo nella letteratura romantica*, by Mario Praz. *Il marzocco*, 29 March 1931.

Praz, Mario. *La carne, la morte e il diavolo nella letteratura romantica*. Firenze: Sansoni, 1966.

Prezzolini, Giuseppe. *Amici*. Firenze: Vallecchi, 1932.

——. *L'Italiano inutile*. Milano: Longanesi, 1953.

——. *The Legacy of Italy*. New York: S. F. Vanni, 1948.

——. Letter to Richard Drake, 5 August 1974.

Quaderni dannunziani, vols. 1–41. Brescia: Fondazione "Il Vittoriale degli italiani," 1955–.

Il regno. Firenze: Enrico Corradini, director, 29 November 1903–5 March 1905; thereafter by Aldemiro Campodonico until the journal's demise in 1906.

Revel, Jean-François. *As for Italy*. New York: Dial, 1959.

Rhodes, Anthony. *The Poet as Superman*. London: Weidenfield & Nicolson, 1959.

Rich, Norman. *The Age of Nationalism and Reform, 1850–1890*. New York: Norton, 1977.

Ridge, George Ross. *The Hero in French Decadent Literature*. Athens: University of Georgia Press, 1961.

——. *The Hero in French Romantic Literature*. Athens: University of Georgia Press, 1961.

——. *Joris-Karl Huysmans*. New York: Twayne, 1968.

Rieff, Philip, ed. *On Intellectuals*. New York: Anchor, 1970.

Roda, Vittorio. *Decadentismo morale e decadentismo estetico*. Bologna: R. Patron, 1966.

Rogger, Hans, and Eugen Weber, eds. *The European Right: A Historical Profile*. Berkeley: University of California Press, 1965.

Romano, Angelo, ed. *La cultura italiana del '900 attraverso le riviste: La Voce*. Vol. II. Torino: Einaudi, 1960.

Romano, Salvatore F. *Le classi sociali in Italia: dal medioevo all' età contemporanea*. Torino: Einaudi, 1965.

Romeo, Rosario. *Breve storia della grande industria in Italia*. Bologna: Cappelli, 1963.

————. *Risorgimento e capitalismo*. Bari: Laterza, 1963.

Ronchey, Alberto. *Atlante ideologico*. Milano: Garzanti, 1973.

Rothenstein, John. *The Artists of the 1890s*. London: Routledge, 1928.

Russo, Luigi. *Carducci senza retorica*. Bari: Laterza, 1957.

Saladino, Salvatore. *Italy from Unification to 1919: Growth and Decay of a Liberal Regime*. New York: Crowell, 1970.

Salinari, Carlo. *Miti e coscienza del decadentismo italiano: D'Annunzio, Pascoli, Fogazzaro, Pirandello*. Milano: Feltrinelli, 1960.

————. "Le origini del nazionalismo e l'ideologia di Pascoli e D'Annunzio." *Società*, May 1958.

Salomone, A. William. *Italy in the Giolittian Era: Italian Democracy in the Making, 1900–1914*. Philadelphia: University of Philadelphia Press, 1960.

Salvadori, Giulio. *Scritti bizantini*. Ed. Nello Vian.
    Rocca San Casciano: Cappelli, 1963.
Salvatorelli, Luigi. *The Risorgimento: Thought and
    Action*. New York: Harper and Row, 1970.
Sarti, C. G. "Fra Giosuè Carducci e Sommaruga." *La
    tribuna*, Roma, 8 April 1910.
————. "La resurrezione di Angelo Sommaruga." *La
    tribuna*, Roma, 6 April 1910.
————. "Ricordi sommarughiani." *La tribuna*, Roma,
    24 August 1923.
————. "Il secondo editore del Carducci: Angelo Som-
    maruga." In Lumbroso, Alberto, ed. *Miscellanea
    carducciana*. Bologna: Zanichelli, 1911.
————. "Sommaruga e le sue idee." *La tribuna*,
    Roma, 11 April 1910.
Sbarbaro, Pietro, ed. *Medico e ministro: lettere di Gio-
    vanni Lanza*. Roma: Sommaruga, 1883.
————. *La mente di Terenzio Mamiani*. Firenze-
    Roma: Fratelli Bencini, 1886.
————. *Regina o repubblica?* Roma: Sommaruga,
    1884.
————. *Re travicèllo o re costituzionale?* Roma: Som-
    maruga, 1884.
————. *Sulle opinioni di Vincenzo Gioberti intorno
    all'economia politica e alla questione sociale*.
    Bologna: Zanichelli, 1874.
Scalia, Gianni, ed. *La cultura italiana del '900 attra-
    verso le riviste: Lacerba, La voce (1914–1916)*.
    Vol. IV. Torino: Einaudi, 1961.
Scaranno, Emanuella. *Dalla cronaca bizantina al
    convito*. Firenze: Vallecchi, 1970.
Scarfoglio, Edoardo. *Il libro di Don Chisciotte*. Napoli:
    Il Mattino, 1911.
Schapiro, J. Salwyn. *Liberalism: Its Meaning and
    History*. New York: Van Nostrand, 1958.
Scrivano, Riccardo. *Il decadentismo e la critica*. Fi-
    renze: La Nuova Italia, 1963.

Sereni, Emilio. *Il capitalismo nelle campagne (1860–1900)*. Torino: Einaudi, 1947.

Seton-Watson, Christopher. *Italy from Liberalism to Fascism, 1870–1925*. London: Methuen, 1967.

Sforza, Count Carlo. *Italy and the Italians*. New York: E. P. Dutton, 1949.

Shattuck, Roger. *The Banquet Years*. New York: Vintage, 1955.

Sodini, Angelo. *Ariel armato*. Milano: Mondadori, 1934.

Sommaruga, Angelo. "Il Carducci e la *Bizantina*." *Pan*, February 1934.

———. *Cronaca bizantina (1881–1885): noti e ricordi*. Milano: Mondadori, 1941.

———. *Giudicatemi!* Firenze: Tipografia dell'arte della stampa, 1885.

Sorbelli, Albano. "I corrispondenti del Carducci." *Pègaso* 4, pt. 1 (1932).

Spadolini, Giovanni. *Autunno del risorgimento*. Firenze: Le Monnier, 1972.

Spriano, Paolo, ed. *La cultura italiana del '900 attraverso le riviste: L'ordine nuovo (1919–1920)*. Vol. VI. Torino: Einaudi, 1963.

Squarciapino, Giuseppe. *Roma bizantina: società e letteratura ai tempi di Angelo Sommaruga*. Torino: Einaudi, 1950.

Stefani, Giuseppe. "Gabriele D'Annunzio e gli irredenti." *Nuova antologia*, 1 September 1939.

Stern, Fritz. *The Politics of Cultural Despair: A Study in the Rise of the Germanic Ideology*. Berkeley: University of California Press, 1961.

Storia dei collegi elettorali. Roma: Tipografia della Camera dei deputati, 1896.

Strappini, Lucia. "Cultura e nazione: analisi di un mito." *La classe dei colti: intellettuali e società nel primo novecento italiano*. Bari: Laterza, 1970.

Symons, Arthur. "The Decadent Movement in Litera-
ture." *Harper's Magazine*, November 1893.
————. "Introduction" in the Georgina Harding
translation of *Il piacere, The Child of Pleasure*.
London: William Heinemann, 1898.
————. *The Symbolist Movement in Literature*. New
York: Dutton, 1958.

Tannenbaum, Edward R., and Emiliana Noether, eds.
Modern Italy: A Topical History since 1861. New
York: New York University Press, 1974.
Thompson, J. M. *Louis Napoleon and the Second Em-*
University of Wisconsin Press, 1964.
Thompson, J. M. *Louis Napoleon and the Second Em-
pire*. New York: Norton, 1955.
Thorlby, A. K. "Literature." *The New Cambridge
Modern History*, Vol. XI. Cambridge: Cambridge
University Press, 1957.
Thovez, Enrico. *Il pastore, il gregge e la zampogna*.
Napoli: Ricciardi, 1926.
Todisco, Antonio. *Le origini del nazionalismo im-
perialista in Italia*. Roma: Berlutti, n.d.
Tosi, Guy. *La Vie et le role de D'Annunzio en France
au debut de la Grande Guerre (1914–1915)*.
Firenze: Sansoni, 1961.
————, ed. *D'Annunzio à Georges Hérelle: correspon-
dance*. Paris: Denoël, 1946.
Trasselli, Carmelo. *Le forche caudine (Pietro Sbar-
baro e Angelo Sommaruga): 1884–1885*. Roma:
Fratelli Palombi, 1945.
Treves, Piero. *L'idea di Roma e la cultura italiana del
secolo XIX*. Milano: Ricciardi, 1962.
Trompeo, Pietro Paolo. *Carducci e D'Annunzio: saggi
e postille*. Roma: Tumminelli, 1943.
————, and Nello Vian, eds. *Lettere di Giulio Salvadori*. Firenze: Le Monnier, 1945.
Tuchman, Barbara. *The Proud Tower: A Portrait of*

the World before the War, 1890–1914. New York: Bantam, 1966.

Ulivi, Giuseppe. *Indice del Marzocco*. Firenze: Vallecchi, 1937.

Valeri, Nino, ed. *La lotta politica in Italia dall'unità al 1925*. Firenze: Le Monnier, 1966.

Vassallo, Luigi Arnaldo. "Angelo Sommaruga." *La nuova rassegna*, 5 February 1893.

Vecchioni, M. "Una lettera inedita di Gabriele D'Annunzio al padre." *L'urbe*, November–December 1952.

Veo, Ettore. "Qualche ricordo su Enrico Corradini all'*Idea nazionale*." *Il marzocco*, 20 December 1931.

Vian, Nello. *La giovinezza di Giulio Salvadori: dalla stagione bizantina al rinnovamento*. Roma: Edizioni di storia e letteratura, 1962.

———. "Giulio Salvadori, scrittore del *Lucifero* e penitente," *Strenna dei romanisti*, vol. 14 (1953).

———. "Un manifesto contro *Le forche caudine*." *Strenna dei romanisti*, vol. 10 (1949).

———. "Sommaruga, ruga, ruga . . . ruga." *Strenna dei romanisti*, vol. 12 (1951).

Vinciguerra, Mario. *Carducci, uomo politico*. Pisa: Nastri-Lischi, 1957.

Weaver, Richard. *Visions of Order: The Cultural Crisis of Our Time*. Baton Rouge: Louisiana State University Press, 1964.

Weber, Eugen. *Action Française*. Stanford: Stanford University Press, 1962.

Webster, Richard. *Industrial Imperialism in Italy, 1908–1915*. Berkeley: University of California Press, 1975.

Whyte, Arthur James. *The Evolution of Modern Italy*. New York: Norton, 1959.

Williams, Raymond. *Culture and Society, 1780–1950.*
  New York: Harper and Row, 1958.
Wilson, Edmund. *Axel's Castle.* New York: Scribner's,
  1936.
Winwar, Frances. *Wingless Victory: A Biography of
  Gabriele D'Annunzio and Eleonora Duse.* New
  York: Harper and Row, 1956.
Wright, Harrison M. *The New Imperialism: Analysis
  of Late Nineteenth Century Expansion.* Lexing-
  ton, Mass.: D. C. Heath, 1976.

INDEX